Gabriel Moran is director of the religious education program at New York University. He is the author of twelve other books, including *Religious Education Development* and *Theology of Revelation.*

NO LADDER TO THE SKY

NO LADDER TO THE SKY

Education and Morality

Gabriel Moran

1817

Harper & Row, Publishers, San Francisco

Cambridge, Hagerstown, New York, Philadelphia, Washington
London, Mexico City, São Paulo, Singapore, Sydney

FIRST EDITION

Library of Congress Cataloging-in-Publication Data

Moran, Gabriel.
    No ladder to the sky.

    Bibliography: p.
    1. Moral education.   2. Developmental psychology.
I. Title.
LC268.M69   1987   370.11′4   85-52001
ISBN 0-06-254591-4

87 88 89 90 91 RRD 10 9 8 7 6 5 4 3 2 1

Contents

Part 1

THE MODERN ETHICAL DILEMMA

Morality and Education

This book concerns experiencing the world without having recourse to the image of a ladder toward the sky. The image of a rope, a chain, a ladder, or a stairway is one of the most widespread images in human history. The fairy tale *Jack and the Beanstalk* is a well-known variation on the theme: Jack climbed the beanstalk in search of wealth and happiness. Religious literature, including the Bible, is especially rich with this image. The Tower of Babel in the eleventh chapter of the Book of Genesis was to be "a tower with its top reaching heaven." And in Genesis 28, Jacob had a dream: "A ladder was there standing on the ground with its top reaching to heaven." Both passages speak of contacting heaven, although the image carries different meanings. In the first passage, humans try building a tower *to* the sky; in the second, the ladder is *from* the sky, with angels of God ascending and descending the ladder.

The modern age and its thinkers dismiss this image of tower or ladder as a childish dream from the distant past. Surely, in the age of spaceships no one is trying to build a tower up to heaven. But fairy tales and religious myths should not be taken lightly: they often embody some profound truth that our rationalistic culture should hear. However, it is questionable whether our contemporaries have even the *capacity* to listen.

My claim is that the modern Western world is tied to the image of a ladder to the sky. Modern Western thought is based on the hope of ascending above the earthly conditions of human life. Religious versions of the stairway or ladder often include the gods descending from the sky. Although modern thinkers see no gods coming down, the image of the ladder has remained. It invites us to climb upward, and in business, government, sport, or war we continue trying to climb the ladder of success in search of the good life.

A dramatic illustration of a ladder upward is "developmental theory" as this phrase is currently used to describe personal and moral change. According to this theory, a person progresses through stages that are "invariant, sequential and hierarchical"; that is, the person goes up the ladder one rung at a time. For three decades the writings of Lawrence Kohlberg have taught us how to imagine and speak about moral progress. For many today, the very meaning of moral development and moral education is Kohlberg's system of six steps upward to the highest stage of moral judgment.

For at least a decade feminists and other groups have severely criticized Kohlberg's system. But given the assumptions of the culture surrounding him, Kohlberg's system is almost impregnable. Effective criticism of it would have to challenge the imagery that presumes that higher is better. Sometimes critics do attack at this point, assuming it is easy to dismantle hierarchical ways of thinking. But movement upward is not easily replaced by another trajectory; some variation on the image of ladder keeps reappearing.

What has slowly dawned upon me through many years of reflection on this question is that the problem is not just the image of ladder, but imagery itself. If imagination means pictorial representation, then all images are suspect when one asks about the direction and meaning of human life. Any thing, object, or condition that one can visualize is inadequate as the be-all and end-all of human beings. But of course we cannot do away with imagery. The human mind is an irrepressible dynamo for producing images. The question is whether we are dominated by those images—any images—or whether our experience is so rich that images are not the controlling factor.

Religious traditions are aware of this problem. Buddhism perhaps goes the farthest in trying to reach an imageless experience. However, Christianity and Judaism, with their emphasis on hearing, also challenge the pictorial imagination. Moreover, religions warn us against being attached to any object, including our own images. Although the claim is frequently made that we need better images of the moral life, imagery may not take us far enough. Images need to be examined within a context of human bodily activity, or else an object at the top of the ladder inevitably returns.

Western philosophy from the time of Plato has been powerfully affected by a bias toward the visual as the only trustworthy sense. Plato's "ideas" were visual forms high above the world. Aristotle, it is said, brought the Platonic forms down from heaven to earth. Knowledge was now conceived to be the abstraction of these forms from the sensible object. In Aristotle the good is the end that can be imagined, sought after, and acquired.

Our modern systems, while seeming to reject Aristotle, absorbed much of his way of thinking. For us, knowledge still means "taking a look," and freedom means the ability to choose the good we prefer. The printing press was one of the most powerful forces that shaped the modern mentality. The movement from knowledge in script to knowledge in print reinforced the notion that knowledge is a visible object fixed in space and distributable in books.

Television, it may be noted, while conflicting in many ways with print, is on the side of print in giving preeminence to the visual sense and the visible object. In the television era we acquire knowledge by looking at pictures on a screen. We should also note that television and its technological associates are still in their infancy. In coming decades they may yet contribute to a different way of experiencing the universe. The computer could represent a greater shift than anyone can yet grasp because it deals in a panoply of relations that shatters our imaginative control of visible objects. So technology might literally return us to our senses—that is, to participating in the world in tactile and auditory as well as visual ways.

But television and computers cannot be trusted to do the whole job. Losing control of visible objects could merely lead to a more incoherent life. We need order in life, an order that emerges from using all our bodily senses. Various kinds of human interaction have to place us in touch with the whole universe. Discussions of human morality require a language that breaks free from the imagery of visible, acquirable objects and instead emphasizes lively, earthy, communal, and politically powerful metaphors.

People often equate image and metaphor. They say "metaphor" when they are really referring to a comparison of two *things*. This reduction of metaphor to image misses the importance of metaphor as governing *how* we think and not only *what* we think. Metaphor is about activity and relations; it includes imagery but is not reducible to image or object. A metaphor is a highly condensed parable: the kingdom of heaven is *like* "a man [who] discovers a treasure, . . . sells all he has, . . . and buys the field." The metaphor is not "God is like a man" but "God is a father who cares for his children." Or God is a mother hen who gathers her chicks under her wings.

The moral life, particularly in recent times, is portrayed as *like* "a man placing hand over hand . . . going up the rungs of a ladder . . . toward the sky." Notice that the image of ladder, rope, chain, or stairway can be present in two or more metaphors. The moral life is like men "building a tower" or like angels "ascending and descending a ladder." In one study of adult development a group of men were asked to comment on a picture that showed a man holding on to a vertical rope. Among men in their early forties, a typical reply was: "I'm not sure he'll make it to the top." Men in their late fifties tended to say: "I think he'll get down all right if he holds on." The image was the same in the two cases, but the metaphors were decidedly different.

I am concerned throughout this book with the metaphors that govern moral life. In this regard I explore in the fourth chapter one of the great secrets of Western history: that the people most successful at taking down the ladder to the sky have been the great religious mystics. These men and women usually distrusted visions, a fact often interpreted to mean they hated the body and the sensual. In reality, though they talked of disciplining the senses, they were acutely alive to the body as the seat of perception. Their lives demonstrated the conditions for living without an escape upward: love for creation, the experience of communion, and immersion in the present.

Mystical language is rich in metaphors that bring into play old and young, women and men, humans and nonhumans, joy and sorrow, the earth and the cosmos. A favorite metaphor of many mystics is that of a woman giving birth. There are objective aspects of pregnancy and birth, but the process that leads to birth cannot be reduced to a visible, acquirable object. So also the metaphors of rushing waters, healing touch, dark abyss, attentive listening, and metal throwing sparks. A moral life conceived within such language has a set of possibilities richer than a moral life imagined to be the acquisition of an object and the protection of my rights.

One of the books that provoked my thinking on these matters is Arthur Lovejoy's *The Great Chain of Being*.[1] A half century after its publishing, Lovejoy's book is still a helpful guide in tracing the Neoplatonic influence throughout Western history. I think, however, that Lovejoy profoundly misunderstands Christianity, especially on its mystical side. He can say of Christianity only that to be consistent it should have followed a Manichean path, choosing spirit above matter. Instead, according to Lovejoy, Christianity followed a path of "fruitful inconsistency." Lovejoy can make no sense of the fact that saintly mystics were often social reformers. Should not Meister Eckhart and Teresa of Avila have disdained efforts to improve this world? I would say that though there is indeed plenty of inconsistency in Christian history, there is also a consistent logic that Lovejoy is blind to, given his assumed categories.

Lovejoy begins his book by assuming a split between "this worldly" and "other worldly." When this language is imposed on Christianity, the implication is that Christianity, insofar as it is true to itself, encourages people to ascend the ladder to the other world, a world higher than this one. Certainly one can find this metaphor in Christian history, particularly in its heresies that imagine spirit above matter. Some popular forms of Christianity make a similar assumption: keep the rules, save your soul, and go up the ladder to your reward in the other world. But Christianity in its richer strands attends to the goodness of creation, the reality of history, and the meaning of incarnation.

Much of modern ethics is a pale version of a badly understood Christianity. Moral education in the twentieth century has been anti-Christian or at least opposed to the version of Christianity known to moral reformers early in this century. But as so often happens to things in reaction, moral education has been attached to what it is attacking and has absorbed its controlling metaphor. Nietzsche flailed away at European philosophy of the nineteenth century as "insidious theology . . . born in a parsonage." Twentieth-century writing on moral education is confident it is not infected with theology. But it still has a ladder up to the sky.

Christianity did in fact appropriate the image of ladder, but in Christianity's governing metaphor all the steps go downward: the ladder is *from* the sky, not *to* the sky. Here is where Lovejoy misses the point of Christianity. The downward ladder is intended to get rid of an upward ladder. In the Christian story, God comes down the ladder but the human journey is not a reversal of that course. To change the metaphor for a moment, in Christianity the river of God's creation flows downstream but humans are not asked to be salmon. In the Christian perspective, the human vocation is to receive and to share. By being present at the center of creation, the human being is the one through whom and in whom the whole world is sanctified. Everything that is, is good, although everything is not yet holy. Humans do not have to go anywhere to find goodness; they do have to stop, be quiet, and listen.

The image of ladder can therefore be part of two strongly contrasting moralities. I am not totally opposed to the image of ladder, rope, chair, or staircase; it is too prevalent in human history to be eliminated. Christian thinkers, starting with St. Paul and St. John, make fruitful use of the image within a metaphor of divine descent. However, even at its best the image of ladder is very limited in the who, what, where, and how it can encompass. A ladder downward all too easily shifts into being a ladder upward. And once the moral life has been reduced to invariant, sequential, hierarchical steps *up* a ladder, then proclamations of divine descent simply conflict with the established way of moral thinking and are peremptorily dismissed. We need breathing space, diversity of visual images; we need divine revelation from every direction and through every sense.

The young Ludwig Wittgenstein finished his *Tractatus* with the famous mystical line: "Of that whereof one cannot speak, one must be silent."[2] The metaphor which Wittgenstein used in this manifesto of rationalism is that of a man standing on top of a wall and pulling up a ladder behind him. Everything that could be stated had been put into words; the ladder of language was now supposed to disappear. In *Philosophical Investigations,* an older and wiser Wittgenstein realized that language does not end that way. Pulling up a ladder does not open the way to some more mysterious reality. Our language eventually fails us, but our struggle is to show with words a reality deeper than words. Wittgenstein moved into the metaphor of "language game" as the way to point to what is beyond images. He drew his examples from such varied sources as mathematics, movies, and sports.[3]

Another writer who discovered the limitations of the ladder is William Butler Yeats. Considering his life at mid course, Yeats wrote:

> Now that my ladder is gone,
> I must lie down where all ladders start,
> In the foul rag-and-bone shop of the heart.[4]

Yeats's metaphor suggests to me a discovery of a set of relations that may be obscured by the climb upward. The relations of men and women, of inner and outer, human and nonhuman, past and future, may emerge from where he lies down, where all ladders start. Our moral vocabulary needs poetic metaphors that will allow us to explore the mystery and the silence, the suffering and the joy of human life.

MORAL EDUCATION

This book attempts to establish a new category of writing, what I call "educational morality." The late twentieth century needs an approach to morality that has been struggling to emerge throughout this century. This approach needs shaping and naming in such a way that the resources of traditional wisdom can effectively be brought to bear upon contemporary life. At the same time, contemporary life may clarify and correct some of the supposed wisdom of the past. My intention, in short, is to open a serious dialogue between education and morality.

The suggestion that we lack books that connect morality and education may seem preposterous. Is not the market place flooded with books on "moral education?" That is true, but it is precisely my reason for reversing the words and asking about "educational morality." In the dialogue between education and morality, I hope to raise a different set of questions than appears in the literature of moral education. In my view, moral education has had too narrow a meaning, both on the moral side and on the side of its educational assumptions. The term "educational morality" has some initial shock value in making us think about our assumptions. I think there is a positive reason beyond mere novelty for making "education" rather than "moral" be the modifier. This book is about morality not as a ready-made object from a church or from an individual conscience, but as something that comes about in and through the educational process. The literature on moral education tends to assume that we know what morality is before we ask about techniques for making it a part of education.

The narrowness of current moral education comes from two flaws in its development earlier in this century. The first is its insistence that morality be kept as far as possible from religion. The second is its assumption that education is practically equivalent to one form of education: schooling. These two working principles have had a compatible but unfortunate marriage in the literature of moral education.

The narrowness of this literature can be illustrated with this summary statement by James Rest:

Historically, there have been two major theories of moral education, the Durkheim tradition and the Piagetian tradition. Durkheim portrays moral education in terms of changing the *motives* of the person. . . . The individual is socialized through direct instruction, example, and group reinforcement. . . . For Piaget, moral education ought . . . to be focused on developing people's understanding of the possibilities and conditions of cooperation.[5]

For a writer to begin by referring to two historical traditions and then to name two twentieth-century European men seems somewhat myopic. Perhaps Rest means to say that Piaget and Durkheim are the twentieth-century representatives of two long-standing traditions, but even that claim does not stand up well. Within a perspective of three thousand years of Western (not to mention Eastern) history, Piaget and Durkheim look remarkably similar. Far from dividing the moral universe, Piaget and Durkheim make essentially the same assumptions about the meanings of "moral" and "education." They differ only slightly concerning the best means to train children to choose the rational good.

To Rest's credit, he does go on to acknowledge that his neat division of the moral universe is not working well these days. "The facts of the matter have forced our hand, and we seem to be stuck with a lot of variables, all interacting in complex ways. If it's true that neither Durkheim's nor Piaget's theory is complete, then we need a more comprehensive theory of moral education."[6] The question is, How far out and how far down is Rest willing to go for a more comprehensive theory? Are writers in moral education ready to reexamine the meanings of both "moral" and "education?"

One of the traits that unite Piaget and Durkheim is an anti-religious attitude. Both men were reacting against what they call "revealed religion." What they were looking for was freedom from ecclesiastical control and the room to explore new moral questions in an increasingly pluralistic society. What Durkheim and Piaget fled to was the dry bones of a rationalistic system of ethics. They applied this system of ethics to the education of children and called the package moral education. Lawrence Kohlberg has continued this tradition into the present. Durkheim, writing at the turn of the century, begins his *Moral Education* with "We decided to give our children in our state-supported schools a purely secular moral education. It is essential to understand that this means an education that is not derived from revealed religion, but that rests exclusively on ideas, sentiments and practices accountable to reason only—in short, a purely rationalistic education."[7]

This presumed choice between "revealed religion" and "rationalistic education" cuts off education in morality from its living roots. The phrase "revealed religion" is itself an invention of modern rationalism. As W. Cantwell Smith shows, no one used the phrase "revealed religion" until the eighteenth century.[8] Religious people do not believe in a *religion* that is revealed but in God who is revealed (and revealing.) If religion were what is claimed as revealed, it would be of interest only to the believers in that religion. But if revelation refers to God's presence in the world, then religiousness can take many forms and there is no neat dichotomy between religion and the rest of life.

If we are to encounter the "whole person" in education, we have to acknowledge the existence of *some* relation between morality and religion. The two have been intimately related since the time when the prophet Amos came down from the hills denouncing injustice; writers in the twentieth century cannot achieve a separation of morality and religion simply by announcing a divorce. Careful distinctions are called for in a setting such as the state-supported school, but an *a priori* and total separation is a self-defeating bias. The crude categories used by Piaget and Durkheim did not succeed in eliminating religion; Kohlberg's references to a natural as opposed to a revealed morality are equally naive and ineffective. Modern ethicists have succeeded only in driving religion beyond the realm of critical thinking. The far right wing of Christianity may indeed talk about a morality "derived from revealed religion," but why cannot sophisticated thinkers of the twentieth century conceive of a different relation?

This book is a study of morality from the perspective of education. It is not a book on Christian ethics, moral theology, or mystical spirituality, but I see no reason to exclude religion in principle when for better or worse religion is part of the arena that needs educational exploration. Moral education's flight from religion has not produced a realistic education in morality. I wish to show later in this book that religion can throw needed light on today's moral problems. Religion does not supply specific answers to agonizing moral problems, but it does provide context, attitudes, rituals, and courage for facing up to our problems. There is nothing wrong with an education in morality that is open to dialogue with religion whenever religious history and religious practice have something to offer.

I said above that in addition to excluding religion, the other deficiency in the modern meaning of moral education is its identification of schooling with education. Here the flaw is almost totally unconscious. Education is simply assumed to refer to the process in which children of a certain age are instructed by one kind of teacher in one setting and in one kind of knowledge. Education is given over to schoolteachers, children, and classrooms. In this context moral education has come to refer to children in school deliberating over hypothetical dilemmas. Perhaps this activity can be called the development of children's thinking about moral problems. But the education of men and women in how to live moral lives is surely something wider, deeper, and longer lasting.

Durkheim's approach to morality is usually called socialization. One might have expected from that term that the family would hold primacy in education and moral education. But in fact Durkheim makes a point of playing down the family's part. According to him, the family deals only in intimate personal relations and is incapable of training the child to the impersonal demands of society. The school, he contends, is the "locus par excellence of moral education."[9]

Piaget's *The Moral Judgment of the Child* is in part an attack on Durkheim.[10] Piaget criticizes Durkheim for making schoolteachers a new priesthood of authority. Nevertheless, Piaget also concentrates on the "school age child" and looks for the development of rational rules of cooperation. The burden of moral education, in Piaget's scheme, is still largely on the schoolteacher and the school. Parents come in mostly for criticism as obstacles to moral development. The task of adults, he maintains, is to design projects of student cooperation and then not interfere with the course of nature.

EDUCATIONAL LANGUAGE

We need a clear distinction between schooling and education; otherwise the schoolteacher is asked to carry an impossible burden of moral education. People will complain that the schoolteachers are not doing their jobs of producing a moral society. Meanwhile, the place of the family, the work site, leisure, and other sources of education for adult and child are neglected. These other settings and agencies do not just disappear if they are not acknowledged to be integral to the meaning of education; their effects can be miseducational. Parents, for example, have a strong moral influence on their children whether or not they are recognized as moral educators.

My distinction between schooling and education in no way disparages schools and their teachers. Schoolteachers perform an invaluable service, but their work is obstructed when schooling takes over the whole meaning of education. It is true that people do not explicitly profess to equate school and education, but the equation has been there for at least a century, and therefore if one does not resist current educational language one ends up by reducing all forms of education to schooling.

As a test of the distinction, listen to the way people use the words "teach," "teaching," "teacher." When people refer to teaching they usually mean schoolteaching. Other kinds of teaching, such as parental teaching or job apprenticing or friendly counsel, must then be judged as strange or lesser forms of teaching. In reality, schoolteaching is a rather late and quite peculiar form of teaching when words have become a reality separable from bodily movements. Actually, teaching is something every human being can do for another. The distinctive contribution of the schoolteacher can be understood and appreciated only within the context of other forms of teaching.

Some people may think the distinction between schooling and education is obvious. Indeed, nearly everyone who speaks about education claims to make this distinction. The issue, however, is whether one makes a clear, consistent, and fruitful distinction. I suggest that a perusal of any educational journal or a careful listening to discussions on education will reveal that the distinction to which everyone gives verbal assent is constantly ignored. When people say "teacher," they usually mean schoolteacher; when "educational curricula" are discussed, the referent is inevitably school curricula; and "adult education" still means that peculiar kind of education given to people outside schools for "school-age" children.

Most attempts to open the word "education" to richer and wider meaning succeed in blurring the edges. Or more radical attempts to make education cover everything end up making it mean anything and therefore nothing. For more than a century the stable core of education's meaning has been tied to the schooling of children. The adult-education movement, beginning in the last century, has not broken the pattern; rather, adult education became the exception to prove the rule, or the weaker form of the real thing: big people instead of children, six-week courses instead of semesters, certificates instead of diplomas. Much the same can be said of the other end of the age spectrum. "Pre-school" education is defined in relation to the one stable form of education that everyone acknowledges: the school.

No current educational language encompasses both three- and seventy-three-year-olds. Furthermore, exclusion by age is only a symptom of education's real problem: that it gets locked into a sphere of reality where it does not belong. Education is not a *product* available in school as is commonly assumed. Education is not a *wider thing* than school so that education would emerge as the school walls are lowered. *Education is a different kind of reality from school or schooling.* While school is a definite institution and schooling is a particular form of learning, *education is not a thing at all but a lifetime process constituted by a set of relations.*

In some respects I am trying to reopen the question that the Progressive Education Movement addressed early in this century. John Dewey and his followers were convinced that education is the key to reforming all of society. Their great hope in education was not entirely misplaced, but they failed to carry through a diversifying of forms for education's mission. Reaction against Progressivism and its idealistic hope in education has not produced any clear alternative that replaces or transcends education. The need for education is even greater than it was at the turn of the century, but the burden of reform through education should not be placed exclusively on the backs of children and schoolteachers.

Most definitions of education try to clear up all ambiguity at the beginning of the discussion. A definition closes off meaning by setting limits. But education is a puzzling and paradoxical process about which we need a continuing conversation. For beginning such a conversation on education, I suggest the following description: *Education is the reshaping of life's forms with end (meaning) but without end (termination).* It is important to retain the paradox created by the double meaning of "end." The human impulse to reach an end (termination) is what makes it so difficult to conceive of education as lifelong. If end as meaning is distinguished from end as termination, then we can talk of ends in an endless process. We cannot have an adequate meaning of education unless these two different meanings of end are kept in tension with each other.

This meaning of education can be clarified by comparing it to what John Dewey calls his "technical meaning" of education. Dewey writes that education is "that reconstruction or reorganization of experience which adds to the meaning of experience, and which increases ability to direct the course of subsequent experience."[11] My description of education has similarities to Dewey's definition of education, but I intend a different tenor. I think one must challenge the adequacy of Dewey's key terms: 1) reconstruction, 2) experience, 3), add, and 4) control.

1) Dewey and others of his time were fond of the word "reconstruction." It is not a bad word, but it is limited to connoting the rearrangement of things in an organized system. In contrast, my word "reshaping" connotes a less aggressive, more aesthetic, and organic change. Education is a reshaping rather than a shaping. Life's forms are not for human beings to invent. The forms are offered to us by history's events and the present environment; our task is to respond and to reshape those forms.

2) Dewey used the word "experience," one of the richest terms in American English. However, he was unable to avoid a fuzziness that led to all sorts of abuses in the name of experience. He spent much of his later life trying to clarify what he really meant by experience. My description refers to life's forms, a phrase that allows of some debate, but it reminds us that education must carefully attend to the concrete, physical, sensual shapes that human beings encounter throughout life. For the human journey is a fragile undertaking attached to precise conditions on the earth that supports life's forms.

3) Dewey speaks of "adding" meaning to experience; I have described education as a process "with end"—that is, "with meaning." My term leaves open the question of what meaning is and how to speak about the human mind's relation to it. But Dewey's verb "add" settles the matter much too quickly and seemingly by an external imposition. The meaning of meaning has to be a central question of education itself.

In saying that education is a process with meaning, one implies some purpose and intentional direction. However, one should not overemphasize the deliberate and conscious intention of the individual concerned. In this regard, most descriptions of education are descriptions of the work of schoolteachers. In schoolteaching an individual sets out to convey a set of meanings; the lesson plan, the syllabus, and the curriculum reflect a deliberate intention to teach someone something. But other forms of education embody human intentionality in a very different way. The reshaping of family roles, neighborhood environments, work arrangements, or sports activity often emerges from many people who are barely conscious of participating in the process.

4) Finally, Dewey emphasizes directing and controlling the future. My description does not exclude future or control, but it focuses on interaction in the present. We get some order in the future by living meaningfully within a process that is ever present, a process that has no end. Education is not preparation for something else; it is a careful response to what living (and its inevitable associate, dying) presents to us.

Dewey's educational writing concentrates on children and schools. In the schooling form it is important that children get the instruments by which they can control some things in the future. But an education that includes more than schooling and school-age children will not set its sights only on life after school. One must acknowledge that to some people the "endlessness" of education sounds like a cry of despair. For people who wish to acquire a rampart against the unpredictability of life and the inevitability of death, the end (termination) of education is highly desirable: the point at which one has the information, power, and control to be on top of things. In contrast, people who discover joy and meaning in the present and in the communion of human and nonhuman life find it unthinkable that education should have a termination point.

MORAL LANGUAGE

As we turn from educational to moral language, we do not enter into an entirely new realm. The word "education" itself carries a moral value. We reshape life's forms because we think we can make them better. Education is never merely neutral, and ethical or moral questions are frequently raised about how education is conducted. I wish to take this point a step further and to propose that *morality and education are essentially the same process.* Morality, or at least moral maturing, is the reshaping of life's forms with end and without end. I suggest that there are three stages in the process of maturing morally:

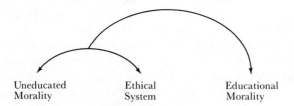

Uneducated   Ethical   Educational
Morality   System   Morality

In the first stage of uneducated morality everyone has a morality, most of which has come ready made. Young children pick up a sense of what is proper and improper within the society in which they find themselves. For children, a traditional way of acting can convey a quite profound understanding of good and evil. Some individuals grow beyond childhood with little reflection, analysis, or conflict of conscience. Although such persons could be saints, one is bound to be a little suspicious of an uncomplicated moral outlook. In this first stage of uneducated morality, the customs, codes, and rituals have not been exposed to a reshaping toward greater meaning. Although this first stage is to be transcended, a thorough immersion in the discipline and ways of a community is the basis of all later morality.

The second stage of the moral life is the dominance of ethical thinking in the form of a religious or secular ethic. As one uses analytical reason to reflect upon morality, one seeks a consistent system of principles or rules. The individual wishes to decide for himself or herself the right thing to do. Ethics in morality corresponds to schooling in education: the definite thing in the middle of the process that can get mistaken for the process itself. Not surprisingly, ethics fits well into classroom discussions. The consideration of principles, rights, duties, and so forth should indeed be part of everyone's education. And specialized courses such as medical ethics or legal ethics belong in every professional school.

The third stage of the moral life is "educational morality." There is no precise age requirement, although this stage does presuppose the ripening and maturing of the two preceding stages. Some people already seem morally mature in their twenties; others in their fifties are still trying to get the knack of it or have yet to be confronted by grave moral crises. The mark of educational morality is one's participation in a language that is bodily and communal. The rituals and symbols reemerge from childhood, having been clarified and reinterpreted by the rational intellect. Moral decisions at this stage are not always agonizing dilemmas; there can be a joy and ease in exercising virtue when it is a lifelong companion.

I would call this third stage "educated morality" except that this phrase might suggest closure. We do not "acquire an education" by which we become morally mature. Education is endless in the sense of

lifelong; so too, moral maturing involves a lifetime of activity. We end-
lessly reshape our moral lives in a process of continuing progress.
When morality is not progressing and we have complacently settled
down to be morally neutral, deterioration of the moral life has set in.
In the ethics of the second stage, movement means progress; but in
the moral life as a whole, regression is always a possibility.

Education and morality imply each other. A genuine education is
necessarily a moral journey; morality can mature only with the stages
of one's education. At the most immature level, morality and education
may be separated; that is, we can talk about a morality simply lacking
in education. Morality is often spoken of in this way when we mean
mere behavioral conformity. The farther along one goes in the process
of human maturity, the closer becomes the relation of education and
morality, so that in the stage of educational morality the two sets of
concerns are almost indistinguishable. The sad fact is, however, that
many people get stuck in the second stage where there is not yet a
unity of principles and life, ethical thinking and moral activity. Well-
schooled people may not be well educated, and ethical-minded people
are not always morally mature.

This problem of getting stuck in the intermediate stage is particularly
acute when ethical theorists rebel against traditional forms of morality.
Ethics does involve abstraction, discursive language, and a search for
universals, but ethical systems need not disparage rituals and moral
codes. If ethicists think that reason is an adequate substitute for tradition, they may eliminate the very context that ethics needs. The language of community, character, virtue, story, and sacrifice does not fit
well into modern systems of ethics. Nonetheless, it is language that must
be reappropriated from religion or elsewhere if there is to be a mature
moral life.

The need for an adequate moral language to describe stages of moral
life might best be seen in an extended example.

Consider the topic of sexual morality. In our society a constant battle
is waged between opponents and proponents of "sex education." From
the very start with the naming of the question, the issue is narrowed
down so that neither side can win the argument. One side works with
an ethic that presumes that facts are preferable to ignorance. The other
side works with a morality that values tradition and is concerned with
behavior. The advocates of sex education protest strongly that they do
not teach "moral values," yet they are obviously teaching the value of
rational enlightenment. The opponents of sex education in trying to
defend the sacredness of the person can sound as if they favor ignorance. The alternatives in sex education are indeed an uneducated morality and a system of ethics. The problem is that we should be dis-
cussing not only sex education but sexual education or sexuality
education. Then we would have the possibility of a third stage: edu-

cational morality. The term "sex education" connotes schools and "school-age" children. While the argument over sex education goes on, the human race has a crisis in sexual education, a process that occurs from birth to death.

Everyone begins with a morality of sexual behavior and sexual understanding that is entangled in myth, fiction, and family rituals. Children are almost totally ignorant of biological facts of sex and psychosocial facts of sexuality. But children nonetheless begin their education in sexuality at birth with the way their parents touch them, the way they interact with brothers and sisters, the way the environment, including the TV set, shapes their early life. Children's sexuality is better shaped if parents have time to read to their children, if husband and wife live in a mutual relation, if physical conditions are aesthetically pleasing. Conversely, any kind of sexual exploitation in the early years of life creates an obstacle for sexual education later in life.

When a child goes to school he or she should learn some crucially important facts about sex. Here is where "sex education" contributes to sexual education if it does not arrogate to itself the whole process. The school is a place to provide biological, psychological, and social facts without the embarrassment often associated with sex. Sexual education is a good test of cooperation between parental teaching and school teaching. Schoolteachers and parents need not always agree so long as they respect each other and are aware of what goes on in the other part of the youngster's life. In sexual education the contributions of family and school are different but complementary.

It may be threatening to parents (not to mention religious officials) that the sex education in the school abstracts from the larger questions of sexuality and morality. However, as one stage in a sexual education, breathing space to look at a few facts is not a bad thing. We should note, notwithstanding this focus on facts, that the school itself has its own mores. Established sexual patterns should not be forgotten as the school attends to "facts." For example, one could ask why most school administrators are men and most schoolteachers are women. That is a significant question in sexuality education even though it never appears in a sex-education curriculum.

This example of job division according to gender is the kind of issue that runs throughout the fifty or sixty years of people's education in sexuality after their high school sex-education course. A sexual education is lifelong, involving a continual increase in factual knowledge but also the reshaping of physical and social behavior. If the approach to sexual morality is a fully developed education, then the mythical and rational stages are integrated within an adult sexuality, and whatever progress is made in adult lives flows over into the education of young children. The attitudes of children are reshaped by the attitudes of parents and other adults.

The modern world loves to talk about sexual liberation; indeed, there is usually more talk than liberation. Sex education supposedly liberates people from traditional restrictions and introduces them to the rational world of sexual enlightenment. Sex education may in fact do that, but it in turn needs liberation into a new world of mystery, awe, respect, discipline, and joy. Sexual liberation means human freedom only if human beings come to love one another and to cherish bodily life. Educational morality is earthy, symbolic, and behavioral; but such a morality can be lost if an unreflective morality is simply replaced by a rational ethic.

In the next two chapters I explore the competing systems of ethics that dominate the modern Western discussion of morality. I argue that the two systems of ethics are not so much false as incomplete, for they both lack the context of a moral life, including any acknowledged relation to religion. These two systems of ethics can be taught effectively in classrooms, but they are not adequate for the whole process of education. After looking at these competing ethical systems in Chapters 2 and 3, I turn in Chapter 4 to what I call a morality of goodness. That chapter forms the background for considering the responsible, the trans-natural, and the private/public as the language of an educational morality.

CHAPTER 2

An Ethic of the Good

This chapter and the next discuss the two systems of ethics that dominate modern discussion of the moral life. One way of contrasting these two systems is to say that the first moves from the good to the right; the second moves from the right to the good. The first system asks about the common good of human life and then asks what an individual's right conduct is in light of that good. The second system begins with the rights of the individual and asks what kind of collective system protects those rights and allows individuals to search for their own goods. What the ethic of rights sees as strength (the distinctiveness of the self), the ethic of the good sees as a danger (lack of togetherness). And what the ethic of the good sees as its advantage (the cohesion of society), the ethic of rights sees as a danger (the submersion of the individual). As an example, compare the ethic that governs China and the United States. China starts from the need for careful social planning, with individuals fitting into the plan. The United States starts from individuals and their rights, with the hope of some collective unity.

The ethic of the good, which is the concern of this chapter, is called teleology, "the science of the end." Many variations on this theme of *telos* (end) have been worked out in modern ethics. For example, "hedonism" holds that the end of life is pleasure. There is no agreed-upon language for dividing teleology into several sub-systems. I will avoid controversies about these divisions and stick to the main idea of a teleology.

A teleological approach to ethics seems to be well grounded in common sense. The ordinary person assumes in daily life that thinking is thinking about something and that choosing is directed toward a desired end. Furthermore, everyone recognizes that to reach destination D may involve moving from A to B to C within a chain of actions. The intended final goal, then, guides the choice of intermediary steps. Those steps are the right ones if they in fact lead to the desired end. This approach to life applies to small decisions as well as large. If I recognize eating dinner as a good thing, I will choose to do that. And buying the food, cooking the meal, setting the table become the right things to do in relation to my goal. If in choosing a career it is a good thing to become a physician, then attending medical school, studying for tests, and going through internship are also good because they lead to my ultimate goal.

These examples and any like them leave some questions unanswered. What is eating good for? Nutrition? What is nutrition good for? Is being a physician the ultimate good, or is there a further good that one's choice of career serves? When one looks at discrete human actions, the idea of *telos* or end seems obvious. Conscious, deliberate actions are directed toward some good. Human activities are purposeful, following reasonable lines of conduct to fulfill the purpose. But can one put together the entire pattern of human activity in relation to an end? Can one say that this pattern—human life—is directed toward some good?

Ancient philosophy and popular religion say yes to this question: they assume that human life goes somewhere. If it does, then the main ethical issue is to discover the good that human life is directed to. Philosophy and religion warn that what we see as an immediate good for part of the self (for example, the sexual drive) may not be in the service of the good of our whole self. We have to find what is really, truly, and ultimately good for every human being and for the whole human being. If we could agree on that, human disagreements would be reduced to procedural ones. In the following discussion I look first at the classical form of teleology, in which the end is intrinsic to human nature. Then I turn to nineteenth-century teleology, in which the end is usually outside the human self. In both of these considerations I note the role that religion has played.

ANCIENT AND MODERN FORMS OF TELEOLOGY

Teleology is usually traced back to Aristotle, who begins his *Nichomachean Ethics* with "Every act and every inquiry, and similarly every action and pursuit, is thought to aim at some good."[1] Aristotle's images and language rely heavily on visual forms. When we make something we conceive it in the mind (the final cause), and then we construct the real object in accord with our mental design. The carpenter has a chair in mind before he makes a chair of wood. The form of chair or boat or dog emerges from the potency of matter when there is a knowing, skillful agent (the efficient cause) to bring out the form. A favorite analogy is the shape of the statue being drawn from the clay.

Reiner Schürmann accuses Aristotle of "methodological teleocracy."[2] That is, he thinks that Aristotle imposes the idea of *telos* where it does not belong, that fabrication is used as the model for *all* activity. In Aristotle, each power of the human body is thought to have an end:

the eye for sight, speech for communication, sex for procreation. The physical organism itself has an overall design or *entelechy*. Each thing, according to Aristotle's metaphysics, has a nature that determines the activities it can perform.

When transposed into ethical terms, the teleological principle means that good activity is in accord with nature. The soul's powers have to be developed according to the purpose and end of each respective power. Each of these powers has to be used in moderation, a mean between extremes. The totality of human powers in proper subordination to one another brings about the good life. Aristotle was confident, then, that he could recognize a virtuous gentleman. The main lines of human happiness could be figured out by the student of human nature.

Aristotle's biggest sticking point for moderns is the implication that if everything is drawn forward to its proper end, there must be a final cause to the universe.[3] Aristotle did not need an efficient cause for the universe; the Greek philosophers assumed that the world of matter was eternal. But a god who draws the world to him as its goal was indispensable to his biology, astronomy, metaphysics, and ethics. Aristotle did not assume, though, that the final end could be made evident to everyone. In fact, we need rules of civility in education and in politics so that disagreeing people can continue their search for the end.

The fact that human beings do search for the end casts doubt on the accusation of "teleocracy." Fabrication does not seem to be the main model in ethics and politics.[4] Aristotle does use metaphors of making, such as the sculptor making a statue. He also uses metaphors where the end is external to the process, such as an arrow shot at a target. Still, for Aristotle the end of politics is not outside the act of politics. And human beings do not invent the end of human life. They have to use the divine spark called reason to get insight into their true and proper end. To act in accordance with reason means to act according to reality. Reason is not encapsulated in the human brain; rather, the human intellect is receptive to the reason that structures the universe.

We get a different picture when we consider the use of the teleological principle in nineteenth-century ethics. At first glance, there seems to be a continuity with Aristotle: the striving after a *telos* by the power of reason. However, the underpinnings of a teleological system had been dramatically altered during the intervening centuries. Reason had changed in meaning from the divine light giving knowledge of the established end, to a human instrument for manipulating the means toward a humanly chosen end. The end was not discovered within the activity itself but is instead an object to be sought after and acquired. An internalizing of reason corresponded to an externalizing of end.

Such a dramatic shift in which reason came to mean the human power of calculation took centuries to accomplish. The history of mod-

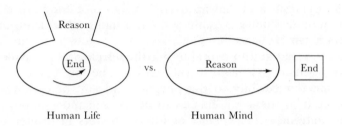

Human Life   Human Mind

ern science is in large part the establishing of a calculative, instrumental, individualistic meaning for the word "reason." Although religious officials have often opposed the rise of technical reason, Western religion played a major part in encouraging a scientific attitude, a sense of trust in nature's reasonableness and in human ingenuity. The line of development can be seen as early as the remarkable essay of Pico della Mirandola "On the Dignity of Man," written about 1485. Pico has God saying to Adam: "A limited nature in other creatures is confined within the laws written by Us. In conformity with thy free judgment, in whose hands I have placed thee, thou art confined by no bounds; and thou wilt fix limits of nature for thyself."[5]

Pico della Mirandola surely thought of such sentiments as Christian; indeed, the words are put in God's mouth. The ideas may have seemed to him only a dramatic heightening of the Book of Genesis. However, from today's vantage point, one can recognize a fundamental change. From an Adam who tills the garden and names the animals to an Adam who is confined by no bounds and may grow into "the higher natures which are divine" there is more than a difference of emphasis.

Pico could not have forseen all the implications of saying in regard to human happiness: "It is given to him to have that which he chooses and to be that which he wills."[6] People in later centuries would take such statements as the literal truth with just one change: God would not be seen as necessary. The "given" did not require a giver; choosing and creating are simply human givens. Reason was not a gift but a human possession. This internalizing of reason has proved to be extraordinarily fruitful in the modern sciences and technology.

The related shift—the externalization of end—can also be traced back many centuries. Christianity played an ambivalent role here, as it did with the internalizing of reason. Christian scholars had devised a complex system of morality, incorporating the inner design of Aristotle's philosophy with a God both more exalted and more intimate than Aristotle's. The end was high above the human and at the same time closer to the human than anything else is.

In its preaching, Christianity spoke with certainty of an end that was established from the beginning and revealed for all to see. The church claimed from the start that Christ is the end, that in him human history has seen its end. The Christian catechism begins with an answer to why God makes us: "God made us to know him, to love him and to serve him in this world and to be happy with him in the next." With this as the premise of an ethical system, the rest is just working out the details. The commandments of God and commandments of the church are the rules to be followed to reach the end.

Christianity, when reduced to formulas for popular preaching, can easily come across as a form of higher selfishness. Reason is put in service of the great prize at the end. The right thing to do is to observe the rules, because the final reward justifies the investment in sacrifice, altruism, and discipline throughout this brief prelude on earth. When medieval theology referred to happiness (*beatitudo*) as the end of human life, there was an inherent ambiguity.[7] Happiness sometimes refers to an activity, an inner realization of a God-designed creation. But happiness can also refer to an acquirable object, something the individual strives after and takes possession of. Both meanings of happiness can qualify as elements in a teleological system of ethics, but the journey to the end involves very different activities in the two cases. Happiness as an object might require forceful action of a person to traverse the distance separating the person from happiness, located at the tip of the arrow, the end of the tunnel, or the top of the ladder.

The nineteenth century carried over some of the medieval meaning of both reason and happiness. At the same time, thinkers tried to situate a new reason and a more tangible happiness on a secure basis. The new reason was thought to supply greater clarity and simplicity without losing the benefits of the old reason. The medieval sense of an ordered universe was presupposed as the new insights of the experimental sciences were applied to that world. Ethics in this new world did not have to depend on the beliefs of Christian teaching but on such things as the "new science of politics" and the abundance resulting from technology. With the release of human potential from the bonds of superstition, and with the channeling of natural powers into better organization, happiness could be brought down from the heavens to the earth.[8]

In the nineteenth century, many people could view ethics as a straight-forward system of rules and procedures. The ethical system had no need of the mysterious design to the universe found in Aristotle, in Christian theology, or even in the economics of Adam Smith with its invisible hand guiding economic development. Everyone is searching for happiness, and the big question is how to reach that happiness here on earth. The people who still believed in a reward beyond this life would have additional motivation for observing ethical rules.

Religion could generally be praised as a motivator of the masses. Of course, the enlightened thinkers knew that religion was no longer necessary because ethics was based on reason alone.

In the eighteenth century, Rousseau and Hume had seen the need for an inborn compassion or pity that gives unity to mankind and impetus to ethical observance. Nineteenth-century thinkers tended to dismiss such concerns as a residue of irrationality. They confidently cleared away all the speculative elements that obscured the simple question of a rational ethic. Herbert Spencer formulates the issue compactly:

Whatever one's point of departure, all moral theory will grant that an action whose immediate and long term results are in sum beneficial is a good action; while an act whose short term and remote results are in turn maleficent is a bad action. The criterion which men use in the last analysis in judging conduct is the happiness or sorrow it produces.[9]

Spencer appeals here to common sense and reasonableness. We all prefer happiness to unhappiness, so any action that takes us toward happiness is good, any action that produces unhappiness is bad. All would agree that a delicious meal makes them happier than a severe tooth ache. Spencer, however, seems to be talking about a known condition called happiness that serves as the guide for all human activity. But *does* everyone know beforehand what human happiness is? How does one total up beneficent and maleficent results unless one has the end clearly in view? What about the possible clashes between immediate and ultimate happiness, or the happiness of one individual in conflict with another?

Nineteenth-century teleological systems do attempt to answer some of these questions with standards for judgment and with mechanisms for negotiation. A name closely associated with this nineteenth-century stream of thought is utilitarianism. The name is peculiar in that it seems to be an evasion of rather than an answer to the question of end. A utilitarian attitude indicates we should do what is "useful," that we should make our decisions as useful means to getting somewhere else. But is not the "somewhere else" the question that must be confronted if we are going to judge that something is or is not useful? The answer is presumably so obvious that the question need not be explicitly asked. We all want happiness; the real problem is getting there: thus it makes sense to concentrate on the means.

What may not be immediately obvious is that concentrating on means to an end can shift the meaning of end. When a *final end* guides *proximate ends,* the final end emerges from within the enjoyment of the proximate ends. In this case, nothing is *merely* means, and one approaches the intermediary and final stages with an attitude of lesser or greater appreciation. But when D is the end and A, B, and C are *merely things for use,* then we may arrive at D with the same calculative and instrumental mentality with which we jumped over A, B, and C. Could people searching for an object called happiness recognize it if they reached it?

Utilitarianism did not itself cause the externalization of end, the reduction of the good to an acquirable object. As indicated above, *telos* as an external thing goes back through Christianity and into ancient thought. But a thoroughly utilitarian attitude cannot act as a critic of whatever becomes *telos*. For utilitarianism is concerned with the means to the end, not the end itself.

Within modern utilitarian thought the good tends to be interpreted in terms of material wealth. Jeremy Bentham, the best-known utilitarian, often sounds crassly materialistic. Bentham begins with the assumption that "every individual seeks to maximize pleasure without limit," a principle by which he intends to be realistic about the basis of ethics. He speaks of human happiness as involving a list of material and spiritual goods, but it is the possession of *material* goods and their accompanying pleasure that dominates his system. "Each portion of wealth has a corresponding portion of happiness. . . . Money is the instrument of measuring the quantity of pain or pleasure." Bentham is aware that some people object to this calculus, but he challenges the reader to produce a better one.[10]

Bentham lived at a time of rising hopes for the spread of private property, free enterprise, and market exchange. A revolution in politics and economics was going to unleash a potential for happiness hitherto unknown. There was little need to discuss what everyone wanted, happiness. The ethical *telos* therefore was "the greatest happiness for the greatest number."[11] The ethical problem was the procedure for working out "greatest . . . greatest." Too many individuals might decrease the supply of happiness; too much happiness for some individuals might take it from other individuals. Of course, if new technology and better organization increase the world's abundance of goods, then the balance of "greatest . . . greatest" has no upper limit. As a favorite saying of economists put it, all the boats would rise with the tide of economic abundance. This hope for a better world through the increase of wealth has not disappeared, but many people today see a dark side in the quest for abundance.

Where Bentham and the other English utilitarians should be given credit is the political implications of their calculus. The concentration upon individuals striving for the good life had the effect of giving recognition to each individual as part of the calculation of total happiness. The political principle was "each one shall count as one." That formula may strike today's reader as innocuous, but it was, and in many places still is, an attack upon class privilege. It has taken a long time to include women and non-whites under the phrase "each one shall count as one." Nonetheless, an egalitarian drive was inherent in this school of ethics. The happiness of each individual is to have equal merit regardless of the age, race, sex, social status, or political position of the individual.

John Stuart Mill, working within the same school of thought, tries to correct Bentham's tendency toward a crude hedonism.[12] Mill argues against the assumption that happiness is a simple matter of pleasure, for pleasure is itself complex. Mill introduces a distinction between higher and lower pleasures. Viewed in one way, such a distinction may reintroduce class snobbery. It could simply mean that listening to music is a higher pleasure than eating pastry, or that listening to a Mozart symphony is a higher pleasure than listening to a popular ballad. From another perspective, however, Mill was looking for a larger context for ethics, a regrounding of ethical thinking in a realm beyond the possession of external goods. Without abandoning the ideal of political equality, Mill reintroduces the issue of "character." The higher goods are qualities of personal life rather than possessions that are owned.

Mill's distinction takes us back to the central ambiguity in the idea of *telos*. Granted that happiness is what each human being is seeking, does happiness refer to the object of the search, or is happiness the activity of being happy? If the latter is the case, then we are thrown back upon the complexity of human life as a whole. The picture of "economic man" with his set of needs that need fulfilling is utterly lacking in psychological, not to mention religious, subtlety. It might be that "the chief thing which the common sense individual wants is not satisfaction for the wants he has but more and better wants. . . . True achievement is the refinement and elevation of the plane of desire, the cultivation of taste."[13] What this idea suggests is not class bias but the need for education, an education that is the reshaping of life's forms "with end and without end."

A utilitarian approach to ethics has generally lacked an educational context for considering the moral life. Ethics needs the perspective of history and of personal development. When there is no sense of historical patterns, utilitarianism will usually seem the best choice at any particular moment. It encourages a spirit of compromise: let's do the best we can for most of the people. Let all the competing parties avoid talk of moral ideals and instead work out a useful compromise. In many political disputes such an attitude is greatly to be desired.

The danger in this attitude is that over a long time the currency of moral discussion is debased. Any compromise becomes acceptable if it is useful in preventing something worse. One life must be sacrificed for the nation to be saved; one nation has to be given up if the dictator is to be appeased; a few lies are necessary to protect important truths; freedom of the press has to be rescinded for the good of the people.

With such an approach, there is no incentive for taking a stand in defense of ideals or of long range improvement. The link across the generations is lost and with it the moral bond to a larger human community. A system that promises the best rewards available to each individual can lead to a decline in the valuable realities that individuals must share, including loyalty, trust, and love.

The failure to grasp this problem rests on the supposition that the goods in question are objects that human beings make, acquire, and use. The ethical question then becomes the fair distribution of these goods. In this view, society is the name for a collection of individuals seeking their own goods, and social happiness is simply individual happiness writ large: when there are more goods there is more happiness.

What seemed clear to the eighteenth and nineteenth centuries was that the masses were being prevented from seeking their own happiness. Even where authoritarian regimes had been toppled, individual ignorance still posed an obstacle. Education in these centuries was understood according to the metaphor of enlightenment—that is, the enlightened ones liberating the benighted ones from a superstitious past. As soon as people were enlightened to their own self-interest, they would begin living with a healthy egotism. Freed from the self-denial that religion imposes, people would find their happiness here and now. As Bertrand Russell puts it: "If men were actuated by self-interest . . . the whole human race would cooperate."[14] The scheme sounds logical: each individual should choose whatever makes him or her happy, and the result will be collective happiness. Certainly that makes more sense than what often happens when people choose what they do not want in order to make someone else happy. The result is that everyone is miserable and no one has what he or she wants.

THE LIMITS OF A MODERN TELEOLOGICAL SYSTEM

Many people sense that there is something askew in this arrangement. They cannot believe that what the whole world needs is a massive dose of selfishness. But simply attacking selfishness, as much of religious preaching does, fails to address the issue. And this approach often has only a spiritualized selfishness as the alternative: sacrifice now because it will bring you a greater reward in heaven. In recent times, a different approach to criticizing this position begins from the relation of person and community. The most telling criticism of selfishness as the ethical basis of economics is Fred Hirsch's *The Social Limits of Growth*. The power of this book lies in its demonstration of a logical flaw in a system that claims to be nothing if not logical.

Hirsch distinguishes between two kinds of wealth: "material" and "positional." The first refers to objects that can be produced and acquired. At any moment such goods are limited, but there is no preestablished limit to the possible expansion of such wealth. If everyone were to work hard and if an equitable system of distribution were devised, everyone would have more goods and—perhaps—be happier.

The second kind of wealth, "positional," is inherently limited. If one's chief desire is to reach the top of one's trade and have the status, fame, and glory of such achievement, one is keenly aware that not everyone can have that good. Part of what makes the good desirable is its exclusive nature.

Consider the example of "a quiet place in the suburbs." When a few people have money, they can move out of town. They then have the goods of serenity, fresh air, and open land; they also have easy access by train or car to the goods of the city: art, restaurants, livelihood, and so forth. But what happens when a large number of people have the money to buy a car and a home in the suburbs? The good that each individual desires begins to disappear because there is an inherent limit to how many people can have a quiet place in the suburbs. As numbers increase, so do noise, pollution, and crowding. Suppose everyone tried to move from the city to the suburbs. Two things would disappear: the city and the suburbs, both replaced by endless sprawl along highways. As material wealth increases, the scramble for positional wealth is likely to increase. And thus we have a paradox that we sense is true but find difficult to believe. As material wealth increases, the more important kind of wealth that depends on relation to others seems to decline. Indeed, for those people who arrived at positional wealth earlier, their good does decline.[15]

Hirsch's main concern is that a doctrine of self-interest must fail in cases where many small decisions are necessary for a shared good of high quality. One of his examples is a bookstore that sells quality books. Suppose this store is confronted by a new mass market bookstore that can undercut prices. If I and others who wish to have quality books available will support the store that sells them, then at a slight cost to myself that good will continue to be available. If enough of us support the store, the price difference will be small enough to justify my investment to have such a store exist. However, my individual decision to support the store is not enough to save it, nor is my decision not to buy there enough to make it fail. My self-interest is best served by buying all the books I can at the mass market store and pay extra only when I have to for books in the quality store. If everyone views the issue similarly, the quality store will fail—even though a survey would find that many people wish to have a quality store available and are willing to make some self-sacrifice for it.

As a second example, consider an all-white neighborhood in which one home owner sells to a black family. Many of the other home owners have nothing against a black family. In fact, individually considered, most of them might prefer an integrated neighborhood. Nonetheless, an individual home owner may feel compelled to sell because the market value, apparently on good evidence, will soon decline. The individual's immediate choice appears to be between an all-white neighborhood on the one hand and a predominantly black and/or financially depressed neighborhood on the other. An integrated neighborhood is not a good available for the individual's choosing. Integrated neighborhoods involve other considerations and mechanisms than the attitude of choosing my individual self-interest at each moment.

Hirsch points out that in cases that require the cooperation of many people—where each decision considered alone is not decisive but where success does depend on all these decisions—the individual faces four possibilities:

1) I do not cooperate; everyone else does.
2) Everyone cooperates.
3) No one cooperates.
4) I cooperate; everyone else does not.[16]

The person who acts strictly on self-interest will choose #1 over #2 and also will choose #3 over #4. That is, the individual quite logically will refuse to cooperate in those things that he or she recognizes as a common good desirable by all. In cases where the choice is between #1 and #2, the individual need not contribute because everyone else seems to be supporting the common good. The individual's best bet is to hope that everyone else cooperates. The results will be that the individual gets all the benefits without sacrificing anything. For example, if a man in the U.S. does not pay his taxes, it will make no perceptible difference in the services he receives, and he also has his money. (The government knows this logic too and therefore has tax laws, but the system still requires a high degree of voluntary compliance.) Self-interest does not lead to voluntary cooperation. In the absence of a coercive law, the enlightened individual would choose not to cooperate in paying taxes or contributing anonymously to private charities.

More devastating are the cases where #3 and #4 are at stake—that is, where one fears that hardly anyone is contributing to the common good. Our tax situation may get to this point, but we already have plenty of examples of public goods that do not have anywhere near the cooperation needed to sustain them. As in the cases cited above, quality bookstores, integrated neighborhoods, mass transit, clean parks, plentiful water, and just about all public services are vulnerable to the logic of self-interest. One can easily feel, and with some justification, that almost no one is cooperating. Whatever cooperation exists among those who cannot flee is not enough to sustain mass transit or well-kept parks. Thus it happens that a highly desirable good will cease to exist because individuals refuse to cooperate, and their refusal is an accurate perception of their own self-interest. The individual can choose to travel by automobile or by poor mass transit; an individual cannot choose good mass transit. And the fewer the number who choose to stay with mass transit, the greater the pressure of increasing cost and of deteriorating environment to make the remaining individuals cease to cooperate. As #4 looms ahead where no one cooperates, who wants to be among the few losers who are left to fight a losing battle? *Everyone knows that everyone else knows* that #3 is unfortunate but that its choice is more enlightened than getting stuck with #4.

In summary, when the *telos* is a commodity that can be made and sold, individual hard work and enlightened self-interest will increase the wealth available to everyone. Adam Smith taught us that "it is not from the benevolence of the butcher, the brewer, or the baker, that we expect our dinner but from their regard to their own interest."[17] When we are considering the goods we make and sell, Smith's thesis has proved to be very serviceable. Individuals who strive for a tangible good and organizations that distribute those goods can provide an increase of wealth for everyone. The choice of self-interest over benevolence, of selfishness over altruism, is realistically supported by plenty of evidence.

When we turn to Hirsch's category of positional wealth, the choice between selfishness and altruism is simply too crude. First, however, it seems that Hirsch's category of positional wealth covers several kinds of wealth that need distinguishing. When he speaks of the quiet place in the suburbs or of getting to the top of one's trade, we are still in the realm of individual self-aggrandizement. The positional wealth in such cases is not a commodity but a personal relation or set of relations. Nevertheless, in the context of moral value there is not much difference. In contrast, when Hirsch deals with the quality book store or an integrated neighborhood, we are in the realm of a communal rather than a competitive relation. That moral value requires some personal sacrifice for the sake of a good that transcends the individual. What is called for is not altruism—the other individual or the group before myself—but a different way of seeing and experiencing the world. The moral foundation for this kind of positional wealth is the cooperative relation of person and community, human group and nonhuman environment. The development of such a morality is found in Part Two of this book.

CONCLUSIONS

The strength of a teleological system of ethics is that it is oriented toward a goal. People want order in the universe, and they cannot live without seeking order in their own lives. As Nietzsche insists: "The fundamental feature of man's will, his *horror vacui: he needs a goal*—and he will sooner will nothingness than not will at all."[18] Much of traditional moral education was concerned with training the will. Religion tries to keep the will going toward something greater than individual pleasure, power, and glory. By taking that route religion sometimes plays a powerful role in building a public order and contributing to economic progress. Religion usually does that, however, in a paradoxical way as it preaches self-sacrifice, devotion to God, and simplicity of life.

Much of modern ethics wants none of that paradox. It takes a pragmatic and reasonable approach to coaxing the individual away from a simple attachment to bodily pleasures. It calls people to recognize the need to build a better world through cooperation. This appeal is a form of the higher selfishness based on the fact that there are finer pleasure in life than indiscriminate copulation and picking food from the trees. Civilization, in other words, is unthinkable unless people set goals, discipline themselves, and work together.

The danger in this civilizing process is that the goals may take on a reality of their own, separate from human life. The machines constructed to be useful begin to govern human choice. Or moral ideals, such as patriotism, loyalty, or justice, can become reified as objects to be sought after or sacrificed to. "Spiritualizing" the goals is not always an improvement; it can lift the goal above the give-and-take of human exchange. One is asked to leave behind body, earth, community, place, and history if one wishes to be perfect. Simple hedonism is not very dangerous as an ethical ideal; it is seldom mistaken for saintliness. In contrast, a flight from the body is regularly taken to be, if not perfection, at least a "higher" state. The lower state in such an outlook is human delight in those pleasures shared with the other animals. The question here is whether higher is better and whether one has to imagine moral progress as ascent to a higher plane.

I have described education as the reshaping of life's forms with end (meaning) and without end (termination). Moral life at an early age means delight in simple pleasures of the body and receptivity to what life offers. The meaning is found in the present bodily experience. A child may have to be given directions by an adult, but as far as possible the adult should cultivate the child's capacity to choose his or her own goals.

Elementary and secondary schools are oriented toward goals of knowledge and skills. The meaning of actions tends to get separated from bodily forms. Youngsters copy math problems from blackboard to notebook. They ferret out the meaning of a short story, or they assess the meaning of a historical event. In the school setting, moral progress is likely to be equated with the movement from rules of conduct that have been adopted unthinkingly to ethical principles whose meaning is understood.

When an adult morality arrives, goals do not disappear, but they are reintegrated with bodily forms. Now meaning is not so much "made" as it is dis-covered in all the interactions of person and person, human and nonhuman. A process of moral maturing without end (termination) has no state or condition that functions as goal. There is always further meaning to be found if we can let the meaning emerge in the interplay of life's forms.

Instead of leaving the body behind, an educational morality recaptures some of the simple joys of the body. As far as we know, only a human being can delight in a fine meal with friends while looking at the ocean and hearing Bach in the background. Only the human being can experience sexuality as symbolic of self-giving love with intimations of life's endless generativity. Having goals is not a bad thing in institutions such as schools and factories. But a teleological language does not exhaust what human life is like when life is experienced at its best. The ordering of people's lives does not require imposing a goal, and the meaning of life is distinguishable from setting a goal for one's life. The emergence of order and meaning in a way that differs from goal orientation is addressed in Part Two of this book. Before examining that line of thought, we look first at the system of ethics that competes with the teleological approach.

CHAPTER 3

An Ethic of Rights

The utilitarian approach described in Chapter 2 still has strong appeal to common sense and to the nonprofessional in ethics. What could be more obvious than that morality is about doing good and contributing to the general welfare? To most ethicists, however, a utilitarian is a mere moralist who is only at step one of ethical thinking. What has triumphed in contemporary ethics is a system based on the rights of each individual. This pattern of ethical thinking is called deontology, the science of duty.

As noted at the beginning of Chapter 2, the two systems of modern ethics have several things in common. One of those is a denial of the classical and medieval idea of an inner design to human nature. Aristotelian and medieval philosophy supposed a fixed end to human development. Modern ethics proclaims our liberation from a preordained or predestined limit. Utilitarian ethics sets about constructing a human happiness as best we can attain it here on earth. Ethical discussion would then concern decisions about the means to happiness, "the only thing desirable as an end."[1] The *telos* or end has to be made rather than discovered.

The deontological ethics examined in this chapter is an attempt to transcend the superficiality of utilitarianism, which does not face up to the radical implications of doing away with "the end of man." "Happiness" is the word smuggled in to cover the nakedness of utilitarianism. If there is any happiness intrinsic to the human being, then there has been no abandonment of the ancient belief in an inner design put there by God or nature. If happiness is simply a name for anything that anyone might choose, then "the greatest happiness for the greatest number" is not really naming anything. Anyone's conception of happiness can be rejected by the next person, so there is no common end toward which individuals move. In this context, ethical questions are not about means to the end but about the absence of an end.

The danger in recent times is that having freed us from the control of God, modern thinking exposes us to the control of whomever or whatever can establish order. The human being cannot live in chaos, so collectivistic societies and state planning are one logical outcome of removing a divine plan from the universe. A small group or even one individual decides for the larger body what is the best arrangement for human happiness. Of course, not everyone will agree with these plans, but those who do not have to learn to sacrifice themselves for the larger reality or else be coerced into agreeing.

This picture of a collectivistic state is what horrifies most modern ethicists. They start from the premise that no one can decide what is good for everyone else—indeed for anyone else. The best thing we can work for is noninterference in the choices of other individuals. Each individual must be allowed to choose his (and only recently, her) own good. In this ethic, there is much to be said about *goods* but practically nothing about *the good*. The only place to locate a basis for understanding what is called good is in the individual human will. As Immanuel Kant puts it, "It is impossible to conceive anything at all in the world, or even out of it, which can be taken as good without qualification, except a good will."[2]

As indicated above, when a utilitarian calculus is used there are sure to be cases of conflict between general welfare and the individual's liberty. The ethic of rights sides with the individual's right to choose. People who commit crimes do have to be restrained from interfering with the rights of others. But nothing takes precedence over the individual and the system of rights that protects the individual. Even criminals have rights that need protection. In this ethical system the happiness of millions cannot be the justification for taking one life.

Daniel Maguire uses an effective if somewhat bizarre example to show the limits of a utilitarian mode of thinking.[3] What would be a sure way to reduce the number of automobile fatalities? Maguire says that one way is to install seats for children on the front bumpers of the cars. Then the automobiles would go slower and the drivers would be more cautious. Beyond doubt, the total number of fatalities would decrease, and very likely the number of children's deaths would also decrease. Nevertheless, as Maguire is trying to demonstrate, we all know there is something patently wrong about the proposal. The very idea of using children this way to get a desired good is morally revolting. Whether we can analogize from this example to capital punishment or abortion I will not pursue here. My point for the moment is that the ethic of rights arises from the premise that human life is special and that the individual human being should not be used as a means to a greater good.

The obvious problem for an ethic of rights is the ground of that premise. Does one simply appeal to a moral revulsion against using a human being as a means? One could claim that the principle is self-evident except that it has not seemed obvious in many places and at many times. Modern ethics values liberty, equality, and justice, but the proof that these values should always take precedence is not easy. The Canadian scholar George Grant writes: "How in modern thought can we find positive answers to the questions: 1) what is it about human beings that makes liberty and equality their due?, 2) why is justice what we are fitted for, when it is not convenient? Why is it our good?" Grant concludes by saying that our inability to answer these two questions is "the terrifying darkness which has fallen upon modern justice."[4]

Since the eighteenth century the two sources seemingly available for justifying the sacredness of the individual have been "revealed religion" and "unassisted reason." In the early modern period it was believed that these two sources said just about the same thing. Biblical religion, it was believed, was an ethic for the masses, while philosophers using only reason could establish a complete ethic. John Locke believed that philosophers could always fall back upon revealed religion, except where it contradicted reason. One had only to open the inspired books and "all the duties of morality lie there clear and plain, and easy to understand."[5]

The task of the ethicist who did not believe in the Bible or who tried to provide ethics for nonbelievers was to use "unassisted reason." The thinkers of that era could not appreciate the degree to which this "un-assisted reason" has been cut loose from its traditional moorings. In its classical meaning, reason had referred to the structure of the universe. The human mind received the truth and conformed to the world. The eighteenth century's dichotomy of revealed religion and unassisted reason was a radical innovation. Not only did religion get placed outside reason, but so also did the revelatory character of truth itself. Reason without revelation (disclosure, unveiling, unconcealedness) meant a reason left to itself inside the human head. Reason became defined as an instrument to move from a premise to a conclusion.

In the eighteenth century the new sciences seemed to be providing a content for reason. The secrets of the universe were being opened up, not through revelation and contemplation, but by aggressive activity on the part of investigative research. Scientists were sure they had the truth because the laws of nature were verifiable by empirical data. Outside the laboratory, what impressed as truth was economic efficiency and technological productivity. To this day science is believed to have the truth because it leads to airplanes, telephones, and television.

Despite the technological marvels of the twentieth century, scientists have been less certain that scientific laws provide knowledge of the existing world. The mathematical formulas are secure, but their relation to physical reality is mediated by a choice among pictorial representations. At best, reason can supply only criteria for the choice. Thus, scientists may choose a picture of the universe that is aesthetically pleasing, but they are aware that their representations are not the reality.

The relation of ethics to modern reason is a complicated one. In neither the early phase of modern science nor in its recent form does scientific reason provide a clear basis for an ethic of rights. In the early period from seventeenth to nineteenth centuries, science was mostly a threat to ethics. Science at that time claimed to explain all reality in terms of physics. It was thought that everything was in principle reducible to the laws of mathematical physics. Even the biological organism seemed to be just a more complex arrangement of matter, force, and energy. If the human being is also reducible to movements of atoms and molecules trackable by universal laws, then ethics becomes a coda of physics. Nineteenth-century ethics is in large part the struggle against the hegemony of physical science. The culmination of this struggle was the assertion at the turn of the twentieth century that "is" and "ought" are in two different language worlds. The physicist can describe what is but must leave to the ethicist what ought to be.

Science has become more modest in the twentieth century, no longer claiming to reduce everything to facts and universal laws. Science thus leaves more room for ethics, but it does not offer ethics much positive assistance. Reason is still locked within the human mind, useful for its technical and instrumental tasks but incapable of establishing the foundation of a human ethic. Science has thereby moved from being the foe of an ethic of rights to being a spectator of ethics' search for a ground to stand on.

KANT AND MODERN ETHICS

Enter what can be called a new kind of reason, a practical reason for handling these problems of human life that neither religion nor science nor classical philosophy has answers for. The starting point for a solution in this approach is individual liberty. The figure who towers over deontological ethics is Immanuel Kant. Classical reason and traditional religion flow into Kant from the eighteenth century. What emerges in the nineteenth century is concern for *autonomy*, the concern to protect the human will against outside interference.

Moderns after Kant feel alone; or more accurately, philosophical spokesmen of the last two centuries express feelings of abandonment, alienation, and anxiety. They live in a universe that is without faith in God and without confidence in theoretical, speculative reason. Ethics is not available by reading the Bible, and ethics is not discoverable by studying nature. The only thing left to do is to construct ethics, to assert what ought to be in the face of what is. Modern ethics often has a kind of lonely grandeur depending on nothing beyond the indomitable will. The burden and the greatness of human choice is that there is no preordained scheme to which the choice should conform.

This kind of ethical thinking is often called individualistic. More precisely, it is a concern with the private sphere within each individual.

The ethical starting point, therefore, is not the individual in his or her personhood, but rather liberty, the individual's capacity to make choices. Central to ethics is the question of a mechanism that allows me to choose my own good and to tolerate a different choice by other individuals. Tolerance becomes one of the supreme virtues of modern times, a sign that one is enlightened and progressive. Any attempt "to impose one's private beliefs" on others is a trespassing of the ethic of rights, a violation of privacy.

Kant grounds ethics in a command or imperative that must be followed if human life is to exist at all. This "categorical imperative" is an answer to the first question of ethics: "What ought I to do?" In one formulation this imperative reads: "Act so that the maxim of thy will can always at the same time hold good as a principle of universal legislation."[6] Because this law is legislated by the will itself, it is not a violation of the will's autonomy. The only law binding on the will is the universal will. The categorical imperative simply joins the individual and universal wills.

What is necessary for there to be willing? One could not universalize lying or murder or cheating. The will could not operate in such a world. Suppose that everyone bribed judges. The effect would be to do away with judges and justice. Every act of bribery is wrong because it undermines justice. If everyone practiced murder, no one could trust anyone else, and the will would be paralyzed. Although Kant concentrates on will, he is not unmindful of *consequences* as important for ethical judgment. His maxim of universalization, as John Dewey notes, is a way of securing impartial and general consideration of consequences.[7]

Kant approaches from another angle in answering the question "What ought I to do?" He formulates the categorical imperative in a way that directly concerns the autonomy of each individual. "So act as to treat humanity whether in thine own person or in that of any other, in every case as an end withal, never as means only."[8] The "kingdom of ends" is humanity itself and the humanity found in each agent. To use a human individual as a means to an end would be to undercut the foundations of ethics.

The principle that we should treat persons as ends rather than means is hard to resist. Does anyone really argue the opposite? Even the people in history who seem to have used human beings as the means for making financial fortunes, winning wars, or advancing science would probably explain their actions in a way that does not violate the principle. No maxim in modern ethics is more often and more piously repeated than "Treat each person as an end and not a means." The principle is taken to be self-evident. Nevertheless, maxims that are assumed to be so obvious as not to need examination often hide the problem they supposedly solve.

In the last few decades some people have in fact begun to question this maxim. The source of this concern has usually been the treatment of animals. If only *human* individuals have the right to be treated as ends, does that mean that nonhuman animals can be treated as a means to whatever human beings desire? A small but vocal minority has been arguing for animal rights.[9] They argue that killing animals in laboratories for experiments or killing animals in the wild for fur coats is immoral. Immanuel Kant, like most morally sensitive people, recognized this concern as legitimate. But Kant had no logical way to work this concern into his system. When Kant considers whether it would be immoral to kill a dog, his reply is that killing an animal is demeaning to the man, even though the animal has no rights.[10]

We seem to be entering an era in which that explanation of animals is deemed insufficient. People's sentiments have changed, whether or not their theoretical rationales have kept pace. Any moviemaker today who shows the killing of animals is quick to explain in the credits that animals were not really killed for the purpose of making this movie. Children never stopped being sensitive to the killing of animals, whether in movies or real life. Movies about the killing of animals that were otherwise sentimental exercises (for example, *Bambi*) became terribly traumatic experiences for many children. Adults today have caught up with children on this point; at least they have great sympathy with some animals who are treated cruelly.

The argument of some ethicists today is that we have drawn the means/end line at the wrong place. That is, the other animals ought to join human beings who have a right to live. I have a great deal of sympathy for the direction of this movement; in fact, I will argue in the following chapters that the movement should go farther than including nonhuman animals. For the present, I would say that "animal liberation" is a symptom of a much larger problem we should be attending to. The current impetus for animal rights is likely to save some rhesus monkeys and some specialized groups that get public exposure. What we still lack is a language with which to think about the whole world of living things in a moral way.

What is at issue is the undermining of this firmest of all principles in deontological ethics, that human beings—humanity as represented in willing agents—is the ethical "kingdom of ends." The most aggressive wing of the animal-rights movement is consciously trying to overthrow this principle as they denounce "species-ism." All animals are equal, and any claim to human superiority is immoral. This line of argument is not likely to be persuasive despite its appeal to the egalitarian spirit. Any form of human ordering is not going to place all animals at the level of human uniqueness. But the case for animals' rights is attractive, and supporting it could undermine the belief that a *person* is the bearer of rights. If there should be a turn to the principle that "all animals are equal," the transition will be a brief one until some group determines, as Orwell's *Animal Farm* concluded that "all animals are equal but some are more equal than others." Force, not reason, might be the basis for new discriminations of differences.

Attacks on "species-ism" are not likely to change ethical systems. The arguments, after all, are by human beings in human language. What is more likely to occur and what already appears in many books is an attempt to patch up Kant's statement of means and ends. In *The Liberation of Life*, authors Charles Birch and John Cobb have put together an extraordinary panorama of empirical data for ethical reflection. The rich store of material is there, including treatment of various animal groups, for a basic overhaul of Kantian ethics. Yet it seems to me they falter when it comes to challenging Kant's language of means and end. They give credit to Kant's principle for its being a big improvement over most of human history during which the rights of the individual were not recognized. Birch and Cobb then go on to criticize Kantian ethics for unwittingly joining forces with utilitarianism. If everything except human beings is mere means, then the main question about everything nonhuman is "What's it useful for?"[11] Everything—animals, trees, art, the past—is reduced to a factor of economic calculation.

Birch and Cobb thus offer a powerful critique of Kant's principle. But having shown the inadequacy of means-and-end thinking, they can only conclude: "What is needed is a new ethic which recognizes in every animal, including humans, both ends and means."[12] In this formula, the nonhuman animals have moved over the line to the side of rights, and the humans have seemingly stepped in the other direction. The authors are trying to indicate a radical shift, but the language of means and end collapses under the weight of its problems.

The distinction between means and end is fundamentally utilitarian. It never belonged within an ethic of rights. No patching up will do, nor is there a simple formula of replacement. Mary Midgely tries several times to replace means/ends with a language of part and whole.[13] At the same time, she does not wish to let go of her Kantian premise. I think that the language of part and whole is no more adequate. If it goes anywhere it would be to some kind of absolute such as Hegel envisioned. Part and whole cannot protect the nonhuman animal world that is Midgely's particular concern. "Whole," like "end," can be an appropriate ethical term; the trouble lies in the way we pair such terms. A language that pairs means and end collapses end into a narrow band of meaning.

The issue of animal rights is a symptom of our failure to grasp the context and meaning of human rights. In what sense is the human being an end? I return once again to my description of education, which is also a description of moral maturing. Education is the reshaping of life's forms, with end and without end. Each activity of reshaping in education is "with end," that is, with meaning, sense, and purpose. Studying in school, praying in church, taking care of children in the home, designing a machine in the factory are not means. To the extent they are educational and contribute to moral maturing they are human activities meaningful in themselves. When a job is only a means to make money, when going to school is only a means to a diploma, when child care is only a means to adult gratification, we have behavior that goes against the grain of both morality and education.

We sometimes refer to activities such as art as "an end in itself." Presumably, the intention is to deny that it is a means, just as Kant's main intention is to deny that a person is a means. But any such phrase remains. ambiguous in our utilitarian culture. To speak of "an end in itself" does not necessarily get free of means/end thinking. The assumption may be that what is an end in itself is the termination point in a sequence. Other things are intermediaries; the end in itself is the stopping point. Here I must emphasize again my phrase "without end" as applied to education and morality. Human activity is without end; it has no stopping point. The alternative to that meaning of end is not means but rather the communion of all things. Each of our meaningful activities is related to other activities involving ourselves, other human beings, and the nonhuman world. When we choose, whether it be love, art, morality, religion or anything else, we do not choose a thing in isolation; we enter a world of participation without end. Everything is somehow connected to everything else, and what the human will calls end at any moment is not a termination point but a way of being in the continuing movement of history.

Only the double meaning of end can keep this paradoxical tension before our minds. Neither part/whole nor means/end but end . . . end. Everything that we may casually consider as mere means (trees for wood pulp, chickens for dinner, chairs for sitting) is actually embedded in some web of meaning. Everything we set up as end (particularly the human individual) is not the *possessor* of meaning, because its meaning is still to be discovered no matter how far and how long we search. The exploration of this kind of morality will require us to use a language of bodily organism, personal community, and ecological system. In contrast, the Kantian ethic of rights does not offer much affirmation of bodily passion, communal solidarity, and ecological unity.

The ethic of rights is not so much about persons as about individuals; its concern is less with personal freedom than with the isolated will. It envisions a world of principles, rights, and duties that if consistently followed would lead to liberty and equality. Within this system the world of animal bodiliness is given short shrift, and that includes the animal bodiliness of the human person. The body is there, of course, but it hovers in the background as possible antagonist. In Kant's ethics, obligation or duty arises out of the conflict between our sensibilities that incline us to egoistic ends and the universal law of reason. In practice, reason becomes a force of resistance commanding us to fight against the easy way of the flesh. Reason protects the will against human passions, starting with our own passions. For Kant, as for John Locke before him, we must "deny ourselves the satisfaction of our own desires, when reason does not authorize them."[14]

This ethic of rights is closely connected to the liberal political tradition. So close is the connection that it is difficult to articulate the ethical issue except in a political context. Modern political discussion concerns a conflict similar to the conflict between selfish passion and universal will. That is, the rights tradition is suspicious of all sources of power outside the will; so large institutions, especially the state, are seen as dangers to individual liberty. Constant vigilance is therefore necessary so that the power of the state is kept as limited as possible. Against the ever-present danger of totalitarian government, the liberal tradition insists on a sphere of privacy. The state and every institution should be kept distant from the individual's right to do whatever he (and now, she) chooses to do.

In this political tradition it is the individual who possesses rights. By means of a covenant or contract that precedes existing governments, the human race established governments to secure the peace and bring about prosperity. The well-known line in the Declaration of Independence says: "We hold these truths to be self-evident: that all men are created equal, that they are endowed by their creator with certain unalienable rights, that among these are life, liberty and the pursuit of happiness." John Locke's formula of rights had been "life, liberty and property," with the third offering a model for the other two. The reason why men put themselves under governments, wrote Locke, "is the preservation of their property, to which in the state of nature there are many things wanting."[15] The state is therefore both the securer of rights and the possible violator of those rights. Particular attention must be given to the arranging of the parts of the government so that while one part is opposing another, the individual can escape the concentrated power of the government.

The U.S. Constitution has attached to it a bill of rights that provides a model for many nation-states. The language of human rights is also used in the United Nations charter and numerous international proclamations. For the United States with its tradition of legal protection of rights, the ethic of rights seems to serve quite well. This nation takes justifiable pride in its idea of citizenship and in its elaborate legal apparatus for protecting the individual. When the government becomes the opponent of those rights, organizations such as the American Civil Liberties Union are quick to jump into the battle on the side of the individual.

In the international arena, human rights are more an abstract idea than a historical tradition. As each U.S. president has to discover, other parts of the world do not approach issues of order and unity through the principles of Locke, Jefferson, and Kant. One might be able to get a unanimous vote around the world that everyone has a "right to life." But that phrase would hide many ambiguous cases that concern the beginning and end of life, the necessities of war and revolution, and the threats to public order or national security.

As one tries to expand the notion of a right to life, the ambiguity can only increase. When rights are claimed for particular goods—decent housing, equal job opportunity, affordable medical care, secure boundaries, democratic government—the very idea of inherent rights sags under the burden of all these expectations. No one is likely to campaign against the idea of rights, but that does not prove there is strong support for the defense of rights. A campaign for human rights everywhere, accompanied by intense concentration on a few individuals or a particular government, may still be ineffective. For it could be missing the context in which the language of rights would carry sufficient moral weight. A higher ethic is not necessarily a better morality.

In the United States we seem to have no other currency with which to discuss moral/political issues than the language of rights. Black rights, women's rights, gay rights, old people's rights, animal rights are just a partial list of recent movements demanding justice for one particular group. Each of these groups may be able to make a case for its claim that it has been unjustly treated. Each of these groups (except the animals) should be able to get the government to defend its basic political rights as citizens. But each of these groups is a symptom that the ethic of rights does not get at the deeper power arrangements that need changing. The political struggle for human rights has to be continued. At the same time, we need philosophical/moral/religious reshaping of our whole tradition to provide a secure foundation for political rights. When we talk of political arrangements, "equal rights" may be appropriate language for describing justice. But a philosophical/moral/religious idea of justice has to work with other categories. Part Two of this book proposes such a language.

JOHN RAWLS AND JUSTICE

For illustrating what I have said about an ethic of rights and to expand my criticism of this tradition, it will be helpful to choose a single work. The choice of a book is fairly easy: *A Theory of Justice* is often cited as the outstanding work of the twentieth century within this tradition.[16] John Rawls published *A Theory of Justice* early in the 1970s and since then has continued to polish some details and answer critics. This massive work is an attempt to bring the great theories of the eighteenth and nineteenth centuries up to date.

I make no claim to summarize here the detailed arguments of this book. A question that might be raised, however, is whether the need for such an elaborate argument results from the assumed starting point and the presumed end point of the ethical journey. That is, John Rawls attempts to provide the mechanism for moving from the principle of liberty to the concrete conditions of a just world. I highlight a few of the central characteristics and also note a few intriguing details that are incorporated into the fabric of the argument.

A Theory of Justice is in part a work of fiction that hypothetically places people in what Rawls calls "the original position." This situation before or above history is one in which people have nothing except the power to choose. How would people make choices about the kind of world they want to live in if they were ignorant of their eventual station in that world? Would not an individual wish to have the necessities of life provided for everyone and to have other good things of life open on an equal opportunity basis? For Rawls, a just way of acting is to choose as one would in that original position, choosing in such a way as to move the world toward a human and just community.

The starting point of Rawls's argument reflects the modern rebellion against a human *end* given by God or nature. In the Kantian world everything flows from the autonomous will. Rawls asserts: "The priority of the self over its ends means that I am not merely the passive receptacle of the accumulated aims, attributes and purposes thrown up by experience, not simply a product of the vagaries of circumstance but always, irreducibly an active, willing agent."[17] The last word "agent" is more appropriate in this passage than the word "self" at the beginning. What takes precedence in the argument is not the self as a full-blooded person but agency: an always-active will. The prospect is exciting but also exhausting. Must the person be always playing agent? Must the person be always active to exist at all?

Notice also that the self has "priority" over its ends but is never without them. Rawls's wish is to develop "the full theory of the good," but to get started he uses what he calls a "thin theory," everyone being related to goods for survival.[18] Here Rawls assumes a utilitarianism for the individual. "A person quite properly acts, at least when others are not affected, to achieve his own greatest good. . . . The principle for the individual is to advance as far as possible his own welfare, his own system of desires."[19] The private world of such choices is not central to Rawls's ethics. The ethical concern is the meshing of those private agencies of choice.

The egoistic agents in the original position meet to vote on the just order of things. "All are similarly situated," writes Rawls.[20] They operate from behind a veil of ignorance about the future destiny of themselves. What they will choose is a just situation. In this world, social and economic inequalities are 1) to the greatest benefit of the least advantaged, 2) attached to offices and positions open to all under conditions of fair equality of opportunity.

Michael Sandel notes that since no basis exists here for the plurality of individuals, then these men are not just similar but identical.[21] And when Rawls speaks of "bargaining" among the individuals he does not mean debate, change of position, and compromise. The logic of the policy decision is so overwhelming that once it has been grasped the vote is unanimous. "The veil of ignorance makes possible a unanimous choice of a particular conception of justice. Without these limitations on knowledge, the bargaining position of the original position would be hopelessly complicated."[22] The second sentence is an admission that bargaining among egoistic individuals is an unrealistic way to pursue a just society. But if one denies real plurality, the decision can be made by acclamation. For David Hume in the eighteenth century, we needed justice because we do not love one another; for John Rawls in the twentieth century, we need justice because we do not know one another well enough for love to be a question.

Rawls is particularly opposed to any vision of "society as an organic whole." He does acknowledge that from his "conception, however individualistic it might seem, we must eventually explain the value of community."[23] How does community come into his picture? "Normally we would expect most people to belong to one or more associations and to have at least some collective ends in this sense."[24] Choosing to belong to an association is hardly what the word community means. For many people, community expresses who they are; that is, a person exists in relation to a community, and a community is the name of a group of persons.

An interesting touch in Rawls's argument is that the contracting parties are introduced as fathers of families.[25] The detail is included to assure interest in future generations. With this seemingly minor brush stroke, Rawls implicitly admits that his rational monads, each seeking his own good, is an inadequate basis for an ethical theory. An intrinsic link to the next generation is needed.

A question, by no means trivial, is why are the agents fathers and not mothers. Indeed, the question of sexually exclusive language hovers over the entire discussion of modern ethics. I have been using male pronouns in the previous pages because that is the only way the argument has gone. *A Theory of Justice* is simply a dramatic example of this sexually biased language. I do not think the bias is correctible by sprinkling "he or she" throughout Rawls's text. Indeed, one would do violence to his argument by referring to the contracting parties as "he or she" because that would introduce a real plurality that Rawls wishes to avoid. Sexually exclusive language could be symptomatic of a sexual bias in the starting point, direction, and conclusion of an ethic of rights.

The ethic of rights assumes the meaning of justice as fairness. Everyone should be even at the starting line and should observe the rules of fair play. Then whoever piles up the most victories is entitled to the rewards. The analogy of a race is deceptively simple. Is the starting point my birthday, or the conditions under which I was born, or the situation in which my grandparents lived? What does access to opportunity mean, and how does a government provide it without interfering in someone's liberty? Should the privileged whose grandparents were robber barons have their goods confiscated?

John Rawls avoids these problems by stepping back from history to the original position where all are equal. His project is to construct a theory and then return to the hard edges of the political reality. In elaborating such a theory he has provided the underpinnings to policies of the liberal state that recognizes a need to help the disadvantaged. Those who accept Rawls's theory of justice see Social Security, Aid to Dependent Families, food stamps, and so forth not as acts of benevolence by the government but as demands of justice that everyone should support. Of course, not everyone is convinced by Rawls's argument. In his conservative critique Robert Nozick argues that unless goods are manna from heaven, there is no way to prove that the rich and the talented should give up what they already possess. I take the point of Nozick's attack to be not the details of Rawls's argument but the kind of argument it is: arguing from an unreal world to the existing conditions of living individuals has little persuasive power.[26]

The utilitarian premise of collective happiness needed to be challenged by the deontological insistence upon rights, principles, equality, and fairness. The resulting stream of ethics has run along a very narrow course, confined by the opponent it was battling. "Given a conception of the good that is diminished in this way [by utilitarianism], the priority of right would seem an unexceptional claim indeed. But utilitarianism gave the good a bad name, and in adopting it uncritically, justice as fairness wins for deontology a false victory."[27] If the good is simply a long list of things that individuals wish to acquire, why is fairness so important? There is some suspicion in the later part of the twentieth century that freedom to choose is not worth much if a high quality meaning of good has been lost sight of. Expanding the choice among soap powders or soft drinks does not seem to lead to liberation. Does access to a good life translate into the ability to acquire commodities?

An ethic of rights invites people up a ladder where everything can be viewed impartially. The educational implications of A Theory of Justice are worked out in Kohlberg's stages of moral reasoning. One matures morally by going up the ladder to the top rung where judgments are based on justice and equality: treat each man impartially. Kohlberg's moral dilemmas can generate interesting debates in an ethics course. But isolated from an overall education in morality, they can be a flight from bodiliness, time, and community. An educational morality discovers meaning in the interplay of life's forms rather than in looking for a principle of justice from which to hang all ethical judgments.

In Robert Nozick's criticism cited above, he uses the metaphor of manna from heaven. His usage has a sarcastic edge to it, but the idea may be far more appropriate than he realizes. The choice may be between discovering gifts from the heavens or building a tower toward the heavens. The human vocation may be to give daily thanks for the priceless goods lying on the earth. This discovery is without end for those who are receptive to the good.

The alternative to this discovery is to attempt to conceive of a grand master plan for a fair distribution of goods. Those who climb up above to get a comprehensive look at liberty and equality may inspire some reduction in the scandalously inequitable distribution we now have. What gets lost in that panoramic view, however, is the bodily and temporal contours. The very old and the very young seem to slide off the ends of moral development. The women and the nonhuman animals are seldom spoken of and therefore tend to disappear. Finally, even the men disappear into active, willing agency. What is left is a system of principles, a theory of justice, and a unity without personal differentiation. If religion is not allowed into the discussion from the beginning, it will make its own way in the end in a murky mystical oneness. Modern ethics in having an ideal end state may sacrifice flesh and blood to the cruel, impersonal god of liberty and equality for all.

Part 2

A MORALITY BOTH OLD AND NEW

CHAPTER 4

A Morality of Goodness

In this chapter and the three that follow, I set out the language of morality and the main lines of a moral system that does not exclude religious influence. The ethic of the good and the ethic of rights are not replaced in this chapter but rather are placed into a larger context. Ethics is a reasonable science, and no one wishes to abandon reason for irrationality. But reason in modern times walks a narrow course from premise to conclusion. The starting place of reason is in a domain that reason does not establish or prove. I am trying to evoke in this first chapter of Part Two the recognition of the goodness which is the ground of reason.

The word "good" has been used repeatedly in the previous two chapters. The utilitarian mind sees little mystery in this term. The good is what all of us desire or, otherwise stated, the good is what would make us happy. The real problem is thought to be devising the effective means to get there. The ethic of rights incorporates much of this meaning of good. It assumes that all of us want certain basic goods: food, shelter, clothing, and so forth. Beyond these necessities, no one knows what would make a particular person happy but one ought to have a right to one's choice in searching for the good life.

The question that is not raised in modern ethics is what makes good things to be good. When the good is defined as the desirable, there is usually just a circle of reasoning. The desirable is good, and the good is desirable. But what is it that grounds the process of human desire for goods? What is the nature of goodness, the quality that good things share? In this chapter I touch on some of the esoteric history of Western thought to bring out the meaning of goodness. Beyond the ethical meaning of good there is a philosophical/religious/aesthetic meaning of goodness that is the basis of a moral life.

While I cite some history, my ultimate appeal is to the experience of ordinary people today. This meaning of goodness is not so abstract as to be obscure to ordinary people. On the contrary, this meaning is almost too simple and too concrete for words. It is not one object among many but the background of all objects and the connecting fabric of all relations. In certain joyful or tragic moments of life this meaning of goodness becomes evident. We think we have things figured out, and then we suddenly recognize something mysterious in the midst of ordinary life.

Consider, for example, what modern ethics calls "altruism." Ethics has no explanation for the fact that some people seem to be intent on willing the good of *other* people. Attempts at explanation generally reduce to these two: 1) it is an illusion because people are actually willing their own good even when they seem to be altruistic; 2) it is a sickness in which people no longer know what is good for themselves. In many cases, what is called altruistic does indeed turn out to be illusion or sickness. But the human race knows that there are other cases where moral heroes, knowing full well what they were doing, have sacrificed themselves for others. And we need not be restricted to a few famous heroes. People regularly go out of their way to help other people and to perform acts that are not egoistic choices.

Durkheim's *Moral Education,* despite its intent to be "rationalistic," still has traces of the recognition that a foundation for morality that is outside reason remains necessary. Durkheim believed that we need "men of substantial intellect and strong will," but he also recognized the place of those who "love to attach and devote themselves to others. These are the loving hearts, the ardent and generous souls."[1] This latter group is what religion used to supply in the past. The passion of religion was a kind of fuel for reason and will. Durkheim proposes that "society" must now take over what divinity used to inspire. Without some sentiment deeper than reason, the bonds of humanity will fly apart.

Perhaps modern ethics has badly stated its dichotomies. Is the choice between intellect and passion, as in Durkheim's formulation? Or is there a meaning of intellect that includes passion, a meaning of intellect that is the foundation of instrumental reason? Is the word "altruism" a red herring, a contrived category invented by thinkers who assume that selfishness is the only normal way to act? Is it possible that the ordinary way to act is to respond to being and its goodness in a way that is neither selfish nor altruistic because we all participate in being and goodness?

The ethic of the good and the ethic of rights both need a ground to stand on, some intimation of a unity that the utilitarian has to assume in the word "happiness" and that the deontologist has to assume in defending the rights of every person. Ethicists of the eighteenth century were aware of the need for this nonrational basis of ethics. David Hume, for example, writes: "It is requisite that there be an original propensity of some kind, in order to be a basis to self-love, by giving a relish to the objects of its pursuits, and none more fit for this purpose than benevolence or humanity."[2] In the twentieth century many ethicists seem to think that this benevolence is unnecessary or is of tangential importance. In Kohlberg's moral development scheme, words such as "love" and "benevolence" are at the lower stages. Benevolence may not rank very high in ethical systems, but I wish to claim that it is central to the morality of everyday life.

The material in this chapter may seem diversionary. A discussion of mysticism seldom shows up in modern ethics. And religion, I have said, is usually excluded in principle. The good is left to fend for itself or has only reason to defend it against all that is outside reason. To enrich a discussion of goods and rights we need to tap into the vein of philosophical/religious history that turns upside down the meaning of the good.

This search for the meaning of goodness involves journeying into frightening lands where the notion of "my own good" is not just slightly modified. Religious traditions in conjunction with certain philosophical and aesthetic experiences challenge the possessive adjective "my." What is called into question is the very existence of the "I" who thinks, wills, feels, and searches. Modern ethics starts from the question of what is right to choose. A more basic question is, Who is the one choosing? More radically put than the faddish issue of self-discovery, the question is, "Is there a self to be discovered?"

When one gets at the more mystical side of religion, the similarities between Jewish, Christian and Muslim, Eastern and Western, are striking. Each religious group has some startling language for its members. To an outsider the language seems at times arrogant, at other times nihilistic. Each of the traditions challenges the human sense of order and meaning, particularly in relation to issues that human beings generally wish to avoid, such as suffering and death. Religion often seems to undermine efforts to improve the world because it constantly reminds us that the future is not ours to decide. It insists that everything, including one's own life, goes beyond the individual's control.

Zen meditation, Jewish Sabbath, Protestant faith, and Catholic sacraments, despite their many differences, have something in common. They let go of the ordinary cause-and-effect pattern by which strenuous effort will supposedly bring us to our desired end. Beyond good and evil, as we ethically conceive those terms, there is some unimaginable harmony. We cannot see it or grab hold of it, but it is available within an appropriately disciplined experience. "One does not get to the end of the world by travelling," says the Buddha. What we have to do is to stop imagining that life consists in travelling to "my own good." If we could do that, if we could recognize that the end is always with us, we would discover that the good surrounds us, is within us, and is beneath our feet.

This discovery or revelation of a power beyond the self and beyond

things has its frightening side. Entrance into this presence means passing into the realm of no-thing. The ground of things cannot itself be
a thing. When people are overwhelmed by this experience, we often
say in comforting tones "There's nothing to be afraid of," not realizing
that this is precisely what bothers them. Probably everyone at some time
has the experience of transcending the set of objects that usually appears as the solidly real. At crucial moments of artistic insight, genuine
love, or the approach of death, the world of solid objects seems to
dissolve. Someone may say then that we are out of touch with reality,
but we have the sense of touching something important, even though
it is not a thing.

Once this all/nothing has been encountered "it" does not entirely
disappear. It eats away at plans for the future, and it demands some
response in the present if we are to continue daily life. Religious rituals
are one response, the freezing of mystical experience into manageable
human actions. Works of art are another form of response to a greater
unity and presence than is conveyed by ordinary reason and discursive
speech. Genuine religious experience and great art *are* morality, not in
what they prescribe or in the messages they deliver, but in simply being
themselves, in being responses to a deeper level of being. Before considering these relations in ordinary experience today, I think it is helpful to consider the mystical strand in history through a few represen-
tative thinkers.

PLATO AND PLOTINUS

A. N. Whitehead made the famous statement that all of Western
philosophy consists of footnotes to Plato. Although that statement may
be true, there are at least two Platos. There is the Aristotelian Plato
whose ideas were brought down from heaven to earth, and there is the
Neoplatonic Plato whose impulse toward unity transcends the world of
ideas or forms. Plato's suggestions in the *Symposium, Republic,* and *Timaeus* that there is a reality beyond the realm of ideas had a delayed
effect upon the history of the West. When that underground stream
of philosophy joined the influence of Jewish and Christian religions it
provided much of the philosophical basis of Western culture until the
eighteenth century.

The Aristotelian Plato is the one better known to most people. Aristotle was a physicist and biologist whose philosophy centered on physical change and on how to explain the conditions that make change
possible. Change, according to Aristotle, requires a permanent sub-
stratum and a form that passes from real possibility to actuality. Like
Plato's, and with even more emphasis, Aristotelian form is a visual metaphor. Aristotle the biologist and physicist is rooted in the world of
physical things and of change toward a final state that has already been
imagined.[3]

As Aristotle's *Physics* exercised great influence over the rise of the physical sciences, so his *Ethics* set much of the direction for the discussion of ethics as late as the eighteenth century. Aristotle's ethics provided a framework for the development of a reasonable code of conduct. The Middle Ages made wholesale borrowings from Aristotle's scheme of moral virtues, a realistic system based on moderation. Unlike the modern penchant for reasoning about dilemmas, Aristotle's ethics was more broadly educational. Its main concern was the communities that are needed to rear moral persons; we become moral by living among moral people.

The problem with Aristotle's approach is not that he was a metaphysical dreamer or that his principles are vacuous in meaning. Nor was Aristotle a rigid ideologue, as were some of his later disciples. Aristotle's ethics is so realistic and practical that although particular concepts may be outdated, there remains much that is of value. But my concern is that the very realism of Aristotle's ethics can obscure the need for a searching inquiry into the foundation of ethics. That inquiry takes us outside of ethics into another strand of intellectual history, but one that Plato also influenced.

The "other Plato" is the one who comes down to us through Plotinus and the tradition called Neoplatonic. This other way of reading Plato turns upside down the Aristotelian world of drawing forms out of matter. For Plato, change and plurality within a class of things implies a fixed form that gives unity to the class. But if many dogs presuppose a unity of form (dogness) and many chairs presuppose one chairness, why leave the ideas themselves multiple? Do not many forms presuppose formness? Because matter is the principle of division and multiplicity, and because Platonic forms are separate from matter, Plato has no basis for keeping the idea of dog and the idea of chair separate. At the end of Book Six of *The Republic*, the Supreme Idea, the Idea of Ideas, arises. Because it is beyond form it is not a being; Plato suggests that it be called Beauty or Goodness. "The good may be said to be not only the author of knowledge to all things known, but of their being and essence, and yet the good is not an essence."[4]

Whether or not Plato is clearly conscious of it, he makes a crucial turn here. From describing the good as that which we desire, he shifts to the good as the author of being. Goodness is that in which all good things participate; goodness or the good is the author of being. This shift is solidified in one of the best-known passages of Western philosophy, the allegory of the cave in Book Seven of *The Republic*. The main image of that allegory is striking: prisoners in a cave who see only reflections on the wall. The prisoners take the shadows for the reality. And if one of the prisoners were freed to go outside the cave he would find it impossible to explain to his fellow prisoners that real people are walking around outside the cave. The prisoners will continue to call real what we outside the allegory know is a mere reflection of what is "really real."

In reading this story we may miss a crucial fact: the people outside the cave are not the cause of the shadows on the wall. The people give particular shapes to the shadows, but it is the light that makes the shadows possible at all. The sun "is the guardian of all that is the visible world, and in a certain way the cause of all things."[5] Plato does not stop with the sun as the ultimate reality; the sun represents the good that can be known but cannot be seen with the eye of the body. "In the world of knowledge the idea of good appears last of all . . . and, when seen, is also inferred to be the universal author of all things beautiful and right, parent of light and of the lord of light in the visible world, and the immediate source of reason and truth in the intellectual."[6]

Plato's question goes beyond the physical into the metaphysical or religious. He raises the question "why," not in regard to one thing or another, but why in regard to anything. Why is there something rather than nothing? Or why is there something coming from no-thing? Plato's answer to that question is best given in the *Timaeus:* "He who constructed the universe . . . was good, and in one that is good no envy of anything else ever arises. Being devoid of envy, then, he desired that everything should be as possible like himself."[7] Goodness overflows itself, creating similarity and partnership.

Plato's answer is strikingly similar to the one that Pinchas Lapide attributes to the rabbinic sages: "Why did God create the world? . . . God created it out of love. Why out of love? Because love is the only thing which has need of a partner, and therefore God created humankind in God's image."[8] Of course, Greek philosophy and Jewish religion were not the same thing. But I think Lapide does not accurately pinpoint the difference when he writes, "We know of no 'God in Self.' An 'aseism' is unknown to us."[9] That characteristic may differentiate Judaism from Aristotle's God who is self-thinking thought, but it does not sharply contrast with "God the fashioner" in the *Timaeus.*

The difference from the point of view of pagan philosophers was law and order. For them, God was "the leader of nature, governing all things by law."[10] The pagans saw the God of Judaism and Christianity as a capricious and unbridled deity. Pagan philosophers were particularly fond of the picture of God fashioning an ordered universe. They read the *Timaeus* without asking about "to be or not to be." This question upsets the order that depends on the visual imagery of forms. The mystical experience, which arises in the early centuries of the Common Era, challenges the Greek sense of order.

The philosopher who made the link between Plato and a mystical/ religious experience is Plotinus. He pushes the Platonic intimations to their limit and is also a meeting point of Eastern and Western religions.

In Plotinus, the One or Good beyond being is the actual source of beings. Everything emanates from this One as from "a spring that never runs dry." Plotinus cites Plato as the master, although he selects his quotations from only the metaphysical dialogues of Plato's middle period: *Republic, Symposium, Timaeus,* and *Phaedrus.* Ultimately, Plotinus disagrees with Greek philosophy's idea or form, the basis of orderly movement toward a desired end. Although Plotinus may seem to assume a movement in the direction of seeing the desired good, he pulls the rug from under sight, reason, and object: "To see and to have seen that vision is vision no longer. It is more than reason, before reason, and after reason, as also is the vision which is seen. And perhaps we should not speak here of *sight:* for that which is seen . . . is not discerned by the seer, nor perceived by him as a second thing."[11]

Plotinus is often understood to be describing an ascent out of matter to a highest level of abstraction. The phrase he is best known for is "the flight of the alone to the alone." Although he does use the image of up and down, the key metaphors concern circling about a center. "Each of our souls has a center. When we are concentrated upon this center, we are fully ourselves and 'in the Supreme.' . . . Through the center of our soul we contact this center of centers."[12] One of his favorite images to convey this circling about a center is a chorus singing a hymn. "We look upon the source of life and sing a choral hymn that is full of God. . . . Sometimes one voice is heard while the others are silent; and each brings to the chorus something of his own."[13] Notice that it is not just the circles of singers but the "choral hymn that is full of God."

One cannot transcend images simply by positing another image; a circle is just as much a visual image as is a straight line. But Plotinus manages to transcend visual imagery by using a metaphor of singing. Hearing becomes a way of encountering the divine.

Tactile metaphors are also abundant in Plotinus. The soul "surrenders" or "abandons itself;" it is "enraptured" or "possessed." The soul is filled with God. The best visual image Plotinus can find for the soul's relation to God is two concentric circles whose centers coincide.[14]

Classical philosophy and ancient religion were troubled by images of an evil god reigning over a preexistent darkness called matter. In such dualistic systems the good is what transcends matter. If present human experience is one of bodily existence, then our best recourse is to flee the body as quickly as possible or as much as possible. The good life turns out to be an inhuman life, or more precisely, the good seems to eliminate humans, life, and world itself. "The ascent of the ladder of created things is, after all, only another name for a progressive *contemptus mundi.*"[15]

Plotinus, as I have noted, is often identified with this ladder of created things that ascends to the heaven above matter. Ironically, Plotinus is the one who succeeded in avoiding the trap; at least he did so better than many of his accusers. The emanation of being, mind, and world soul can be imagined as a movement of flowing out and flowing down. The overflowing of life is the very meaning of good. But there is no corresponding motion in the opposite direction; God does not throw down a ladder that human beings climb one rung at a time. The metaphor is one of overflowing goodness that, as participated in by the creature, puts the creature in immediate contact with the spring that never runs dry. On this point, Plotinus agrees with rabbinic writing: "From earth to heaven is a five hundred years' journey; yet when a man whispers or even meditates a prayer, God is at hand to hear it."[16]

The strange thing about Plotinus's solution to the darkness of matter is that at first sight he seems to worsen the problem. For Plotinus, as John Rist notes, matter is "wholly negative."[17] Those philosophers who have tried to lessen the influence of matter or make it into a hazy darkness have not found a positive basis for creaturely life. The creature is still thought of as "contaminated" by matter. In Plotinus's bold solution, matter does not exist at all as a being or a substrate. Matter is the limit in the being of material things. Instead of being a verbal trick, this solution is a recasting of classical thought in a framework different from the fashioning of forms in eternal matter.

This solution requires us to let go of the visual metaphors in which shape is drawn from *materia:* stone, plastic, clay, or any stuff at all. Classical thinkers could not imagine things dependent for their existence on an act creative of being. When any of us try to grasp in visual form the creation of something, we start from a preexisting something. But the metaphysical question is to be and not to be. When the act of to be can be entertained and experienced, then the good is not an object to be looked at and acquired. Goodness is in the act of overflowing, welling up at the center of ourselves, of every living thing, and of the cosmos. Although matter does not exist, every material thing is unique, good, and worthy of respect. Everything is good because everything participates in being and shares being with others. For the full flowering of this philosophical/religious attitude, we turn to two great representatives of the Christian Middle Ages: Thomas Aquinas and Meister Eckhart.

AQUINAS AND ECKHART

The Dominican preacher Eckhart, whom history knows as The Master, has often been viewed as a misplaced Buddhist sitting in splendid isolation in the fourteenth-century Rhineland. Twentieth-century scholarship has to some extent rectified that picture and situated him in the stream of Western philosophical history that runs from Plato to Heidegger, though more exploration of the biblical basis of his thought is still needed.[18] And his close relation to Thomas Aquinas comes as a surprise to people who have stereotypes of metaphysics and mysticism. Nevertheless, both of these thinkers in distinctive ways carry through the insight found in the Neoplatonic tradition.

The Neoplatonism in Thomas Aquinas had largely been obscured until the Thomist revival of the twentieth century. It had been possible to read Aquinas simply as an Aristotelian. Aquinas did absorb into his philosophy-theology the Aristotelian language of moral virtues and physical causality. Thus, one can read the first part of the *Summa Theologica* as a description of a supreme being who is the efficient and final cause of the universe. However, in the prologue of the *Summa*, Aquinas writes, "Because we cannot know what God is, but rather what God is not, our method has to be mainly negative. . . . What kind of being God is not can be known by eliminating characteristics which cannot apply to him."[19] The assumption that someone is building a rational system up to an explanation of God does not stand up well when that person says he is setting out "to investigate the ways in which God does not exist."

The exterior elements in Aquinas have an Aristotelian look, but the overall framework comes from biblical and Neoplatonic ideas. What governs the movement from God is the axiom "The good is what is diffusive of itself." Aquinas saw both the biblical account of creation and Plotinus's emanation from the One as manifestations of the principle that goodness overflows itself. For Aquinas the problem was to preserve God's freedom to create, which seems to be denied in Plotinus's emanation. The problem is solved for Aquinas by the Christian doctrine of the Trinity, in which goodness overflows within God's life itself. The created world is not an entirely separate object but rather a participant in the act of "to be." In the movement that goes out from God and back to God, humans do not climb the ladder of good things up to God. The human being is the "shepherd of being," the center of creation. Human goodness is a participating in God's overflowing goodness.[20]

One of the great ironies in Western history is that this philosophic stream was accepted into Christianity through the channel of an anonymous Syrian monk who was mistakenly thought to be an associate of St. Paul. The authority attached to this person, Pseudo-Dionysius, made possible the adoption of Plotinus's insights. Dionysius combined the incarnational theme of the New Testament with the goodness beyond being in Plotinus's philosophy. The reason for creation, Dionysius says, is that God "had been cozened by goodness and affection and love, and led down from his eminence above all and surpassing all, to being in all."[21] Thus there is "plentitude of being." Once there is creation, goodness requires a variety of creatures or a hierarchy of beings. In Aquinas's view, "God has instituted each and every single nature in order that it not lose its own uniqueness."[22] And for the human being, the specific way of imitating divine goodness is the act of understanding.

For Aquinas, understanding is the birth of word, or perhaps better, the birth of speech. Besides word (*verbum*) Aquinas uses a visual metaphor (*species*) in reference to understanding. However, understanding is *through* these species, not *of* them.[23] We also need sensible pictures (*phantasmata*) through which and in which understanding occurs, but understanding is of the real, not pictures of the real. Conceptual and sensible pictures arise in the course of making judgments of what is and is not. For Aquinas, the act of understanding is simply an overflowing of life. When matter does not limit spirit and spirit is not outside itself in space and time, then spirit is present to itself. Presence to self of a spiritual being is intellect.

The "will" in this system is not a faculty separate from intellect; the will is the inclination that naturally follows upon understanding. The human will is neither the origin of what is good nor the direct cause of any good effects.[24] Morality is not centered in choices of the will so much as in the letting be of being that flows from goodness. The process of understanding/love is in one sense not an activity—that is, is not the accomplishing of change in the world of objects. Nonetheless, in a deeper sense of activity, understanding/love is the most genuine act of the human being.

Meister Eckhart takes Aquinas's description of understanding/will and pushes it to the limit. Intellection in Aquinas is still tied to the language of reading, seeing, and intuition. God is implicitly "seen" in everything we know.[25] Eckhart does not deny this position, but he introduces a language of "divine abyss" and "nothingness." Neither God nor intellect is a thing: therefore it is proper, even if shocking to some ears, to speak of God or intellect as no-thing. Eckhart wishes to shake up rationalistic philosophy's metaphor of onlooker. He wishes to get to the "naked unity of the soul" that, rather than looking at God, yields to God's embrace. Eckhart wants to lay aside the "thought of God" so as to make room for a "godlike God" or "the Godhead."

When Meister Eckhart got into trouble with church officials it was not his Latin treatises on theology that were the problem but his sermons preached in the vernacular German. Preaching, with its aural/oral nature, is consistent with the attempt to transcend visual imagery. "Again and again 'God' must be spoken of in order that the realm of the silent experience of the 'Godhead' be able to open. The experience of the 'Godhead' is not possible if 'God' cannot first become and unbecome in the speech of man. . . . Godhead emerges in its unity as the limit of what can be said."[26]

These sermons of Eckhart were, according to the charges of the Inquisition, "confusing the unlearned." No doubt there is some truth in that accusation, but it does not explain why people flocked to hear him. "Unlearned people" were stirred by what Eckhart's learned opponents saw as esoteric and confusing doctrine. Eckhart was not engaged in building an abstract, theological system. His metaphors, far from being flights into high abstraction, are rooted in daily experience. Like most mysticism, Eckhart's preaching is attentive to the concreteness of things. "Philosophical language proposes to speak of reality without touching it; mystical language seeks to divine reality as if by touching without seeing."[27]

Eckhart's governing metaphor is pregnancy and birth. That process has visual aspects, but it is not an object that can be seen and possessed. The language of pregnancy, which Eckhart probably took over from the mystic Mechtilde, is as intimately physical as language can be.[28] Thomas Aquinas uses this language to link speculation about the inner life of God with the working of the human intellect. Eckhart brings this language into direct experience. "What help is it to me that the Father gives birth to his Son unless I too give birth to him?" With a slight shift in his metaphor, he encourages each of his hearers to become the Virgin Mary, giving birth to God in their souls.[29]

Eckhart's use of earthy metaphors is a paradox, considering that for him, as for Plotinus and Aquinas, matter does not exist. Creatures can be called nothing in that they possess no being of their own. Instead of matter's being kept in its place as a dark shadow to the spiritual world, Eckhart sees matter as a sign of the radical finitude of all creatures. "I do not say that they are either important or unimportant but they are pure nothing."[30] Not surprisingly, this statement was one of the propositions condemned by the Inquisition. Indeed, if one considers Eckhart's statements in isolation from one another, a case could be made not only for his lack of orthodoxy but for his lack of sanity.

Eckhart's sermons can be understood as sane if they are taken to be a scheme of moral-religious development. In mystical literature there is a journey, often described in an odd number of stages: three, five, seven, nine. The reason for the odd number is that the stages are a dialectic of positive and negative moves together with a final stage pointing to a unity beyond dialectic. At a first stage, a person possesses objects, uses goods, acts for self-improvement. At a last stage (third, fifth, seventh, ninth) the person may seem very similar in possessing, using, acting, but now the possessing is lightly, the use is with gratitude, the acting is for justice's sake. Between the first and the final stages are several cycles in which the person is weaned from an attitude of possessiveness and self-centeredness.

At the beginning of the mystical journey one is invited to lead an ethically good life. This stage requires letting go of evil attachment to destructive forces. This step is relatively easy, and most people can accomplish it. There is widespread support from the world at large for the movement. The person thus reaches a plateau of moral living in which he or she follows a reasonable code of conduct. The ethical-minded person is praised as an upstanding citizen and held up as a model for others to imitate.

The step beyond the ethical is more difficult because it challenges the limits of reasonableness. The author of the *Cloud of Unknowing* tells the reader to "forsake as well good as evil thoughts."[31] One has to be "detached" from the good things of life, an attitude looked upon skeptically by the practical-minded ethicist. Nevertheless, once this stage has been reached there is likely to be a grudging admission that it is all right for some people. Many people can appreciate that ascetic detachment from everything can issue in a beautiful and fruitful life. The person is now ready to see everything as an embodiment of God's presence.

Just when it seems that the journey is complete and that the final joyful unity has been reached, the great test comes. Beyond the luminous presence of God is the dark abyss of Godhead. Beyond the attitude of letting go of everything is the letting go of letting go. The "letting be" at the center of the soul finally occurs when all human effort ceases, even the effort to act effortlessly. Activists may scoff at what seems to be passivity and defeatism. Nonetheless, most people do catch a glimpse of "letting be" at moments when it is apparent that human efforts are futile. Such a moment can border on total despair, but it can also give birth to a new kind of hope that rests on more than human choice.

The crack of ultimate truth closes quickly, because that truth is not a shaft of light but impenetrable darkness. Rufus Jones thinks that Eckhart's "theory of the abstract infinite . . . lands him in the deepest, darkest agnosticism and nescience." Jones is correct on one point regarding Eckhart's teaching: "We arrive nowhere."[32] The final good, according to Eckhart, is the unknowability of the hidden divinity: "When the soul crosses over she sinks down and down in the abyss of Godhead nor ever finds a footing." Jones is wrong in calling this an "abstract infinite." What we have instead is a communion that goes beyond a unity of things. In the bottomless abyss of Godhead is the original unity of all and nothing.

This experience of communion—all in all—implies a passionate quest for a justice that restores unity. The relation between mysticism and revolution is not the unfathomable puzzle it may at first seem to be. Revolutions come from people whose passion for life is not attached to things of the present moment. A contemporary Marxist, commenting on Eckhart, writes: "A subject who thought himself in personal union with the Lord of Lords provided, when things got serious, a very poor example indeed of serfhood."[33]

Efforts to reform or revolutionize human conditions are always prone to violence. The mark of true mysticism is that it gradually reduces violence through a discipline of removing the deep causes of violence. The test of the mystic's commitment to the good that overflows from goodness is whether he or she resists violent actions and works to remove those conditions that breed violence. Seeking justice is inseparable from having compassion for every living thing. "What is spoken of here is to meet with gentleness, in true humility and selflessness, everything which comes your way."[34]

IMPLICATIONS FOR MORALITY

What is the connection between this mystical language and the problems of everyday morality? Is this language of Eckhart and other mystics irrelevant to the lives of most people? My contention is that the morality of mature people, an educational morality, must include an element of the mystical. Few people deserve the name mystic, but everyone eventually encounters the kind of experience that Eckhart and other mystics explore with dazzling language. Movement beyond an ethic of good and an ethic of rights requires a conversionary movement when we let go of every possession, even the possession of goods and rights. But we had better not try letting go prematurely lest our supposed progress turn out to be a mental sickness or a fraudulent mysticism.

Despite the dangers of misunderstanding this mystical element, the meaning of the good that is embedded in this tradition needs to be recognized. It is a meaning of good that has only the faintest echo on both sides of ethical disputes today. And yet, this meaning of good is not unknown in the most ordinary experiences of life. Despite the protests of some schools of thought, people still speak of "a good person" or "a person of good character." They usually do not mean that such a person wills his or her own good. Rather, people sense a flow of life out from that person and see no constriction or diminishment on the part of the person who gives, serves, loves, and shares. There is immediate experiential data for the medieval maxim: All that is good is diffusive of itself.

This meaning of the good is implicit at the beginning of life's journey; that is, the child is a natural mystic. But the full flowering of the good that is consciously received as gift and freely willed so as to overflow into other lives usually takes the better part of a lifetime. The mysticism of the child may seem to have no effect upon morality; indeed, the young child seems egocentric and selfish. It takes four or five years for a child to grasp that there are other centers of personal autonomy. The very young child does not plan strategies to get to the good things in life. The intellect and will are mainly concerned with recognizing what is and responding to what is given. Reality unveils itself, each thing being a wonder that has a name even if all the distinctions are not clear between fact and fiction, living and nonliving, human and nonhuman. For the young child, what is, is. In the Zen formula: The mountains are mountains, the rivers are rivers, the trees are trees.

What may seem like mere tautology is in fact the basis of rights language. Each thing deserves to be treated as a unique being with its distinct characteristics. Each thing has a dignity and deserves respect because it exists. A humanly made object has less autonomy than a tree, a dog, or a person. What the humans make, humans can use: a chair, an aspirin, a TV set. But even within humanly made objects there are gradations. A Vermeer painting deserves more respect than subway graffiti; a crafted Shaker chair from the nineteenth century has more right to exist than much of today's thrown-together furniture.

The religious traditions of the West had much to do with establishing the sacredness of the individual and the inviolability of "his" rights. Immanuel Kant, as noted in the previous chapter, was a major bridge from Christian piety to modern ethics in recognizing the individual as end. Only lately has concern been expressed that Kantian ethics turns the nonhuman world into mere means for human autonomy. The animal-rights movement is trying to extend the idea of rights to include nonhuman animals, but this agenda is too narrow. Rights language needs grounding in the recognition that *everything* participates in being, goodness, dignity, and autonomy. The Jewish and Christian traditions had the right principle from the start, but they failed to develop sufficiently the moral place of the nonhuman creature. As a result, the "man" at the center of modern ethics is the isolated, aggressive male individual rather than men, women, and children living in communal relations.

The recent period of modern ethics thus correlates with the intermediary stage of personal life. That is, the older child and the younger adult tend to be *ethical agents*. Things are put at the service of the reasoning, willing, and active individual. To adapt the Zen formula: The mountains are not mountains (they are obstacles to highway development); the rivers are not rivers (they are sources of electrical power); the trees are not trees (they are wood pulp for the printing press). The good or rather goods are not revealed to us; instead they are made, acquired, possessed, consumed.

When we have an ethical attitude we gauge each action carefully, totaling up benefits and drawbacks. As we sacrifice any bit of self-interest we take pride in our good deeds. We feel that someone should praise us or reward us because we are better than certain other people who are selfish. We also feel confident that if everyone followed our example and acted within the rules of good conduct, this world could be made a good place to live in. Probably most of us spend most of our lives in this attitude of trying to choose the good instead of the bad and trying not to interfere in the choices of other individuals.

The stage beyond the ethical stance is in some ways a rediscovery of the childlike attitude. Once again the Zen formula is true: The mountains are mountains, the rivers are rivers, the trees are trees. If such a stage of peacefulness and unity does not arrive before we are confronted by death, the act of dying usually illuminates the limitations of goods and rights. We carry out of life what we carried in: no possessions at all. But one of the last demands of the dying is for "dignity"— that is, to be recognized as a unique, existent individual. Dying teaches us the severe limitations of ethical concepts, but at the same time it teaches that rights language does have a meaning to the last breath of life. I return to the issue of caring for the dying as one of my extended examples in Chapter 8.

Recognition of a morality of goodness often comes much earlier than death. For some people, the first grave illness is the occasion; for some, retirement from a job shifts their perception of the good; for many, falling in love, getting married, and giving birth to children are the manifestations of goodness as the overflowing of itself. The will becomes more integral to the movement of the body so that one is not always struggling to stay on a diet, to repress one's anger, to pretend interest when bored, to obey civil laws, and to make hundreds of other choices that we know are good things to do. Such choices come with more ease and more joy even as one is acutely aware of the suffering and the evil in the world. To be morally adult is to know that the world does not divide into good and bad things, right and wrong choices. Every choice we make is contaminated by side effects that we cannot escape. If we let the choice flow from the center of our receptiveness to being and in resonance with fellow travelers on earth, our actions will have a gentleness that lessens the violence in the world.

In not being attached to the merits of our good deeds we are also not overwhelmed by guilt at our failures. In the mystical teaching of both East and West, we are to do the best we can but never for the purpose of a reward. Religious traditions are remarkably unified on this point, although it is a paradox that has often been misunderstood. Good actions flow from the person who has stopped trying to be good and has instead discovered a deeper meaning of will and a different source of energy than choosing through clenched teeth. Those who are looking for earthly or heavenly rewards are distracted from appreciating the things themselves. Thus, John of the Cross states a typical sentiment of mystical tradition: "You should do your good actions in such a way that, if it were possible, God himself would not know you were doing them."

Mystics are accused of fleeing the world and not facing reality. But the accusers are often in the business of storing up goods to protect themselves from suffering and death. The truth is that the mystic not only "faces reality" but embraces it, or rather, is embraced by it. What is fled from is the trivializing attitude of grasping at goods that the human being cannot carry beyond death, or demanding rights to the exclusion of all other creatures. The moral and mystical journey is not to ideal and spiritual forms above the world but to the deepest, darkest center of the material cosmos where goodness bubbles up in gentle, just, and caring attitudes.

In such experiences of goodness there is some resonance across religious lines and also across the modern boundary between religion and secular life. Contemporary scholars need to listen to religious traditions, even though learning from religion requires patience. Religious symbols are not easily translatable into other languages. One must participate *to some degree* in the language of religion for religion's meaning to become manifest. One need not join the religious group, but one needs to be sympathetic and receptive while also having analagous discipline and experiences in one's own life.

What, for example, does the Sabbath in Judaism mean? Jewish religion says that in six days God created everything and each day pronounced "it is good." But on the seventh day he created the Sabbath, and that is holy. Beyond the good that men and women rightly seek is a whole other realm. One reaches it, paradoxically, by doing nothing, by taking rest from one's labors. In the Deuteronomic tradition of the Hebrew Bible, Sabbath is also a symbol of the struggle for justice. If there is to be true rest, the laborers, the animals, and the land itself must be allowed to rest. A new social order with a better distribution of wealth is required for Sabbath experience. And paradise can therefore be described as Sabbath without end.

Can contemporary men and women make any sense out of this complex Sabbath symbol? They may not be able to do so unless they have some Sabbath experience in their own lives. But if they do have sufficient peace at the center of their lives, the trans-ethical meaning of good, the goodness revealed in every good thing, becomes obvious.

From the opposite direction, defenders of religion have to work at an educational pattern that would test religious traditions in relation to today's experience. For some religionists, words such as "experience" and "education" are red flags. These people believe that submitting the pure word of God to education and experience corrupts the one true way. The potential dangers for religion should be acknowledged, but education need not be reduced to schooling, where religion does not fare particularly well. Nor should experience be reduced to experimental science, which has a limited taste for religion.

Religion should have its appropriate place in both schooling and non-schooling aspects of education. Indeed, religion helps to keep that distinction alive, reminding us of the part that family, work, and leisure play in education. Religion can neither dictate answers before the journey begins nor submit to preestablished criteria of modern sciences. We need a language of educational categories that can mediate between religion and the secular ethics that dominates the school world. In the following chapters I consider some language that might be adequate to today's moral questions while also being open to the wisdom embodied in religious ritual and doctrine.

CHAPTER 5

Responsible Morality

Uncovering the mystical strand in history shifts the discussion of morality to different ground. The mystical experience can create acts of heroism, self- sacrifice and devotion to causes. People who advocate the mystical/religious life can rightly point to the dramatic effects of this impulse in history, for mysticism has often been the source of powerful and fearless struggles against injustice. But even as we praise mystical experience, we might still be wary of people who call themselves mystics. It is one thing to catch a glimpse of the underlying oneness of the universe; it is another thing for an individual to announce that his or her life is permanently esconced beyond the plurality and ambiguity of the human situation. Most of us live most of the time in the intermediary stage of both receiving the good and struggling after good things.

A life based exclusively on giving can have its own illusions and arrogance. Jesus said that "it is better to give than to receive." He could have added "but it is better to receive than not to receive." Precisely for the sake of giving by others, it is important to receive. In mutual exchanges, every giving is receiving and every receiving is a form of giving. In the previous chapter I emphasized the "givingness" of being and goodness. But the overflow of life requires that there be a recipient. Human beings are capable of both receiving and giving in mutual relations. That is, the impulse of love and care is set in a context of reciprocal activity. Education has to look to creating such exchanges of power. The agents in the exchange need not be equal in all respects, but without some balance and proportionality in the exchange, any intended mutuality is overwhelmed by the actual flow of power.

Religions in general, and Christianity in particular, often encourage a selfless devotion to God and neighbor. But the *agape* of outpouring energy always seems to run downhill: "Love your neighbor" turns into the *eros* of teleology or the right of deontology; the dazzling moral imperatives of the New Testament become the church laws of the fourth century; the fire of Luther's *sola gratia* passes into Lutheran scholasticism. To fight against the decline from first fervor, institutions create esoteric and exoteric levels of membership. The great religious power is saved by separating it from the masses. In Christianity, for example, the "evangelical counsels" went into the monastery while ordinary Christians were left to follow a prosaic ethical code of basic duties.

When preachers and moralists tell their listeners to love their neighbors, many people try to follow this commandment by making the neighbor the object of patronage and pity. Carol Houselander describes a woman as "one of those people who live for others, and you can always tell the others by the hunted look on their faces." The act of giving can turn perverse when power goes only in one direction. Vincent de Paul told his disciples to comport themselves so that "the poor will forgive you the bread you give them." That is not an extreme expression of an overly humble saint but an essential reminder for anyone who tries to do good for others.

The word "charity" has acquired bad connotations because of its association with a one-way grant to those who cannot help themselves. When someone is in immediate need of food or shoes or bandages, a one-way charity may be the only recourse available, but a continuing fare of such actions is not morally beneficial to giver or receiver. Friedrich Nietzsche, that monumental hater of Christianity, sensed that there was something important here that had been corrupted by Christianity. Nothing repelled him more than the pity that Christianity bequeathed to modern ethics: "I realized that the morality of pity which spread wider and wider, and whose grip infected even philosophers with its disease, was the most sinister symptom of our modern European civilization."[1]

Religions of both East and West advocate compassion for the world's poor and suffering. Compassion, meaning "to suffer with," suggests not a pity directed at the weak but a sharing between those who *appear* to be strong and those who *appear* to be weak. The sharing of suffering reveals weakness in the strong and strength in the weak, and consequently new meanings of both "strong" and "weak." If we respond to the other as fellow sufferer, we can begin the process of channeling power in a human form. Whereas pity is the act of an individual that solidifies the inequitable distribution of power, compassion is a mutual action that protests systematic oppression.

Responsibility is the category that seems to me to have the best chance of expressing the relations that constitute the moral life. The human being's central characteristic is to respond or to answer. Nearly everyone acknowledges the place of responsibility in moral life. In fact, the first problem with responsibility is that it is praised on all sides; no one gives speeches in support of irresponsibility. But a moral term that everyone praises is likely to be a vague and safe generality. Our first task is to resist several twentieth-century narrowings of the term.

A first example of reductionistic meaning for the word "responsibility" is found in Max Weber's writings. Weber is a key figure in twentieth-century thought; he is a writer through whom the word "ethics" finds its way into the contemporary Christian seminary. Weber uses the word "responsibility" in contrast to "an ethic of ultimate ends." In this distinction, there are "two maxims of conduct . . . fundamentally different and irreconcilably opposed."[2] The ethic of ultimate ends is concerned with the "otherworldly" and is the province particularly of religious believers. Weber's favorite example is the Sermon on the Mount, the collection of sayings in which Jesus, among other points, admonishes his listeners to love their enemies and turn the other cheek. The ethic of responsibility, in contrast, is very much "this worldly." It is concerned with managing with our highest reasonableness our daily affairs in this sinful world. Weber does bring these attitudes together in the man who has a political vocation, one who does not lose idealism while calculating the realistic consequences of actions.

Weber's division of responsibility and ultimate ends has had widespread and lasting effect within philosophical and Christian ethics.

In this chapter and the following ones I take strong issue with Weber's dichotomy and his peculiar use of "responsibility." My intention is to place responsibility at the center of all morality. The Sermon on the Mount is a startling but realistic demand for a response to everyday moral problems.[3] Weber saves the Sermon on the Mount by turning it into otherworldly idealism, a pious collection of sayings that most people need not respond to. On the other side of the divide—the lower half—Weber's distinction reduces the meaning of responsibility to reasonable compromises that calculate "foreseeable results in one's actions." Of course, in this sense almost everybody is responsible, the word indicating a minimum demand upon a reasonable individual.

A paradoxical result of Weber's distinction is that "ultimate ends" are not ultimate enough. However high and idealistic these ends may be, they are still imaginable, conceivable, and nameable. But in the Sermon on the Mount, Jesus' reign of God is not a thing to be acquired; it is a set of relations. The ever-widening and ever-deepening meaning (or end) of these relations is without end (termination). The ultimate end of morality is "world without end. Amen."

Because responsibility has a limitless potential, a responsible person might be difficult to handle. Suppose that many people really did respond to the most profound teachings of Moses and Isaiah, Jesus and Paul, Gautama and Sankara. Would we be comfortable with such people? Society and its leaders are quick to clamp on a safe stereotype of how a responsible individual acts. And collectively, the phrase "responsible society" came to refer to some reasonable reforms in society but "nothing too outlandish."

Max Weber was trying to get at a needed distinction between the demands of the immediate situation and some unimaginably greater good. Unfortunately, he came at the question backwards, influenced by patterns of classical thought and Christian teaching that had placed God in another world and relegated care of this world to a temporary duty of "fallen" creatures. But the proper way to come at responsibility is to start with the total, concrete, unique situation of a person. This situation contains within itself the history of the person, the history of his or her family, the history of the human race. Within the ecological matrix of the present, every responsible action reverberates without end. Responsibility is not securely anchored by a set of ideals outside the ambiguities of history. Nor is responsibility a neatly calculable way of living without recourse to sacred depths, mystical eruptions, or divine inspirations. The anchoring of responsibility and the relevance of religious categories are to be gradually discovered through a responsive attitude that does not have a preestablished safe limit.

As an example of a contemporary religious writer who unduly limits the word "responsibility," John Howard Yoder is an interesting case because he is one of the most provocative, insightful, and original writers in Christian ethics today. Yoder regularly takes issue with the category of responsibility as a bad compromise between the demands of Jesus' teaching and the realities of today's world.

Because Jesus is not meant to be taken as normative for political ethics, it is said, we must obviously, consciously, properly get our ethics elsewhere, from a "responsible" calculation of our chances and our duty to make events come out as well as possible. This substitution of nature or history for Jesus as the locus of revelation was justified by the claim that Jesus had nothing to say on the subject.[4]

Instead of his making the sharp contrasts he does in this paragraph (Jesus as normative vs. responsible calculation, Jesus as locus of revelation vs. nature or history), Yoder's own interests would be better served by recovering a deeper meaning of responsibility. When, for example, Yoder explores the "household codes" of the New Testament and shows that they are much more demanding and more in sympathy with Jesus' teaching than has generally been presumed, the idea of responsibility is just what is needed to carry out this rethinking.[5] In regard to these commands addressed to slave and slavemaster, husband and wife, parent and child, one must ask responsible to whom, responsible to what, responsible when, responsible how.

In one place Yoder does show the possibilities of the word "responsible." In his view, what most of the world calls responsibility involves exercising offices of violence. Yoder says that for the followers of Jesus

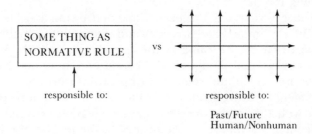

it may happen that "the most effective way to *take* responsibility is to refuse to collaborate, and by the refusal to take sides in favor of the men whom that power is oppressing.[6] In this use of the term, Yoder does something creative and helpful with the word "responsibility." He indicates that being responsible does not always mean doing the reasonable and expected thing that society asks. It can mean responding to wider and deeper forces in ways that society's leaders may brand as irresponsible.

In the passage quoted above, Yoder seems to have no uneasiness with the word "normative." He sets "normative" against "responsible." There is indeed a conflict between "normative" and "responsible"; Christian writing of the twentieth century has unwisely chosen to go with the former. It seems to me that Yoder's quarrel ought to be with the word "normative," which sets inherent limits to the person of Jesus and his teachings. "Normative" suggests that finally there is something, some object, some fixed point against which being and truth, person and goodness are to be measured. Responsibility, in contrast, suggests that *no thing* can be a final norm, that response is without end.

Yoder's portrait of Jesus in the synoptic Gospels is of a political radical who requires responsibility without end. Jesus preaches against turning anything into an idol. People's lives are not to be judged by submitting them to an impersonal standard. Once anything in the world is "normative" responsibility is domesticated to mean acting according to preestablished "norms." If, however, responsibility takes precedence, then reasonable calculations, traditional rules, and prophetic demands can each play a part in morality. But the teachings of Jesus and of other religious figures as well as human inventiveness and exploration have implications without end. The frequent conflict in Christian history has been between church teachings as normative and the radical call of Jesus to responsible action. Response to that call always has reverberations beyond the church.

I take one more contemporary writer, Carol Gilligan, to illustrate a reductionist tendency in the use of responsibility. Gilligan has been an effective writer on moral development, offering penetrating criticism of Kohlberg's theory.[7] Contending that Kohlberg's system is sex biased, Gilligan has found in her own studies that most women address moral issues in ways that do not score high on Kohlberg's testing. Women, Gilligan finds, ask about intention, context, and consequences; they are especially concerned about the violence inherent in many human situations. Gilligan frequently calls this approach an "ethic of responsibility."

This ethical approach is predominantly but not exclusively associated with women. Gilligan does not erect an impenetrable barrier between a male and female morality. She finds that people can and do switch from one moral perspective to the other. My concern is the way she names her two perspectives.

Whereas justice emphasizes the autonomy of the person, care underlies the primacy of relationship. Thus, justice gives rise to an ethic of rights, and care engenders an ethic of responsibility.[8]

This quotation sets forth her usual contrast: justice on one side, care on the other side; autonomy on one side, relationship on the other side; rights on one side, responsibility on the other. The consistent contrast is between justice/autonomy/rights and care/relationship/responsibility. I return at the end of this chapter to the unwise contrast of justice and care. For the present I am interested in her close association of responsibility and relationship.

That responsible and relational go together is something I wish to argue for. I have said that to be responsible is to answer to whomever and whatever we are related to. I have also acknowledged that responsibility is often made into a safe and controlled category that law-abiding citizens possess. The word "relation" has suffered a worse reduction, almost disappearing into the abstract noun "relationship." The way the word "relationship" is used today blocks our perception of how wide and deep our relations go.

"Relation" is one of those words that should indicate process, dynamism, movement, activity. But as those very words illustrate, we use nouns rather than verbs, thereby suggesting that the referent of such terms is an object. Thus we can forget that a relation is that in which one participates, not a thing one possesses. "Relation" has always shared with many other words the tendency toward reification. But "relation" in the last few decades has had a much worse fate, moving to a second level of abstraction in the omnipresent word "relationship." One actually hears people say, "I'm looking for a relationship." What they are saying is that they are looking for an idea about relations or a system to classify relations. They are apparently not looking for a person as friend, lover, or spouse. One can *have* a relationship but one cannot have a person.

In contemporary speech the word "relationship" nearly always signals two people. However, this peculiar relation cannot be called interpersonal because if one or both parties "*have* a relationship," this is different from *being in relation* to another person. The word "relationship" seems to have emerged when many people were unsure whether they wanted a spouse or a lover. Relationship has become a convenient abstraction for something everyone should have and something that can be dropped when no longer convenient. This distancing of the other person into the category of relationship is a major obstacle to experiencing that person as the other pole within a relation of mutual exchange.

Carol Gilligan is not particularly to blame for the spread of the word "relationship." However, because Gilligan is especially concerned with persons being turned into objects, it is regrettable that she does not see that the word "relationship" narrows and reifies the meaning of relation. In one essay Gilligan complains of "relationships" being treated as "holding environments" and the dichotomy of egoism/altruism being "embedded in a particular perspective toward relationship." In this essay she several times says "there are two ways of speaking about relationships."[9] It would be more helpful to say that there are two ways of speaking about relations: one abstracts from the concrete situation of two persons, henceforth speaking about *having* relationships; the other plunges deeper into the human and nonhuman relations that constitute each of our lives.

The worst thing, therefore, with the word "relationship" is that it collapses the meaning of "responsible" before we have barely begun to explore our relations. To respond requires a personal center, and it is preeminently in the presence of other centers of personal activity that we discover mutual relations. If such mutual exchange continues for any period of time, it gradually encompasses more and more of what each party is related to. A test of whether I love my friend is whether I love her children, though I need not love them in the same way or to the same degree. Nonetheless, to be lovingly related to a person who is at once mother, daughter, Italian, Catholic, schoolteacher, Bostonian, and Red Sox fan is to meet a multitude of relations, human and nonhuman, in the one I love.

RESPONSIBLE TO AND FOR

For exploring the dimensions of responsibility we need first to distinguish between "responsible to" and "responsible for." Otherwise the meaning of questions about responsibility is murky. Take, for example, this interview in the book *Habits of the Heart*.[10] The interviewer is Steven Tipton; the interviewee is a woman psychotherapist.

Q: So what are you responsible for?
A: I am responsible for my own acts and for what I do.

Q: Does that mean you're not responsible for others, too?

A: No.

Q: Are you your sister's keeper?

A: No.

Q: Are you your brother's keeper?

A: No.

Q: Are you responsible for your husband?

A: I'm not. He makes his own decisions. He is his own person. He acts his own acts. I can agree with them or disagree with them. If ever I find them nauseous enough, I have the responsibility to leave and not deal with it anymore.

Q: What about your children?

A: I . . . I would say that I have a legal responsibility for them, but in a sense I think they are responsible for their own acts.

Is this woman responsible, or irresponsible? From the interviewer's line of questioning I would gather he cannot believe the callousness of the woman's answers. It does not seem to occur to him that he is asking the wrong question or that he is not getting the answers he thinks are right because he is not asking the question he thinks he is asking. In the several pages of the book where this woman is described, she comes across as a highly responsible person who loves her husband and children, works hard at her professional vocation, and is involved in all sorts of activities.[11] The interviewer can conclude only that since she is not the moral monster that her answers suggest to him, she must be confused, "caught in some of the contradictions her beliefs imply. She is responsible for herself but she has no reliable way to connect her fulfillment to that of other people."[12]

Nothing that the woman says about responsibility contradicts the description of her life. The interviewer does not seem to grasp the difference between "responsible to" and "responsible for." The basic question is *responsible to:* that is, To what and to whom do you answer? If the interviewer had asked: Do you respond to husband, brother, sister, children, I am sure the answer would have been yes to each.

As to the question, What are you responsible for? the woman is quite clear that she is responsible for her choices and for the direct results of those choices. Most of us forget that beyond some immediate behavioral effects we can take neither credit nor blame for what goes on in the world. We ought to choose as best we can and attempt to carry through on the choice. Our attempt to take on responsibility for all kinds of things and persons beyond our control is a way of avoiding the decisions we should be responsible for. Are you responsible for breaking this dish? The person may say: Yes, I carelessly placed it on the edge of the table where it should not have been. Are you responsible for killing this child with your car? The driver may say: I was observing the speed laws; no one was watching the child; I braked as quickly as possible. Are Christians responsible for the holocaust? The Christian may say: I am not responsible for Christian attitudes that contributed to the rise of Nazism; I *am* responsible for resisting those elements of Christianity today.

Are we responsible for anyone besides ourselves? Only insofar as others cannot decide for themselves. When a person is incompetent to make a needed decision, someone who is concerned with the welfare of that person has to decide. In the case of the dying we have no hope of restoring the person to responsibility for himself or herself. In other cases where persons are hurt or in need, we try to restore them to their own responsibility. Even severely retarded persons can be helped to take some responsibility for their own actions. If I unneccessarily take responsibility for another person, substituting my will for that person's will, I am treating the person as an object.

The most common case where substitution does and should play a role is with children. In the interview above, when the question is about her children the woman hesitates and then attempts a distinction. I think she does not find the words she needs in talking of "legal responsibility." True, parents do have some legal responsibility for their children, but that is because there is a real difference between young children and adults regarding responsibility. Every parent does sometime substitute the wisdom of age for what otherwise would be a disastrous choice by a child. Of course, parents sometimes substitute in too many decisions, not allowing a child to make mistakes that would be good learning experiences. Or parents forget that their seventeen-year-old is no longer a seven-year-old. Whatever the mistakes that are made and the negotiations that are needed, the principle is clear: We should be responsible for other people only to the degree and for as long as they cannot be responsible for themselves. And because *things* cannot decide for themselves, we are responsible for them, too.

Notice the strange tendency to reverse this responsibility. I have said that generally we are not responsible for other people; they should decide for themselves whenever and however they can. We *are* responsible for things: trees, rivers, mountains, and earth cannot decide their fate and depend on human responsibility. We often assume that the opposite is the case, that we are responsible for people but not for things. In the interview above, the questioner asked about brother, sister, husband, and children. He never got to any things. Perhaps if he had been aware that we are responsible for trees, rivers, mountains, and earth, he might have asked a question that deserved an unqualified yes.

Our confusion about what we are responsible *for* is tied to our failure to ask the prior question: What are we responsible *to*? The answer to that question is "Everyone and everything." In principle, nothing can be excluded. We cannot embrace the whole world at any moment, but we still have to be open to learning from any source that might present itself. Each thing that comes within our awareness deserves a response within a set of gradations. Figuring out how to mesh the multiplicity of responses is the task of moral judgment. The past says one thing, my father tells me something different, and a schoolteacher says something different from both. How can I act responsibly? I am *responsible for* being *responsible to* the truth available to me. My *responsibility to* is limitless, while my *responsibility for* is tightly circumscribed.

A responsible morality is therefore a relational morality, not in the faddish sense of "having a relationship" with another person, but in recognizing the many relations in which we participate. Here is where religion can play an important part in morality. Religion is, if anything, relational, the activities that acknowledge the bond of creation to its creative source. Religion's concern is that we do not miss any of the important relations: divine/human, past/present, living/dead, man/woman, adult/child, animal/animal namer, garden/gardener, and so forth. Each of these relations has its own narrative description in a religious tradition. The human and nonhuman creatures are historically related in Jewish or Buddhist or North American Native religions by stories that have their own distinctive twists and yet some similarity across religious lines. Through parable, proverb, and epic poetry, men and women are reminded of their many relations on this earth and their relation to powerful forces beyond earth.

For moral purposes, religion gives special attention to one relation: the relation of possession. Religion could be described as a critique of the human propensity to acquire and to own. The mystical attitude, which we explored in the previous chapter, acknowledges that the human vocation can include taking over, constructing, holding, and using. But when we enjoy the fruits of our labor there has to be detachment, a light grasp of things. And sometimes we need a willingness to step back and appreciate things as they are, a readiness to share whatever we have because it is ours only on loan. If we are not blinded by a possessive attitude, we will discover that everything that is, is good and that to the extent that anything is, it has some right to be.

For several centuries an ethical-political language of "human rights" has been in the air. Are such rights ontologically stamped on the baby by God, or are they the product of a social contract? A morality of responsibility says: neither. Rights emerge from response, but they are not bestowed by society. They are inherent in the being of things in response.

The human being is by far the most responsive of earthly beings and deserving of the most respect. The human being in turn is the guardian of the rights of other creatures and has to make fallible judgments about gradations of rights. A monkey has greater rights than a mosquito; a redwood tree has greater rights than crabgrass. In between such extreme cases the lines are often blurred when a choice is to be made. Many species of life are threatened with extinction, and human choices have to be made whereby time, energy, and money are expended to save one species rather than another.

Mary Midgely in arguing a case for animal rights begins with the statement "We can have duties to people, but not to things."[13] Throughout Western history nonhuman animals have been considered more like things than people and therefore have had no rights. She argues that we should redraw the line so that all animals as bearers of a sentient, feeling life with purposes of their own have rights.

Midgely correctly notes that response can be made by nonliving objects: a tree, a boat, or the earth responds to our touch. However, she quickly dismisses this meaning of response as irrelevant to moral responsibility and proceeds to her concern with animal rights. I would suggest that although the response of objects is of less moral relevance than animal response, objects should not be immediately excluded from moral concern.

Is it nonsensical to speak of a duty to a river or to a painting? Considered in total isolation, such duties may be meaningless. But our patterns of response are always within a human community that has a past as well as a present, and within an environment with a wealth of accumulated meaning. The past lives in the present by way of artifact; the present living environment is always sustained by nonliving environment. Our duties may therefore include protecting the river from pollution and protecting great works of art from economic exploitation. We are responsible *to* things and we are responsible *for* things, and these two come together in the need to care for things.

Does this usage of "right" and "duty" evacuate the terms of their firm, historical meaning? Not unless we assume that rights and duties are attached insignia. Attributing rights to people, monkeys, and rivers does not mean that all three are equal. On the contrary, it invites us to use our best insights to understand the complex differences among things. Our moral language generally remains too crude and too blunt, letting us off with drawing a single dividing line that dismisses everything below the human as right-less. But responsible morality places human response and human rights at the center. Concentric circles expand indefinitely around the human. Circumferences far removed from the center bear only a trace of the language of rights and duties; nevertheless, the human listening at the center cannot on principle exclude any class of things.

Religion's powerful contribution to human rights lies in its critique of possessiveness. Religion affirms an individual's human rights by denying anyone else the right to own that person. Since religion challenges an ultimate right to possess *anything,* the possession of another human being is in religious terms a blasphemy. Modern ethics has gone on a dangerous path of basing human rights on the right to ownership. The individual is placed in isolation with "his" property, and the possessive instinct is encouraged rather than disciplined. We should not be surprised that a society which comes to rights by that route comes up short on the rights of women, black slaves, or animals. Rights do not trickle down from powerful men on top; rights have to emerge from communities of men, women, children, and nonhumans who realize the need to share our common gifts and to protect specific rights to assembly, free speech, fair courts, affordable housing, and so forth.

RESPONSIBLE COMMUNICATION

The respect for a legal tradition of rights is part of our being responsible to the past. It would be the height of arrogance to assume that the past has nothing to say to us. Tradition, as Chesterton says, "is the extension of the franchise to that most obscure of all classes, our ancestors. . . . It is the refusal to submit to the oligarchy of those walking around."[14] The most dramatic instance of tradition is religion. If laws of nations are to be enforceable, governments have to attain a quasi-religious aura. Governments that try to exist by reason alone or by external threat will probably be short lived. Religion has a lot to teach governments about forms of communication.

Religious traditions that have existed for thousands of years cultivate a sense of ritual. Moral authority can never be separated from ritual. Religious commandments sound unbending and apodictic ("You must. . . .") and usually are in the negative ("Do not steal," "Do not lie. . . ."). To the outside spectator such rules seem life-denying, and obedience to rules is often called legalism. To the devotee, however, the rules are a fence of protection around the community's life. Rules can be experienced as a liberation from self-centeredness, an experience that is difficult to come by in today's world.

Even the ritual rules that seem to have little moral import may have a hidden meaning for morality. Anthropologist Mary Douglas, referring to dietary laws in religion, says that reformers often try to get rid of rules that seem irrational to the outsider and inconvenient to the insider. But, she says, that is just the point of such laws; they bind the members of a community in a ritual unity. Of course, we do need communication across historic divisions; but immediate clarity among the billions of humans, not to mention the lions and lambs, is not available. The individual person still needs a community with a sense of ritual, past, and place as the basis for attempts at worldwide communication. Reasonable ideas, discursive speech, and orderly sequence always have to be in tension with bodily organisms, habitual behavior, and traditional rituals. Douglas concludes "that those who despise ritual, even at its most magical, are cherishing in the name of reason a very irrational concept of communication.[15]

When we respond to the past, it is generally to an object, code, or ritual whose meaning is fairly well fixed. But such meanings are not finally set, so a process of continuing reinterpretation is to be expected. The meaning of the biblical text, for example, continues to yield new meaning many centuries after it was composed. In this process codes and rituals, if not texts, do change over a long time as constant modifications occur with application of code or ritual in the present. Wisdom is to be found in the present, although the contemporary community may sometimes be mistaken about where its true wisdom lies. No major monument of tradition can be casually tossed aside, but the wise men and wise women of today's community have the right to speak respectfully to past and to future.

The process of responsible communication in the present is far more complicated to describe. My response to another calls forth a response to my response. In turn, I respond to the response to my response . . . *ad infinitum.* Each response is weighted by history and is also made in expectation of responses in the future.[16] We can manage conversation because we get to know the meanings of words and gestures through years of interpretation. However, even with friends and family we sometimes misinterpret activities and respond inappropriately. And when we feel ourselves among strangers and we distrust a process of responsible exchange, there are certain to be cries for equal rights.

Where people respond to one another in a communal setting with an experience of mutuality, equal rights is only occasionally the issue. When men and women live in mutual relations they discover differences not contained in the word "inequality." Where adults and children meet in mutual exchange, real inequalities are revealed (physical size, historical memory, economic power), but the movement of the relation is toward lessening the inequalities. This principle is not an argument against feminism or even against a children's-rights movement. Some historic inequalities do need righting, particularly women's rights to a fair share in the economic order. But without some sense of community, some trust among people, some recognition of what nature and history have given us, the demand for equality cannot succeed. The attempt to meet the demand will often lead to the courthouse instead of to the best, even if fallible, response we can make to familial, neighborly, civic, schooling, and job situations.

Beyond a fairly small circle of people we find it extremely difficult to decipher all the messages coming at us. We usually do not know the message sender well enough—whether it be CBS news, IBM, the U.S. government, OPEC oil, or the Kremlin—to place any one action in an interpretive context of past and future, direct and indirect reference. We need to rely on rules and laws as clues to the interpretation of meaning. If we have no hope of understanding the actions of a threatening person or organization, we are forced to rely on a system of laws mechanically applied. We demand utter clarity on the part of our adversaries just when the conditions for gradual clarification of meaning are absent. When we lack a relation of mutual exchange, every person and every organization tends to become menacing.

These steps of distrust, misunderstanding, and accusations of irresponsibility are regularly played out in international exchanges, particularly where long memories are the fuel of today's distrust: witness Northern Ireland, the Middle East, Central America. The U.S. and USSR have continually played out the pattern. An example is the 1983 clash over the shooting down of the Korean airliner.[17] The whole pattern was displayed on international television. Both sides accused; both sides dissembled. When the Soviet Union more or less admitted what they had done, they said that the U.S. was "wholly responsible" for the destruction of the airliner. To most people in the U.S. the statement was so preposterous as to be beyond belief. However, if one is interpreting and responding not only to the moment but to decades of distrust, the responsibility for evil can always be seen in the other's activity. Suppose that one's initial point of reference for interpreting an event is the dropping of the first atomic bomb. The resulting interpretation of who is the cause of evil in the nuclear age may be biased but not absurd. The U.S. starts from different reference points, perhaps the sentiments of the Declaration of Independence and the Stalinist years of the USSR. Not surprisingly, in this interpretation the U.S. comes out blameless.

The fact that response entails interpretation in both breadth and depth does not offer great solace at the level of international conflict. But the hopeful side is that a break in the cycle of distrust, misinterpretation, and accusation can start a new cycle of growing trust. And in responsible communication, the breakthrough need not be a mountain of new information. A seemingly minor gesture can let in a crack of light: a ballet company, a piece of music, a child's letter, a personal friendship among leaders. The moral life does depend on the fragile and fallible responses of human beings to those rituals and gestures that represent goodness.

Few of us can directly influence international problems, but we all need to extend mutuality and responsibility to more than parent, spouse, and a few friends. Such work with a wider public takes time, patience, and effort. One has to untangle lines of communication to find signals that the other party is not totally closed. Human beings do not "build" or "make" a community. What they can do is take down the specific obstacles that they or previous generations have erected against the emergence of community among persons who are capable of responding to one another with knowledge, care, and affection.

RESPONSIBLE JUSTICE

The several strands of this chapter can be brought together through reflection on the idea of justice. In contemporary discussions of rights, the virtue of justice is constantly invoked and the assumption is regularly made that justice means equal rights. "Treat each man impartially" is the call of modern ethics. The material in this chapter leads to the following conclusions about the supremacy of justice: 1) justice presupposes a moral condition that has been disrupted; 2) the language of equality and inequality is inadequate for a description of justice.

David Hume in the eighteenth century pointed out that justice is not the first moral principle. Justice is not needed, says Hume "if every man has the utmost tenderness for every man, and feels no more concern for his own interest than for that of his fellows."[18] Hume believed that the family approaches this situation, and elsewhere "the stronger the mutual benevolence is among individuals, the nearer it approaches" to the situation where justice is not the concern.

As I suggested above, where father, mother, and children live in mutual relations, there are few cries for justice. Where true friendship exists, the same thing can be said. A friend who insists on paying his half of a dinner check when someone is trying to express affection can disrupt fraternity in the name of justice.[19] Once we go beyond the family and intimate friends we all wish to have protections of our rights, that is, guarantees that we will be given equal treatment when we are functioning as individuals in relation to concentrations of power. If I am applying for a job in a corporation or if I am tried for a crime in a court of law, I look for impartiality, or at least I wish not to be faulted on the basis of sex, color, religion, and so forth.

David Hume's appeal to benevolence as the condition presupposed by justice suggests a connection to the philosophical-religious attitude described in Chapter 4. A morality of goodness does not start from a quest for justice but from the goodness of all things and the "non-envious" character of the good. If everyone were to respond wholeheartedly to the need for care and love, justice would be unnecessary. Of course, the world is not perfect, a fact crystal clear to the morality of goodness which is not a looking at the world through rose-tinted glasses. The historic religions are very realistic about the shortcomings of human beings. True, religions that talk of original sin, fall from grace, or corruption of human nature are always in danger of turning their mythical story of human beginnings into a jaundiced metaphysic. Nonetheless, religions both East and West are acutely aware that there is a wrong that needs righting and that a passionate commitment to fight injustice is needed.

Justice is a seeking to restore the unity of benevolence. Such unity is beyond human vision and not directly under the control of the human will. However, an original concord can be intimated in profound moments of love or art. And a reestablishing of harmony can be hoped for and worked at. The effort to secure human rights for the vulnerable and oppressed is no small part of seeking justice. Precisely to make those rights secure, justice has to mean a reduction of violence and the reconciling of enemies. Martin Luther King, Jr., refers to a non-symmetric response to violence that will eventually win over the oppressor. King draws here on the biblical meaning of justice as a reconciling unity. We must *do* justice in response to the covenant with all creation. Justice in Jewish and Christian traditions does not center on obeying the law but on faithfully responding to the possibilities of wholeness, completion, and unity in the cosmos. We must care for each existing thing and work for its proper relation to everything else.

The view of justice proposed here is at variance with both conceptions that George Grant contrasts as the traditional and modern views of justice:

The view of traditional philosophy and religion is that justice is the overriding order which we do not measure and define, but in terms of which we are measured and defined. The view of modern thought is that justice is a way which we choose in freedom, once we have taken our fate into our own hands and know that we are responsible for what happens.[20]

Grant's contrast in this passage creates an unbridgeable gap between traditional and modern views of justice. He also gives over the word "responsible" to the modern meaning, as if the traditional meaning excluded interaction, interpretation, and human initiative. A responsibility for oneself and a responsibility to everything is compatible with what both traditional and modern views assert. Responsibility means neither being resigned to fate nor taking it into our individual hands. Responsibility means knowing our human limits and knowing that we can always improve the human situation. We do not invent justice, but we are responsible for contributing to its emergence.

Modern writing on justice does closely associate the word "justice" with individual rights. The tradition from John Locke in the seventeenth century to John Rawls in the twentieth is a powerful one. No individual or group today can simply overthrow this dominant meaning of justice in ethical-political discussions. However, one can protest its inadequacy and point out the individualistic, rationalistic, and male biases in this modern tradition. Earlier or non-Western meanings of justice can be invoked as correctives to the equating of justice with equality, rights, and impartiality.

Lawrence Kohlberg's use of justice is a dramatic case of the modern assumption that one must rise above body, community, and temporality to reach the principle of justice. Kohlberg does have to acknowledge that there is something beyond justice, some state or condition that is the source of justice. Kohlberg can only look for that state on the next rung up the ladder. Up there everything—including the person—disappears into a mystical unity.

Kohlberg's system is extremely vulnerable to the kind of feminist criticism Carol Gilligan has brought to it. Gilligan finds among girls and women a different focus to moral judgment. Her use of the word "care" is an insistence on the values of body, community, and time. She is rightfully wary of creating a new single system of moral thinking and prefers to describe a morality of dual perspectives. However, any effective reform of modern ethics has to challenge the dominant assumptions about justice. Carol Gilligan does not do that insofar as she regularly refers to "adding to Kohlberg's focus on justice a complementary ethic of care."[21] A complement of care, especially among women, fits all too comfortably the nineteenth- and twentieth-century stereotypes of justice.

Gilligan misnames her two perspectives, justice and care. What she describes under these two terms is a tension between attachment and detachment, unequal treatment and equality. But the word "justice" should be reserved for what transcends this split and points to reconciliation. A simple way to see the difference between justice and equality is that while it is quite possible to argue that inequality is sometimes appropriate, no one argues for the value of injustice. Justice subsumes equality and inequality, attachment and detachment. And most important, justice arises out of care, the attentiveness to the needs of each bodily thing. To speak of a complementarity of justice and care is to imply that justice is care-less or unfeeling.

Gilligan is suspicious of any speaking of "caring justice" because she believes that this collapses the duality too quickly and allows care to be absorbed into a system controlled by justice. Gilligan's suspicion has foundation; it is no easy thing to fight the forces that control justice. But like Socrates arguing with Thrasymachus in the first book of *The Republic*, one must fight for justice by (among other ways) resisting those who equate it with an existing unjust system.[22] Thrasymachus says cynically that justice is "the rule of the stronger." Socrates cannot deny that that is often true when people talk of justice. Nevertheless, Socrates insists that we must fight for what the word "justice" means. That meaning, Socrates says, is "to each according to its due." We do not have in existence such a state of justice, and the Thrasymachuses of the world helpfully remind us of this fact. But we need a word that expresses what perhaps once did exist and what we hope will exist in the future.

The religious traditions are once again helpful and realistic. Human beings cannot invent a just world. No individual or planning group knows how to translate Socrates's formula "to each according to its due" into a fair and compassionate social system. But all the religions insist that we are capable of recognizing terrible injustices. Although it is not our vocation to leave the world a just place, it *is* our task to reduce injustice. We often lack the knowledge, power, and skill to create a just order, but we all have the knowledge, power, and skill to say no. We all have the capacity to lodge protests of one kind or another against obvious injustices. Outrage at unjust acts does not depend upon a complex capacity to make abstract judgments. It depends on a sensitivity to all living things and a simple recognition that the violent destruction of forms of life is senseless and immoral. To develop this foundation of morality we must examine the place of the natural in the moral life.

CHAPTER 6

Trans-natural Morality

The word "natural" is one of the most ambiguous and confusing words in the English language. People generally assume it is a simple, straightforward word when they use it, and they use it frequently. One possible strategy would be to advocate avoiding the word, but even if avoidance were possible that would merely push the confusion elsewhere. We are confused about the natural because we are confused about morality and about the human vocation. If we can sort out the confusing overlay of meanings in the term "natural," it may lead us into a fruitful discussion of morality.

I begin with an illustration of how the idea of natural shows up in confusing ways at the center of moral debates. Samuel Gorovitz quotes from an essay of Paul Ramsey on the need to recover a sense for "man" as a "natural object."[1] Ramsey maintains that procreation is a course of action "natural to man, which cannot without violation be disassembled and put together again." Ramsey concludes that "the proper objective of medicine is to serve and care for man as a natural object, to help in all our natural 'courses of action,' to tend the garden of our creation." Samuel Gorovitz disagrees in the strongest possible way: "It is time this sort of argument was laid permanently to rest. That something is natural has no moral force." Gorovitz proceeds to distinguish three meanings of natural, none of which, in his estimation, helps us to decide about morality. Gorovitz concludes that Ramsey's "invocation of the concept of the natural only obscures the point that there are morally desirable and morally undesirable actions, and we must strive to discern the difference between them on reasonable grounds, not on purported grounds of naturalness. I do not understand why this confusion about the moral significance of the concept of what is natural persists as widely and tenaciously as it does."[2]

The confusion that Gorovitz deplores will not disappear by simply dismissing the issue as he does. The natural has had moral significance for centuries, and it continues to be important. In this chapter, I attempt to articulate a meaning of "natural" in morality that is different from both Ramsey's and Gorovitz's.

Both Ramsey and Gorovitz draw from defensible meanings of "natural," and each has a truth worth defending. However, both authors overstate their cases. Ramsey argues that human procreation should not be "disassembled." His argument may apply to the *in vitro* fertilization and embryo implantation he attacks in the article, but what about the wish to modify, control, alter, restrain, or otherwise influence procreation? The relevant moral question is the limits of such change, whereas Ramsey's language seems to resist all change. For his part, Gorovitz wishes us to discern desirable and undesirable actions "on reasonable grounds, not on purported grounds of naturalness." But reason has to reflect on what is non-reason, on bodily activities whose structures are not infinitely malleable. Gorovitz, however, does not address the relevant moral question of the relation of the natural to what transcends the natural.

My use of the term "trans-natural" indicates the direction of my argument. Human morality is always both natural and more than natural. The central moral issue is how to go beyond the natural without going contrary to it. This project is not something one may or may not choose; it is inherent in the human condition, which is why the human being is ineluctably a moral animal. Trans-natural is just one more variation on my description of the moral and educative process: the reshaping of life's forms with end and without end. We do not invent life's forms, but we do influence them for better or worse through transforming action.

This chapter is not a defense of "natural law." Although one might make a case for the term, it is tied to historical connotations that make it unrecoverable at this time in history. Even the Roman Catholic church, one of its great defenders in recent times, generally uses other language today. The Second Vatican Council and the encyclicals of subsequent popes speak of personalistic anthropology rather than of natural law. But even as one tries to transcend inadequate language it is important to understand how terms have functioned in the past and how some previous language is still implicit. The idea of the natural has by no means disappeared, and its meaning requires clarification.

THE HISTORY OF "NATURAL"

In trying to unravel any confusing word, etymology is always of some help. A word may travel far from its original meaning, but it never entirely severs itself from that root. In the case of "natural," the root meaning is particularly important: natural is what is given by birth or origin. For ancient peoples the line between living and nonliving was not absolute, so the nonliving were thought to have a constitution similar to that of the living. An organism, it seemed obvious, had a nature: a definite form with its own natural tendencies. So too the nonliving world had natures, or at least there were forms for each thing. Although the human mind has difficulty grasping the nature of things, some patterns are evident in the living organism. An animal is born, grows, declines, dies; the given structure of its physical constitution governs its activities throughout its life.

Aristotle towers over much of Western history in influencing the idea of nature and natural. His reputation suffers from the narrow-mindedness of his later disciples, but Aristotle himself was a careful observer of behavior. He was a biologist interested in the details of the *bios* sphere. Mary Midgely rightly praises Aristotle for being the biologist among moralists, seeing the world as a continuous organic whole.[3]

Aristotle did not think that we can simply abstract universal ideas and then proceed to live by deduction alone. Although the teleological principle implies that everything moves toward an end and that the rules for proceeding to this end are inscribed in nature, Aristotle's ethical and political thinking reflects a modesty and a need to work at detail. Given the subsequent meaning of "natural law," some contemporary commentators, such as Hans-Georg Gadamer, separate Aristotle from natural-law tradition. The practical judgments of the human mind require knowledge of bodily behavior and historical precedent. Aristotle's understanding of the virtuous life depended heavily on the Hellenic culture around him.

After Aristotle, "nature" took on a more abstract meaning. Especially among the Stoics, a kind of generalized abstraction called nature begins to emerge. Nature has to do with the recurrent patterns of the universe and the fate against which human beings struggle. In Boethius's synthesis of Christian and Stoic thought, he makes no appeal to animals for his meaning of nature. For the Stoics, God was a "leader of nature, governing all things by law."[4]

The twelfth and thirteenth centuries saw a renewed interest in animal activity as the meaning of the natural. Some scholars bemoan this medieval interest in animal behavior as the reason why natural law became an unimaginative reduction of human morality to fixed rules of conduct. The bigger problem, however, was not the medievals' interest in animal behavior but their misinformation about animals. Scientific information was laced with myth and fancy. Knowledge of the procreative process was minimal or often wrong.

The Protestant Reformation in calling for a return to the Bible took special aim at what then passed for natural law. Luther and Calvin absorbed assumptions of their time about nature's order, but they insisted on the need for the word of God to enlighten sinful hearts as to the necessities of a moral life. Within some parts of Protestantism—Puritans of North America, for example—natural law made a comeback; reason and nature had considerable autonomy within the idea of a biblical covenant.[5] For the most part, though, Protestant Christians down to the twentieth century have been suspicious of claims to base morality on anything outside the biblical word of God.

The rejection of natural-law morality was not the same as a rejection of nature. Protestant Christians no less than Catholics affirmed that God had created the Book of Nature. As all of Christianity struggled to come to terms with the new sciences, nature seemed to be the bridge for relating science and religion. The period of the seventeenth and eighteenth centuries, then, is most responsible for the confusion in the meaning of "natural." The confusion was to a large extent intentional, or at least scientist and theologian preferred the ambiguity of nature to the hostility that was likely if the confusion were cleared up.

Putting it very simply, the pagan philosophy to which the enlightened could appeal against Christianity, had enough in common with Christianity to enable a substantially Christian ethic, based on a substantially Christian conception of human nature, to survive the repudiation of much, or even all, Christian doctrine. And this was assisted by the ambiguity of the term "nature" which retained its reassuring suggestions of normativeness, and transcendence of merely human fashions, yet could range from the teleological to the purely descriptive, from the scientific to the mystical."[6]

In the early period of modern science, nature functioned as a kind of substitute deity. Modern science was thought to be the discovery of the laws of nature. "God said let there be light, and Newton was made." The hope was that as the laws of nature were discovered, "man" would be improved as well. The creation of social science at a later period embodied the continuation of this hope. But the peculiar language of modern science always pitted "man against nature," pointing to a conquest and a submission of nature by "man." From that opposition no advance in comprehending the laws of nature would itself suggest moral improvement. Science was the study of an objective realm outside the human.

As I pointed out in Chapter 3, modern ethics had to go on its own in the nineteenth and twentieth centuries. It stepped outside modern science, reason, and the laws of nature. Freedom of the will is taken to be a peculiar hole in nature. A gesture of defiance is called for in the "man" of freedom who now stands outside nature. Existentialist "man" becomes the other side of objective science. The eighteenth-century Declaration of Independence makes its appeal to "the laws of nature and nature's God." Compare that to Sartre's Orestes' saying to God: "Outside nature, against nature, without excuse, beyond remedy, except what remedy I find within myself. But I shall not return under your law; I am doomed to have no other law but mine. Nor shall I come back to nature, the nature you found good. . . . Nature abhors man, and you, too, god of gods, abhor mankind."[7]

The claim that "man" is outside the laws of nature or in conflict with such laws is the strange dilemma that early modern thought bequeathed to the twentieth century. Perhaps existentialist "man" feels so lonely because he defines himself without reference to the other animals. What is beginning to develop in the later twentieth century is a new alliance for exploring the relation between human organisms and the cycle of nonhuman life. Moralists, biologists, ecologists, feminists, and others have a stake in reflecting on human limits and the ecological system. The scientific study of animals is a needed corrective to both the medieval tendency to accept limits of nature too readily and to the early modern tendency to pit "man" against nature. The human animal is distinctive among the other animals, but it has to find its kinship with nonhuman animals to be able to exercise wisely its distinctive vocation.

As a way of summarizing this history and of sorting out the different meanings of "natural," it is helpful to see "nature" in contrast to related terms. Throughout Western history, "natural" has always been paired with some other term. These correlations suggest a human ordering that goes beyond nature but not entirely beyond it. The following four pairings do not exhaust all possibilities, but they at least indicate the main emphases throughout the centuries.

1) *Natural and Personal.* The distinction between nature and person emerged out of the Christological controversies in the early church. Christian thinkers developed a language (not without bitter controversy) to express a distinction between the Jesus of Nazareth whom they experienced and what they affirmed him to be. They formulated a belief in a divine nature and a human nature within one person. The same distinction of nature and person was used in the Christian doctrine of the Trinitarian God.

Greek philosophy had no comparable distinction between the *what* and the *who*. Once introduced, though, this distinction became the basis of a creationist metaphysic. Each nature or essence participates in the act of being. Notice that a "natural law" here would not mean acting according to a form that has a preordained end. Rather, it would mean unique participants in the act of being, realizing their selfhood in a unique way. The Christological and Trinitarian controversies do not engage much of today's world, but the tension between the natural and the personal still underlies many of our moral dilemmas. In the care of the dying, for example, who I am may be in considerable tension with what is happening to my organism.

2) *Natural and Supernatural.* The distinction between nature and supernatural grace runs throughout medieval thought and continues until at least the nineteenth century. This pairing has some relation to the preceding one, but it more directly pertains to a religious transformation of all creation. Theologians saw all of history in the light of

the Jewish and Christian narrative of sinful humanity being divinely transformed. Thomas Aquinas presented the most integrated picture of a graced world in which human nature stands open to a fulfillment by divine grace.

By the time of the Reformation and Counter-Reformation, the medieval synthesis had collapsed. Nature and grace were seen in juxtaposition: two layers, the lower visible to everyone, the higher visible only to those having faith. This caricature, which Christian writers unfortunately acceded to, lost the tension and the inner unity between grace and nature. The questions became: Does grace build on nature? Is nature corrupt? Is the proper Christian stance "to act against nature"? With such questions, the range of possible answers in a Christian moral theology were severely limited. The discussion was of concepts that were by definition about things above our natures. Twentieth-century theologians such as Henri de Lubac and Karl Rahner pointed out that a grace that is beyond experience bears strong resemblance to no grace at all.[8] The tension continues in moral life. A twentieth-century religious person has to ask how saintliness, moral heroism, or simple loyalty is to be imagined and how to imagine the tension between bodily structure and transforming unity.

3) *Natural and Historical.* A distinction between nature and history governs much of the modern era in the West. Many other variations on this distinction have emerged: natural and social, natural and cultural, natural and political. The laws of nature refer to the realm of necessity, whereas history connotes freedom. There is a sharp division between the physical sciences in their search for universal laws, and history with its contingencies, novelties, and great men.

As was pointed out above, history is often equated with "man" or man's exclusive possession of free will. It was thought that only man conceived of ends and operates with purpose. Metaphors of conquest became the way to describe the relation of history and nature. In Francis Bacon's image, "man will put nature to the rack and demand answers." The great hope of the seventeenth, eighteenth, and nineteenth centuries was that "men" would make themselves "masters and owners of nature." The only feminine image that has played a major part in this dichotomy is the contrast of nature and nurture. Although this contrast suggests cooperation rather than opposition, the language of nature/nurture is still an unhelpful split in looking at most human issues.

4) *Natural and Artificial.* The distinction between nature and artifice is by no means new, but it has suddenly emerged into prominence during the last two decades. The amazing part of the story is the near reversal in evaluating the two realms. In 1920, "plastic" was a word enthusiastically used to praise human possibilities; fifty years later, "plastic" was a code word for phoniness. The sudden upgrading of

what is natural and the corresponding downgrading of the artificial are a sign of pessimism about what modern science has wrought. The atom bomb is the chief symbol of disillusionment with science, although a Frankenstein view of science did not seem to spread throughout the culture until the 1970s, capped by the near disaster at Three Mile Island. Now we have grave suspicions of living on top of an ecological time bomb. Dupont of Delaware is still making chemicals, but it would not dare today to advertise its contribution as "better things for better living through chemistry."

Artifice refers to what human beings make. The human animal, instead of resting in nature, insists on making art and inventing devices. In United States history, technology has always been our glory: progress is our most important product. However, there has always been another side to that history, a nostalgia for unspoiled nature. Tom Paine in the eighteenth century wrote, "America has demonstrated to the artificial world that man must go back to nature for information."[9] Throughout the nineteenth century we had numerous attempts to go back to nature or at least to flee from the evils of urban civilization. Thus, the recent disillusionment with the artificial and the praise of what is natural is not a new phenomenon in U.S. history. Of course, few people totally despair of science and its technological benefits. They drive their cars to the supermarket, where they can buy natural bread with no artificial preservatives and natural light beer.

In summary, as "natural" is paired with each of the four terms above, its meaning shifts across a wide range. Natural as opposed to personal has quite a different meaning from natural as opposed to artificial. A natural diet, for example, is presumably not an impersonal diet or a non-nurturing diet. In the late twentieth century we are heirs to all of these meanings of "natural." When anyone uses the term it is likely to have several of the meanings in a confused relation. The dizzying ambiguity of the idea is not likely to cease. We do not get clarity by simply defining what the word means.

The good news of the late twentieth century is that we have better data than past centuries had about the behavior of animals and the complexities of the life cycle. These data are important as we try to maintain a coherent pattern of meaning for nature and to close the unhealthy dichotomy between "man" and nature. We are entering an era no longer enamored by the "conquest of nature." If we can avoid despair in our attitude to technology, resisting romanticized notions about a return to nature, we will be able to explore the human vocation at the limits of nature.

THE HUMAN VOCATION

Classical philosophy and ancient religion were well aware that the human animal holds a peculiar position in the world of natures. As

G. K. Chesterton was fond of saying: "Man is the only wild animal. It is man that has broken out."[10] The human being has always broken out of nature—to a degree. Speech, technology, and urbanization create a gulf between human and nonhuman animals. Nonetheless, birth and death have not been eliminated, and these two are more than points at the extremes of life's journey. Birth means entry into the world of physical organisms with given limits. Death, which the human animal anticipates throughout life, is a driving force of human efforts at self-protection.

The human being is the speaking animal, the animal who makes promises. Because human hopes and fears can be extravagant, it is not only a wild but a dangerous animal. It has always been a player with fire, testing the limits of what is given by the cycle of birth, growth, decline, and death. Having "broken out," the human being has to try finding order on a new basis. A humanly restored order is never only a natural order; on the other hand, human order can never entirely dispense with the natural. In the quotation at the beginning of this chapter Samuel Gorovitz denies any moral significance to the natural. Considered in isolation, "natural" may be morally neutral. But the heart of human morality is the relation between the natural and what is not natural.

When we say that something is natural we often mean that it is widely done or that it is a regular occurrence. When the sun rises in the morning and the moon in the evening we assume that nature is on course. Scientific laws of nature help us to determine and then to predict what will happen. We know, for example, how gases will react in relation to heat and pressure. Contemporary scientists admit that such laws are not universal truths but rather statements of extremely high probability. All the oxygen could move to the corner of the room and leave everyone in the room to suffocate, but the probability of this happening is so infinitesmal that we do not worry about it. We generally live in confidence that nature is regular and predictable, even, for example, in the case of earthquakes whose occurrence we do not yet know how to predict but whose imminence is apparently known to some nonhuman animals.

The animals are not only part of nature; they are the origin of the idea. The behavior of nonhuman animals fits with recurring patterns. A bodily organism in a particular environment has a range of possible activities. Behavior outside of that limit would destroy the species. For example, every species has a limit to the number of offspring supportable by its environment. These recurring patterns of the animal world may not be evident from a few minutes or a few days of observation. But a pattern that continues for years or centuries can be called natural to the organism or natural to the organic patterns of an environment. We thereby move from "natural" as a word meaning what regularly occurs to "natural" as what has to be. We expect animals to act in accord with their natures or the way they are. Cats are not supposed to bark; birds ought to fly; giraffes should have longer necks than hippopotamuses.

When we introduce the term "human nature" we should be aware that we are using shorthand for a complex combination of ideas. I will write it as human-nature for a reminder that we are not really referring to a class of things called natures, one of which is the human. Rather, we are referring to the human in its place among the animals as "the wild animal that has broken out." The human being's range of activity is immeasurably extended, although it still has limits (often not obvious) that it cannot transgress without serious harm.

The term "human-nature" indicates both the natural inborn structure and the human capacity to transcend the organismic. Concerning inborn structure, humans should be interested in learning what they can from their nearest neighbors. The behavior of chimps or dolphins does not dictate what good human activity must be; however, the behavior of nonhuman animals may suggest limits that cannot be disregarded. What the animals have regularly done for centuries is probably good for them. Animal behavior in accord with nature has lessons to teach the human species provided that humans have the humility to learn.

In much of modern history, humans have been curiously ignorant of the actual behavior of the animal world. One could go farther and say that humans deliberately remained ignorant so they could project their own worst tendencies on the animals and prove that "man" and beast are hardly related at all. The closest acknowledged relation was our saying that an irresponsible individual was "acting like an animal." Humans flattered themselves with the assumption that they are reasonable whereas beasts are vicious. A favorite example of an image expressing a negative and despairing view of life was: "Man is a wolf." Ironically, we have come to discover that wolves are paradigms of steadiness and good conduct. They are faithful spouses and parents, they respect one another's territory, they keep clean, they seldom kill except for food, and when they fight each other they do so only to the point of a ritualized act of submission.[11]

The point of this description is not that humans should be just like wolves or any other animals. The human being is the wild animal whose order has to be a restored order, one that is achieved through cooperation. But the wish to be as far as possible from the animal world leaves the human being ignorant and vulnerable when it comes to solving conflicts that involve space, bodies, and emotion. A knowledge of bodily rituals might act as a restraint to the human capacity for all-out triumph—and destruction—when conflict occurs.

What animals regularly do is at least preliminary evidence for accepting their activity as part of human-nature. Anything that is truly natural can be incorporated into human-nature. But it does *not* follow that what is absent from the other animals cannot be part of human-nature. I have said that the peculiar term "human-nature" refers both to what is natural and to what is beyond (that is, transforms) nature. When we say "natural" in reference to human activity we are often referring to this tension between *what* a human being is and dimensions of human activity that are personal, gracious, historical, or artificial. When religious groups say that "human nature is corrupt or fallen" they need not imply an elaborate theory about a corrupt thing; they can be describing a fairly obvious set of activities that issue from the tension between the natural and trans-natural.

Human-nature thus often functions as a moral phrase, a bridge between what is given us to work with and what morally results. This distinction, it should be noted, is not the false dichotomy of *is* and *ought* that has plagued twentieth century ethics. The question raised at the turn of the century was "how to derive an ought from an is," how to move from fact to prescription.[12] The answer to this question is that you cannot do so. But the question assumes that a) we start from facts, that is, morally neutral statements, b) we need to have prescriptions of what to do in order to have morality.

On the first point, concerning facts, we never start from bare facts. Even in the physical sciences our descriptions represent choices among ways of representing our relation to the world beyond us. Facts (from the Latin word for "to do") are a combination of what we have discovered and what we have formed in language. As the human element comes more into the forefront of the facts (in history, social studies, politics) our language has more of moral valence. A dinner is not the name of an object; it is what human beings need and enjoy. A home is less a physical plant than a human dwelling place. A friend, a parent, a game, a rape, a blackmail, a fraud are names of human realities that both describe what is and reflect a moral stance already taken.

On the second point, concerning "ought," it is misleading to suggest that the point of morality is to tell people what they ought to do. The assumption seems to be that there is an end point to be reached and there is only one way to get there. That is the way "natural law" was sometimes interpreted: each thing or person must act in this prescribed way because that is its nature. However, in a responsible morality, response is to everything and everyone, to each reality according to its appropriate place in the cosmos. What limits the response is the organic dimensions of the responder and the particular aspect of the universe being responded to. In practically all cases, there is a variety of appropriate responses. Morality is not a set of prescriptions of how one ought to live; it is a living with respect for what birth, past human lives, and the present nurturing environment provide for our response.

Writers who gleefully announce that "you cannot derive an ought from an is" usually draw the conclusion that ethics is about choice, rights, principles, and tolerance of differences. However, a responsible morality is not concerned with telling us what we ought to do but insists on what we ought *not* to do. A lack of prescriptions does not mean that anything goes or that choice makes right. Some things that human beings do are wrong and deserve condemnation.

A morality with "don'ts" may seem to be a negative view of life. Actually, a few clear prohibitions free us to explore many possibilities. We do not know what a perfect diet is, but we need to know and we can know what poison is. Once we have excluded poison from our diet, we can explore varieties of food. We can constantly improve our diet and discover that there is no such thing as a "perfect diet." Would anyone complain that his or her freedom to eat is violated because poisonous foods are eliminated from the supermarket? Generally speaking, no; even the most ardent libertarian does not care to drop dead after taking a poisoned Tylenol. In practice, we, or a consumer protection agency, make distinctions about how poisonous something is and what purpose traces of poisonous materials might serve. As this example suggests, moral reflection moves backward from the worst case to borderline cases. We can recognize some activities as dreadfully wrong (poison in the Tylenol, razor blades in Halloween apples, cyanide in the city water supply), and then we argue by way of analogy about less obvious cases. Spraying a crowded supermarket with an automatic rifle is clearly wrong. Shooting a man who is trying to rob the supermarket manager is somewhat similar, but the differences demand that we examine all the details before judging the action.

The central moral issue should now be clear. The human vocation is to go beyond the natural but not against it. In morally good activity we do nothing out of accord with nature; we do not reject, oppose, or destroy the natural. The human vocation is gentle transformation that does no violence and may even improve the natural. My term "transnatural" refers to all realms of the non-natural that are not unnatural. The personal, the gracious, the historical, and the artificial are not natural but they need not be unnatural, a term that connotes contortion, violence, and at least in the long run, destruction. Smoking tobacco may have once seemed a harmless gesture of human inventiveness; time and medical tests have shown it to be unnatural.

The distinction between non-natural and unnatural is similar to that between nonrational and irrational. The latter term connotes incoherence, craziness, violence. But some people who do not abide by contemporary standards of reasonableness are not crazy. Many artists and religious people go their own gentle way within their own set of nonrational concerns. A person who refuses to accept the rational processes of a government agency may only seem to be irrational; he or she may be fighting the premise of the system in a way that makes eminent sense. A Greenpeace raft taking on a Soviet whaler is not an irrational act; it is an act of defiance that appeals to a moral sense of life and chooses not to go the route of reasoning. Salvador de Madriaga has written that the most widespread religious doctrine is the belief that God is not utterly mad—a far cry from the belief that God is a reasonable fellow just like you and me.

With the distinction between non-natural and unnatural in mind, we can state the foundation of morality: What is unnatural is immoral. Very simply, anything in direct opposition to the natural, leading to its destruction, is morally bad. The caution must be immediately added that this statement is only a starting point. Without a wealth of experimental data we cannot jump to conclusions about sex, medicine, eating, dressing, and most other things. John Boswell points out that shaving, regular bathing, and wearing wigs were activities once thought to be unnatural.[13] We have discovered that some supposedly unnatural acts really are not that way, but this is not to say that the category unnatural is becoming depleted. Pouring radioactive chemicals in a river is an unnatural act although our moral language has not caught up to the practice.

In Chapter 8 I examine homosexuality as a case in point where the word "unnatural" has traditionally been used. In this chapter it may be helpful to use sexuality as a general area for reflection upon the trans-natural. If one asks, "What is sex for?" the most obvious answer is: procreation. Ask a biological question and you get a biological answer. Nature in nearly all the animals makes a direct connection between sex activity and procreation. If one asks "What is human sexuality for?" the answer might be: a variety of things. That response is the route that sexual liberation generally took in both church and secular law. A more startling answer to the question "What is sexuality for?" would be that it is not *for* anything. It is a pattern of responses that has neither end point nor an object to be attained. That answer would have the advantage of forcing us to look at sexuality itself and at all of its variations. Some of what human beings have been doing for centuries may be dastardly. But if we are frightfully ignorant of data we cannot distinguish between what happens to strike us as outlandish and what is truly unnatural.

The two Kinsey reports in the middle of this century revealed data that surprised almost everyone.[14] Alfred Kinsey, who had been a student of insect behavior, simply counted the sexual activities of people. He was castigated by moral and religious leaders for either counting wrong or for merely counting rather than evaluating. Over the years, though, the accuracy of his numbers has stood up well. As for evaluation, moral issues are not resolved by counting. Nevertheless, a knowledge of how people actually behave is preferable to ignorance when making moral evaluations. Knowing that millions of people perform a sexual activity provides some perspective in gathering further information as to whether the act is unnatural. In contrast, first encounters with sexual activity are often shocking. Many a child has thought that its mother was being treated violently on the basis of the moans coming through the bedroom wall.

Sexual activity, like other forms of play, involves closeness to danger. A high-wire walker, a marathon runner, an outfielder diving for a catch perform at the limits of endurance where a false step can be disastrous. Like all the animals, human groups have rituals to work out their fears, drives, and potential violence. Unlike the other animals, humans put elaborate creativity into their rituals. However complex the game, human play is a tension between physical demands with an element of danger and rituals that diffuse violence.

As human beings play at being sexual—that is, as they reorder the sexual tendencies they have as animals—they need rituals and practices that may look irrational and unnatural to the spectator. Sexual activity often does turn violent; there are natural limits that should not be transgressed. Mary Midgely, distinguishing between what she calls a weak sense of "natural" (regular occurrence) and a strong sense (morally acceptable), writes: "That consenting adults should bite each other in bed is in all senses natural; that schoolteachers should bully children for their sexual gratification is not."[15] She means that while both activities regularly occur, the first is within the boundaries of a human transforming of natural sex but the second is a violent contortion of sexual life. We might, of course, wish to know precisely what she means by biting each other. Presumably she means a playful nip rather than someone sinking teeth into flesh until blood flows.

We can confidently say that sadomasochism is immoral. However, that label does not take us very far. For moral judgments about particular acts, we need precise data and a large context. A ritual that moves in the direction of reducing violence may be acceptable moral behavior in lives previously racked with violence. Rituals of being tied up or spanked could be part of working through unresolved sexual feelings. On the other hand, rituals that are leading to an increase of violence may need moral resistance even though the individual act of sexual coercion may seem minor. A man's hand on a little girl's thigh can be a vicious intrusion.

THE TRANS-NATURAL AS NON-VIOLENT

Immanuel Kant was right in seeing the need for an imperative rather than a general principle at the base of morality. The imperative is an ought not: Do violence to no one. Innumerable distinctions and further data for working out the implications of this imperative are needed, but it provides the two things necessary for an adequate moral posture:

concreteness and universality. Every human being has a concrete referent for the word "violence." Granted that whether or not some acts
are violent is debatable, it can still be said that an atomic explosion is
violent, hatcheting someone in the head is violent, hitting a guard rail
at eighty miles an hour is violent, raping a five-year-old is violent—
and plenty of other concrete cases are not hard to come by. The imperative is universal in that "no one" refers to all human beings, including oneself and, further, it refers to nonhuman others.

As we try to imagine what this imperative means in practice, the
difficulties of living nonviolently loom as unimaginably complex. Every
society known to have existed has forbidden indiscriminate killing. Each
society, however, works out compromises to discriminate among kill-
ings. Frequently one's enemies are called something other than human
(white men are allowed to kill savages); a Nuer mother kills her deformed baby because the society says it is not a human baby but a
hippopotamus. The world divides into "my people" and the others;
under certain conditions the others may be killed.

Moral critics within a particular society take issue with these conven-
tions and compromises, sensing that there is a continuous texture to
the web of life. Very few people are ready to extend the recognition
of life's claim to every cockroach and mosquito. The Jain monk goes
the farthest in that direction by wearing a gauze mask and sweeping
the ground before him. This attempt to avoid killing insects is extreme,
but for those who claim to respect life, there is no obvious basis for
drawing a line between organisms to be respected and others that need
not be.

Christianity at its most mystical and sacramental goes farther than
respect for insects. As I have noted in the previous two chapters, the
Christian mystic sees nonliving objects as also deserving of respect. The
human vocation is to listen respectfully and to respond nonviolently to
river and rock as well as to tree and animal. Humans cannot avoid
putting their foot into the ecological system. The moral question is
whether they act in tune with the cycles of nature or whether they set
out to exploit, conquer, and subdue.

Western culture would seem to have a lot to learn from the Eastern
ideal of compassion for all living things. Perhaps today the East also
needs the scientific information of the West to make a nonviolent
stance realistic and effective. If a species proliferates by the billions, it
is unclear why one's moral energies should be focused on not killing
one member. If nature itself has cycles of birth and death, the killing
of a creature is not necessarily a moral calamity. Attention would seem
best directed to the complex cycles of life and death, so that human
actions are not violent intrusions into these precarious balances. A compassion for the members of one species can produce results that lead
to their over proliferation that then undoes the balance in the envi-

ronment. More moral energy might also be directed at changing po-litical-economic systems that indirectly cause great suffering.

When human knowledge is far out of proportion to what we are tampering with, violence is likely to be unleashed even though we plead that violence was not intended. Nuclear power is the chief symbol today of human beings dangerously playing with a toy they do not really understand and certainly cannot control. Discussion of how to store radioactive waste lacks all sense of proportionality, considering only that nation-states may last a few centuries while the half life of the chemicals is tens of thousands of years. Modern medicine is another area where we are confused about technological possibilities. Geneticists should not be prevented from any scientific exploration, but the tech-nological experiments ought not to outstrip what is firmly known.

We live in a world of considerable violence. Nature achieves balance and harmony, but not without explosive conflicts. The human beings are often the recipients of these explosions. Perhaps nature cannot be accused of doing violence to humanity, but the results nevertheless are suffering and chaos. If humans better understood the doings of nature, the effects of flood, drought, earthquakes, cyclones and other "natural disasters" might be lessened. But some kinds of nonhuman violence have always been with us, and the problem of human violence is added to these. Whatever the roots of human violence, it has been present in every age and among every people. Some people seem much less vi-olent than others, but no one is entirely removed from violence.

The important conclusion to this omnipresence of violence is that the moral imperative "do violence to no one" is always carried out in resistance to many tendencies in the opposite direction. Morality re-quires not just reasonableness but courage, discipline, and stamina. And if that be the case, we should not be surprised when we sometimes fail. The recognition and acceptance of our own failures make it easier to understand the failures of other people. The act of forgiveness is an indispensable part of all morality—forgiveness of others and forgive-ness of ourselves. We forgive by doing good to others, opening again the mutual exchange of power that has been disrupted by an act of violence.

It is not our task to create a totally nonviolent world, but we are called to lessen the violence in a violent world. We can try to do violence to no one, and as we find that most of our actions are contaminated by violence, we will be led to activities that modify our sense of "try." Through cooperation with other humans and with nonhumans, through openness to forces that transcend the earth, we will discover that freedom is a kind of response. We will still make mistakes, but we will be moved away from gestures of domination and exploitation that underlie human violence. With less human energy spent on conquest and subjugation, more energies of a healing kind might be released among all the earth's inhabitants.

CHAPTER 7

Private/Public Morality

A morality of goodness, besides being responsible and trans-natural, is public. It contibutes to the welfare of others and prepares the world for the next generation, which is at least some of the meaning of the term "public." Like "natural," "public" is a quite confusing term, although its history has fewer sharp turns than the history of "natural." "Public" has almost always been paired with a single term: "private." The meaning of "public," therefore, has been what is non-private. The history of the relation of public and private has one dramatic shift in the course of Western culture as well as a contemporary malaise about where to go from here.

The question that always must be asked of such a term is whether it is worth arguing about. In this case, the word "public" has thousands of years of history embedded in it and continues to show up in numerous important discussions. Furthermore, the rich meaning I argue that "public" should have is sufficiently present in many of its usages that the task is not hopeless. Like the word "responsible," "public" generally gets reduced to a single thing rather than being a complex set of relations.

The first problem is the reduction of "public" to "governmental." This tendency is very strong in the United States, where today "public policy" nearly always means the policy of the government. Likewise, "public school" in the U.S. means a governmental and tax-supported school (a British public school would be a private school in the U.S.). Public transportation is mass transportation under the government's aegis. The same language holds for public welfare, public housing, public toilets, and hundreds of other items: public is what the government does.

This equation might not be so bad except that it is combined with a historic distrust of governmental power. "Private property" is taken to be sacred; the government's role is mainly to stay out of the way. *New York Magazine* recently did a story on new immigrants to the U.S. One immigrant says: "What a wonderful country this is. You can say anything you want and nobody cares." Indeed, "nobody cares" is a fine description of what happens when "public" means government and government is kept from intruding. If your interest is freedom of speech, it is wonderful that nobody (including the secret police) cares. If you are a welfare mother with four children and no job, "nobody cares" is a bitter commentary on the arrangement of private goods and public noninterference. Private wealth/public squalor is not an inexplicable mystery that the U.S. cannot shake off. It is the basic division of things whether one is talking of housing, transportation, recreation, or toilets. Enough money gets you private goods; poverty gets you public doles.

This chapter is not a jeremiad on the maldistribution of wealth or an argument for a more liberal welfare policy. In the twentieth century, "liberal" and "Democratic" have usually meant a more benign view of government and therefore a larger welfare role for government. "Conservative" and "Republican" have usually meant a theory of getting the government "off our backs." My argument about the meaning of "public" is outside this debate. I am interested in the historical background that gave rise to this political situation and the possibility of uncovering a meaning of "public" that is not equivalent to government, whether viewed from left or right.

The assumption in most political debates today is that the choice is between individual and government. Increasing the power of one is presumed to decrease the power of the other. Thomas Jefferson wrote that that government is best which governs least and the best government would be no government at all. Of course, Jefferson assumed that churches, schools, and civic organizations would provide governance of another kind. He also envisaged a nation of farmers, each of them self-sufficient on "his" own plot of land. The changes in the late nineteenth century upset this dream of individual self-sufficiency. With the great concentrations of money and wealth, many individuals were ending up unproductive, criminal, or sick. Thus was born the age of progressive reform and the language of morality we are heirs to in the present age.

Two quite different things went under the label of progressivism. The two agreed in their concern about the incapacity of the individual to cope with the emerging world of big corporations and complex technology. One wing of progresssivism consisted of organizational theorists who calculated economic improvement with a cold efficiency. The way to improve the lot of individuals, they argued, is for experts to organize the individuals for better competitiveness. The other wing of progressivism consisted of populists who advocated compassion for the downtrodden. Experience in groups would blend the individual into better social relations. One of the few places where both kinds of progressive reform had their chance was the public school. The organizational experts began to arrive as early as the 1870s, slowly changing the school system into a massive bureaucracy. John Dewey's reform, with its concern for group activity and community relations, came later. The key term in this reform is "social."

Outside of the schools and liberal Protestant churches the language of social reform did not get very far. But it did supply a rallying cry for moral reformers to the left in the twentieth century. "Social" became a way to differentiate liberal, and conservative approaches to morality. When liberals say "social" they mean "nothing less than social"; when conservatives say social they mean "nothing more than social." That is, the liberal's use of "social" presumes that the enemy is individualism, so that "social" means getting to the heart of the problem by transcending the individual. The conservative's use of "social" assumes that the enemy is a lack of true individuality, so "social," meaning group conformity, is no help and is perhaps a danger. Liberal and conservative agree that "social" is the alternative to "individual" and that morality is to be discussed as individual or as social.

I wish to argue that the language of individual vs. social, like individual vs. governmental, is inadequate. Christian writers who are fighting against the "privatization" of Christianity speak of "social ethics." They might do better to talk about public morality and its complex set of relations. Public morality has a place for both governmental bodies and social relations, but both of these must be kept in their place, that is, at the service of the public life of men, women, children, and non-humans. The history of the relation of public and private does involve the history of the rise of the social. I outline in the following section the two main forms that the division of private and public has taken, and how the modern concern with the social may be a key to a new relation of public and private.

THE HISTORY OF "PUBLIC" AND "PRIVATE"

Our meanings of "public" and "private" derive in large part from the ideal of the Greek city state.[1] The *polis* contained both the privacy of the household and the public domain of political life. The family household was caught up in the necessities of life and was regulated by the power of the father. Equality did not apply to membership in the family: man, woman, child, and slave occupied distinct levels of family existence. The family, insofar as it was forced to labor for survival from day to day, was the realm of necessity; hence the word "private": to be lacking in something (from the Latin *privatus*, "deprived"), specifically, to be lacking in freedom.

The family's lack of freedom was "natural." Someone had to cook the food, clean the house, chop the wood. The human animal has to labor for its survival. Someone and something had to shelter children until they were ready to engage in mutual exchange with their elders.

The private realm was a dark world, a place of shadows where some things went on unchanged generation after generation, and some things were nurtured until they were ready for emergence into the light.

The public realm, in direct contrast to the dark necessity facing domestic life, was the place of light and freedom. Those citizens who could leave behind the necessary labors of the household did so. They stepped into the arena of political discourse as the free men of the *polis* (city). Here there was radical equality with one's peers, a fact that did not exclude a striving for excellence by individual men. Aristotle's definition of the human being as "the animal capable of speech" refers directly to this political realm.

Public life was preeminently a place of dialogue and debate. Human beings either achieve order by the use of speech or else resort to violence. Political life in the Greek ideal is the use of civility, rationality, and discussion without end. Decisions that are reached after careful reflection benefit the whole *polis*. The Greeks, as is well known, distrusted democracy, the rule of the *demos* or masses. A humanly ordered world requires disciplined thought and careful choice by small groups of people with common interests. Politics is speech that maintains distance between people but is about what *inter-ests* ("is between") them.

This ideal of public and political life had only a brief flowering in practice, but some of its idealistic hopes lived on in Western history. The founders of the "new science of politics" in the seventeenth and eighteenth centuries took some of their inspiration from the *polis* and Greek philosophical ideas. The great hope of freedom was raised aloft. At the same time, the U.S. Constitution reflects a fear of rule by the masses, building in safeguards such as indirect voting for president and senator as well as restriction of the franchise.

Some of the characteristics of modern government suggest a shift that had occurred in the nearly two millennia between old and new politics. The individual was now at the forefront, suspicious of large concentrations of power. As the *Federalist Papers* explain, the genius of the U.S. system was its design to divide these powers and to play them off against each other. Even in a large republic, or especially in a large republic, the individual has a series of protective covers: division of state and federal power, division of bicameral legislatures, division of executive and legislative branches.[2]

Among the founding fathers of the U.S. republic there was high respect for public life. Public life had to draw the man of courage and dedication to its service. If the new experiments in polity were to succeed, there had to be thoughtful people who would be concerned with what *inter-ests* the whole community. A constantly widening pool of talent was available as the franchise was extended to more groups.

The celebration of the individual and the protection of individual rights had the effect of moving the ideal of freedom into the area where it had been lacking, that is, the private. This expansion of freedom would seem to be progress, except that progress in privacy's freedom was matched with suspicion about government's interfering in that freedom. In almost an exact reversal of the Greek ideal, "private" became the realm of freedom and "public" became the necessary instruments for the protection of privacy. There are still two realms, but the private is now the valued one.

"SOCIAL"

One way to trace this remarkable shift in the relation of public and private is to examine the rise of society and the social. Our word for "social" comes from Latin, and it originally refered to a group that was formed for a specific purpose. The meaning is still evident in our word "association," a voluntary grouping of people who are interested in medicine, trucking, stamp collecting, or any of a thousand things. The Greeks did not have a term that precisely coincides with "society," the generalized and abstract meaning that emerged in Latin. Individuals in modern times belong to a collective and comprehensive unit called society. Hannah Arendt, who is much concerned in her writing with the rise and the domination of the social, credits the Christian church, or perhaps one should say blames the Christian church, for a major part in the rise of the social.[3]

Christianity set out to create a bond among all people who are called by God. The divisions between Jew and Greek, man and woman, slave and free man, were to be transcended in the Christ figure. Christianity therefore resisted the split into private and public sectors. On the private side, the Christian movement refused to be confined to the shadow life of the single household. Even when private houses were used for churches, the liturgy brought the household into contact with other households and into relation with the principalities and powers of the universe. On the public side, Christianity did not see itself as a political movement involved in dialogue, debate, and compromise. Transcending the split of private and public, Christianity claimed to unite people by a bond of charity or a mystical body. The church took over the word "society" from other associations of the time, such as the funeral society to which it was compared in Rome. But beyond all particular societies, the church saw its mission to be *the* society of all people.

The Christian movement triumphed only in part. The world did not get swept away in the endtime where all things would be united in Christ. Neither did all people respond to the gospel announcement and become part of a universal church. The hard divisions of Greek and Jew, woman and man, slave and free man, remained visible even within the church itself. As the church developed its organizational structure, it took on elements of political debate and factions. Perhaps because of an unwillingness to acknowledge its human limits, the church resisted the idea of political machinery in its exercise of power. When Aristotle was rediscovered in Western philosophy, the political did not have the distinctive elements it had in the Greek *polis*. Hannah Arendt sees as a disastrous change the line she attributes to Aquinas: "Man is naturally political, that is, social."[4] Individuals now lived in societies, the imperfect society of the state and, as later ecclesiologists formulated it, the perfect society of the church.

When the modern world came to birth in the seventeenth and eighteenth centuries, the social was an established category. The church was now one society among others or, rather, one claim within a more comprehensive society in general. As the church's ideal of unity receded, the vision of a common humanity to which all individuals belong nevertheless remained in place. Study of the past and discoveries of other lands helped to create a sense of fraternity despite the diversity of culture. If you scrape away all the accretions, it was believed, you would find a noble and primitive example of individual humanity.

The ominous side of this vision of sameness was the implied control of individual life. Society could be a kind of church without Christ, where everyone is expected to behave with proper decorum. The struggle for freedom in Europe and North America was centered on the overthrowing of political despotism, but the struggle for freedom from "social conformity" also began. The individual was now acutely aware of "himself" and his behavior as he confronts a collective unity of the social.[5] The meaning of social behavior is nicely captured in this newspaper story: "A father tells his three year old to behave. The child responds: But daddy, I am being haved."[6] We tend to laugh, assuming the child has misunderstood the word "behave," whereas in fact the child is very attuned to the original meaning: to be "haved" (had). Either I have myself or others have me—that is, the anonymous mass represented by "social roles" controls me. In relation to behavior the alternatives are the private choice of the individual or the coercion of social collectivity.

For the last several centuries, discussions of freedom have generally started with the will and the need to protect the privacy of the individual. The family, somewhat illogically, has been on the private side of the modern divide. A free man should be surrounded by his family: his wife, his children, his servants, his house, his goats and sheep. The belief has been strong in Protestant Christianity that the family is the one "natural" associaton.[7] Every other form of human organization is at best the family writ large. Classical thought and medieval theology would have found this projection of the family image peculiar. And it does not entirely fit into the glorification of individual liberty.

THE POSSIBILITIES OF THE SOCIAL

From the above considerations we can draw some conclusions about the historical effects and the possibilities of the social. As I understand Arendt's treatment, she is completely pessimistic about the emergence of society. Recall that society did not come about as a third element but as an alternative to public and private. I think we have to consider both the good and the bad possibilities in this development, first on the private side and then on the public side.

The good news for the private household is that labor was brought into the light. The people who had performed the burdensome tasks throughout the centuries got a chance to improve their lot. Slavery was bound to disappear once it was subjected to social criticism. A respect for individual humanity finds it intolerable to own other people. Others who were not slaves but had carried out necessary labors also received help from the light that society brought.

I cannot imagine glorifying a situation in which the majority of people were not "free men." Before the rise of modern technology, the necessities of life may have seemed to require that most people live poor, laborious, and unfree lives; ancient Athens needed as many as four slaves to liberate one free man. We no longer think that God established this order and that it is unchangeable. Today's society with its technology holds out the possibility of a more humane order. Buckminster Fuller used to say that each U.S. citizen has the equivalent in technological help of 150 slaves. In such a social order, men can recognize women as full human beings with rights. Children can also be acknowledged as persons who bear rights even though children still require a set of protections and restraints.

The bad news for the private sphere is that the family's distinctive character may be blurred. The relation of parent and child may sink into the fuzziness of "social relationships." Twentieth-century society is not as convinced as seventeenth century Puritans that the family is a "natural association." Marriage has become more like other voluntary contracts, dissolvable at the wishes of either party. Children are now acquiring more say in divorce proceedings, but overall progress for children in today's society is dubious. I think that Arendt's concern on this point is a legitimate one:

The more completely modern society discards the distinction between what is private and what is public, between what can thrive only in concealment and what needs to be shown to all in the full light of the public world, ... the harder it makes things for its children, who by nature require the security of concealment in order to mature undisturbed.[8]

Christopher Lasch in *Haven in a Heartless World* attacks the social sciences and social workers as the enemy of the family.[9] I think he overstates the case and that the family is not in the dire condition he assumes it to be. Nevertheless, the family does need to resist the embrace of its helpers, the social experts who wish to fix up each family to fit society's image. The television set, turned on an average of seven hours a day in U.S. households, is a symbol of society's conformity. Even without a Big Brother looking into the living room, we still feel a pressure to conform to television's dictates: the right clothing, the right cereal, the right speech pattern, the right Christmas doll, the right way to raise children.

On the public side, the rise of society also has good and bad effects. On a positive note, the public sector can be stabilized and better ordered by institutions that complement the state and its politics. In the U.S., voluntary organizations mediating between individual and government have made a crucial contribution. As government becomes unavoidably large and impersonal, people need to find their identity in face-to-face associations that contribute to a sense of well-being and control. Larger associations can sometimes provide a sense of participation in public life.

Two examples of such organization are the university and the sports team. The university's role is to contribute to the political order without itself becoming political. It is to be a zone of free speech that is given specific political protections against interference. We reserve the special word *politicize* to describe what happens when an organization such as the university is turned into an arm of state politics. The line is sometimes a fine one between a university responding to social needs and a university no longer exercising a critical function. Good universities, whether they are called private or public, are social institutions that relate the individual to public service.

The sports team is a social group that is especially important to U.S. cities. A baseball or basketball team may do more for racial integration than any number of governmental decrees. A city's sense of well-being can be tied to the fortunes of its hometown team. Despite the sports industry's getting caught up in big-time economics, the game itself remains a communal, quasi-religious activity. Thousands of people associate around an event that intensely interests them. Although spectatorship is sometimes disparaged, being a spectator can be a participation in excellence, and learning to be a spectator is important for political life.

On the negative side, political life faces a threat similar to the family's: the social tends to swallow its friends. Politics has tended to become national housekeeping, with the executive branch of government being called "the administration." In the U.S. one might look to the Senate as the place where a political body is articulating the nature of our lives together. The fact that half of the Senate's members are millionaires could mean that these leaders are freed from life's necessities so as to engage in deep reflection and high powered debate. The additional fact that they are nearly all white and male suggests a limitation on any political debate and a tendency for the body to resemble a rich social club.

Communist governments certainly score no better on this scale. The picture that the Soviet Union conveys is that of an endless string of male administrators engaged in national housekeeping. Karl Marx's hope for the "socialization of man" and the "withering away of the state" is often ridiculed in light of the gigantic bureaucracies in communist governments.

However, Marx may have been right in an ironic way. The political life of the state has indeed withered away by being absorbed into the social form called bureaucracy. Marx was naive about the question of administration. He did not count on the state/politics being replaced by a social system that is not particularly conducive to the freedom of the individual. Bureaucracy is a system of government in which no one is in charge, a condition that individuals do not experience as liberating.[10] On this point as on many others, Marxism is a peculiar reflection of Christianity: the proclamation of mystical or social union is followed by the growth of cumbersome administrative mechanisms.

Another drawback when social swallows the political is the failure to appreciate *things*, especially those things that exist from one generation to another. The ethical and political debates of modern times concern the primacy of individual or society. The supposition that beyond the individual man there is nothing but groups of men is a peculiarly myopic view. These days women are insisting on a change of language to include them. That step is a partial correction, but the change must go much further to include the nonhuman. Politics is speech that is about what *inter-ests* us, about the things that stand between humans in the context of a world that outlasts each individual speaker. Politics cannot be reduced to individuals talking about their "relationships" or to self-interest (a term nearly self-contradictory).

Human activity is response to past as well as present, to things as well as people. Political decisions should be guides to the men, women, children, and nonhumans who share the earth. Both the formations of the earth, including mountains and water, and humanly made objects, such as art and architecture, situate the individual as an actor in the great narrative of humanity. Place, for example, has special importance in one's sense of political and public life. Place is where communities have sunk roots, and place shapes social, political, economic and religious lives. A community exists when an individual can go to the same place regularly and be confident of meeting the same people. In Hannah Arendt's words: "Only where things can be seen by many in a variety of aspects without changing their identity, so that those who are gathered around them know they see sameness in utter diversity, can worldly reality truly and reliably appear."[11]

A NEW RELATION BETWEEN PRIVATE AND PUBLIC

Having examined the good and bad possibilities in the emergence of the social, we can now suggest a new relation between public and private. Any proposed relation must be historically rooted and at the same time realistic for today's possibilities. The classical meaning of freedom located it in the public realm, and that is a truth not to be abandoned. But the modern meaning of freedom concentrates on the private realm of an inner self; this modern conviction also has the ring of truth. Somehow these seemingly opposite truths have to be reconciled. Before I attempt a reconciliation, notice the inadequacies in classical and modern meanings of freedom. In the classical ideal, a minority of men arguing in the political assembly constitute the public. In the modern development, freedom's locus, instead of being broadened, is narrowed even further: to the individual's inner life. The meaning of public is left to go begging mainly to government or society.

Suppose, first, that the meaning of public is extended from one man or a minority of men to include all men, women, children, nonhuman things of earth, and humanly made objects. Suppose, then, that privacy is not an additional realm but the inner depths of those realities. Freedom is found in the interiority of every human being, and at least traces of freedom exist among nonhuman animals. The modern revolution reversed the realms where freedom is located, but the problem is *realm*. The too-narrow realm of public freedom was narrowed even further to a realm of private freedom (a man and his family). An isolated sector was mistaken for an inner depth. An inner depth to freedom's privacy actually requires a wider public than does either classical or modern meanings of public.

Is there any realistic hope of accomplishing this second major revolution in the relation of public and private so that the two are not conceived to be mutually exclusive sectors of reality but rather the breadth and depth of every activity? Such a change is difficult, but under today's pressure the modern dichotomy of private space and public space is collapsing. The result will be either a healthier unity in which the valuable aspects of public and private are preserved, or else a noisy and superficial blurring of privacy and public exposure. The functioning of social organizations is one of the keys to determining which direction we will go.

The language of social and individual is an inner structure of the private/public relation. Because social means a collectivity of individuals, the social and individual do vary in inverse proportion. Individuals need the help of social organizations lest the individual be isolated in his or her solitude. Social groupings can be very helpful, especially when kept in tension with state or party politics, for the individual does need protection against intrusion by the government. However, the individual may also need to resist subtle intrusions by social organization, because membership in a social group does connote some lessening of individuality.

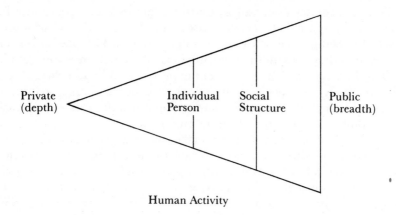

Human Activity

What is difficult to suggest in the above diagram is the fact that private and public vary in direct, not inverse, proportion. The relation is an aesthetic one whereby the universal is embodied in the particular. A great piece of art delves deeper and deeper into the particular so as to manifest a universal truth and beauty. Hamlet is every person even though he is one fictional character in one time and one place. The Guérnica can be any human suffering although it is one man's rendering of one human conflict. *The Marriage of Figaro* is one man's beautiful music that touches a chord about all injustice. A morality of goodness acknowledges that every person, every living thing, every object could reveal ultimate truth if we had the capacity to receive.

This aesthetic principle suggests what is lacking today for a truly private-public morality: ritual. We often try to reach beyond our aloneness by means of technological devices, but the result is often mere "public relations" or publicity. Consider what happens when a television camera intrudes upon private sorrow. An individual's grief is suddenly exposed to thousands of eyes that happen to be looking at the 11 P.M. news. The effect is a kind of obscene exposure that interferes with a person's needed privacy ("How do you feel about your daughter being murdered this morning?"), and reduces the public meaning to one more filler on a news show while revealing almost nothing about the world we share.

In contrast to the blinding exposure of television, a well-done funeral liturgy is both private and public. A centuries-old ritual enables one group of people and individuals within the group to reach out in the direction of all humanity. At the same time and in the same public gestures, private sorrow is allowed, even encouraged. The ritual provides that deeply felt sorrow will not run out of control or withdraw a person from ordinary functioning (although it may provide for a short, clear-cut time for such withdrawal).

We are starved for public rituals that would allow us to experience joy, sorrow, compassion, and a hundred other emotions we cannot feel unless we have public forms of expression. Occasionally television does succeed in being a public ritual. A funeral of a world leader or a sporting event sometimes does unite millions of people in some genuine feeling. Most often that happens unexpectedly, although careful technical planning can facilitate the experience (for example, a funeral). When television tries to manipulate national feelings (for example, the Super Bowl), the result is often an emotional flop.

A private/public act of morality makes us aware of personal response as uniquely our own. No one else can decide for me; my freedom to choose is both a burden and a gift. A private/public act of morality also makes us aware that we are part of some great, unimaginable unity. My personal decision is a response to everyone and everything. Since I cannot examine every side of every issue, I am driven deeper into my personal conscience to listen more intently for a universal truth. A choice to help one person in one needed way can be more public than starting an organization that is supposed to serve millions. Writing a book that will be read by a few thousand rather than by a million readers does not mean the author is uninterested in reaching a wide public. The public includes future generations who might better be served by a book's affecting profoundly a few readers of the present generation rather than by its being this season's publishing sensation.

For enhancing a private/public morality, the social has to be open on both ends—that is, open to political, economic, and ecological structures on the public side and open to individual idiosyncrasy and contemplative quiet on the private side. When the word "social" preempts the moral coin, as has frequently happened in the twentieth century, social activism can be both narrow and arrogant.

People who are active in social programs should not jump to conclusions about people who are not. The opposite of social action is not necessarily political apathy or indifference to public affairs. Cranky individualists and unusual religious groups can be telling us that there are many ways to oppose injustice. Some people avoid the sociable and the socializing because they sense the negative meaning of social: the conforming of one's behavior to the dictates of society. Skepticism about "social reform" can be a helpful reminder of the wisdom of the ages not to put all our trust in human remedies.

With this caution in mind that social reform is not the ultimate answer, we can affirm that protest, socially organized if possible, is at the heart of private/public morality. People who say that the "merely social" is not enough for true spirituality have a responsibility to show the connection between spirituality and the hunger for justice. Consider this glib pronouncement from a widely read book: "The wise aspirant to eternity will recognize no hope of a better social order in his endeavors, for he knows that the expectations of men are incapable of satisfaction. . . . Christians are those who act under the permanent rule that the ways of God are not the ways of men."[12] The partial truth in this statement is offered as an excuse for doing nothing to reduce injustice. True, the ways of some "men," especially those who flagrantly violate justice, are not the ways of God. That is why other men, along with women and children, must act to resist injustice. Wise aspirants to eternity know that we can always hope for and we can constantly realize a better social order even if it remains immeasurably different from whatever God has in mind. None of the great religious founders offered a plan of social reform; but Jesus, Moses, Gautama, and Muhammed gave impetus to personal transformation that has reverberated and must always reverberate in the social order.

Social organizations have to transform public life but at the same time avoid politicization. A university, church, or professional association has to observe rules of fair play in influencing a wide public. Since the government is itself one of the elements in public life, it can prohibit only the most flagrant violations of fair play; it cannot say exactly how the game of moral influence is to be played. Any group claiming to be a moral watchdog has to pay attention to issues of fairness, propriety, and balance. The moral approach needs to be an educational one that respects the individual consciences and explicitly acknowledges the great diversity of public life.

As an example of social action, consider the attempt to improve television. Anyone who does not like a program can send a letter to the producer, the network, or the advertiser. Such action is praiseworthy as civic responsibility. If many people organize their protest, their voices will be better heard; they may even decide to found an organization called "Morality on Television." The danger of such a pressure group is that they may focus too narrowly on their particular likes and dislikes. A small number of people with a large amount of money can have unfair influence on the programming available to all.

A similar example today is the "targeting" of political candidates with large amounts of money from outside the political district. Anyone, including a church official or a religious body, has a right to criticize a politician. During a political campaign any group may organize opposition to a candidate. However, if the opposition is around a single issue or if the procedures are inappropriate for that particular kind of organization, the result is a subversion of the political process. Church leaders should try to educate their people with discussion of a wide range of moral issues in politics. If a church official issues a letter to be read on the Sunday before an election telling people how to vote, the tactic will probably be self-defeating both politically and religiously. As a moral critic, the church is weakened by a noneducational approach that assumes that "to teach is to tell," that the way to moral improvement is to tell people what to think.

The unfortunate result of fairness violations is that they lead to a call for churches and other religious bodies to stay out of the public order. During the 1980 campaign the *New York Times* ran a lead editorial entitled "Private Religion, Public Morality," the prelude to many editorials on the same theme throughout the 1980s.[13] As the title indicates, the *Times* advised religious groups to get out of the public forum and stay where they belong: in private. "The proper boundary between political and religious advocacy . . . can be found only when secular morality is given precedence over all religious morality." The *Times* distinction, though apparently clear, fails to describe the U.S. of the past or the present. For a church the choice is not private household on one side and party politics on the other. A church is, among other things, a social organization with the right to advocate its moral position in public.

The *New York Times* editorial and most political discussions speak of a wide disjunction between "private religious belief" and public secular morality. Elected officials are especially cautioned against letting their private religious beliefs influence their performance as "public servants." What disappears in this tidy division is the variety of ways in which personal convictions influence public performance. Religious conviction is indeed private; any genuine religious activity touches the interior depths of a person. But a religious *belief* is of its nature public; it connects the individual to history, language, and a tradition of moral wisdom. In some cases, the religious belief (for example, God's creation of each individual) has obvious moral relevance; in other cases (for example, the necessity of baptism), the doctrine's moral relevance is apt to be unclear to outsiders and perhaps to many insiders. An educational morality should be able to illuminate those connections.

In the case of religious beliefs influencing legislation, groups must agitate for political change on the basis of a present or a hoped-for consensus. This term "consensus" does not necessarily mean one hundred percent unanimity nor a bare fifty-one percent majority. Usually the level of agreement for a working consensus is somewhere between those two numbers. Minority groups, religious and otherwise, are always advocating positions that they believe are good for a wide public. If these groups work toward a consensus through educational means and appropriate lobbying, no one has grounds to object to the influence of "private religious beliefs." The civil rights movement is a case in point. The energy for the movement came in large part from religion; however, it was directed at an emerging consensus about fundamental rights within the U.S. legal system. The fact that many black leaders were ordained ministers was not an obstacle to a truly public morality. Supported and spurred on by their Christian beliefs, they used appropriate political means to advance a moral cause.[14]

As for the individual office holder, let him or her be judged by competence of performance. Suppose that polls indicate sixty to seventy percent of the population favors the death penalty. A governor who refuses to sign a bill for the death penalty can expect criticism. If the governor's position is a moral one related to his or her religious beliefs, then those religious beliefs are part of what the electorate should scrutinize. A governor's religious beliefs do not provide him or her with an automatic answer to any political decision, but any real religious convictions must influence the outlook and the stands one takes. The political system provides, among other things, legislative override of the veto, news-media criticism of the governor's position, and voter rejection of the governor at the polls.

At a time when government and business are in great need of people with deep personal convictions, we get cries for a separation of the private and the public. What such a separation produces is people who have neither much private life nor much that can serve the public. As a result we get the individual who is on display most of the time and who reacts to opinion polls. But the person who listens for a wisdom beyond today's cliché and who risks unpopularity by speaking a hard truth is not easy to find.

Part 3

EDUCATONAL IMPLICATIONS

CHAPTER 8

Three Moral Issues

This chapter examines three topics that are in the daily news: the control of birth, the care of the dying, and homosexuality. Each of them is the subject of spirited, often bitter, controversy in places that range from the dinner table to the Supreme Court. Each of the three deserves not just a chapter but a book of its own; and, in fact, hundreds of books have been written on these issues. My reason for presumptuously dealing with all three topics in a single chapter is that something might be revealed by comparing these complex issues to one another. The separate discussion of any one of these three issues today is often frozen in categories that obstruct further clarification.

In these three areas, the ethic of the good and the ethic of rights show their inherent limitations. We need a morality of goodness with its wider and deeper context. The previous discussion of responsible, trans-natural, and private/public morality should throw light on these disputes. I am not so naive as to think that my brief arguments will solve the contemporary problems and bring agreement to the conflicting parties. But I do think that some of the points in dispute are badly stated and that my material on responsible, trans-natural, and private/public morality suggests directions to move in and more effective modes of arguing. For example, in all three areas the words "private" and "public" are regularly used as part of the argument. Almost never is there awareness that this is a complicated relation that is itself in a process of change today. My treatment of these three topics is intended to be, at the least, an illustration of the fruitfulness of the material discussed in Part Two.

There is no morally neutral language with which to state these problems. If we could agree on how to state the question, we would have agreed to a large extent on the answer. This is dramatically illustrated in the abortion dispute, one part of the issue of controlling birth. Referring either to a "fetus" or to "an unborn child" leads to, or has already assumed, different moral positions. Even the choice to speak of "procreation" or "reproduction" usually reveals a pattern or moral thinking.

In this matter of language, it is significant that "abortion" itself is a negative word, and yet hardly anyone avoids its usage. That kind of fact may suggest one of the starting points for moral discussion. Are there any things people agree on, even the usage of the word to describe the issue? If so, that fact might lead into some areas of common concern that are obscured as people try to support their side of the issue. In the remarkable study *The Politics of Motherhood*, Kristin Luker discovers common concerns of the most militant people on both sides of the abortion dispute. For example, both are concerned about the quality of parenting. At the least, Luker is able to penetrate some of the stereotypes and show another side of the group on both sides of the dispute.[1]

I. THE ORDERING OF LIFE AND THE CONTROL OF BIRTH

The heading of this section is a necessarily complicated phrase to remind us of the large context within which human control of birth occurs. Debate on abortion is the center of the dispute today, but that question presupposes attitudes and practices that extend throughout the moral life. Through most of Christian history, writers and church officials assumed a continuity in the morality of the use of any devices to control birth.[2] Abortion was wrong because all use of sex that was intended to be non-procreative was wrong. Today in most discussions a sharp line is drawn between abortion and other means for controlling birth. Even most Roman Catholics make a disjunction at this point, though official church teaching does not. That strategy of drawing a sharp line has the advantage of lessening the area under dispute. Its drawback is that morality cannot be cut up into manageable segments. The abortion dispute sometimes appears to be reducible to one controverted fact: whether or not the fetus is a person. But if a seemingly simple question of "fact" has not been resolved, and if there is no imaginable way in which the parties will agree on a criterion for establishing the fact, then probably the clearly stated question in the manageable area of dispute does not help us make any progress.

Perhaps we would do better to place abortion back into a continuous relation with other questions of controlling birth and ordering life. That means talking not only about "birth control devices" but about sexual activities of all kinds, sexual education, and biogenetic experimentation. Indeed, the questions of "life" go out in expanding circles to human issues of capital punishment, war, poverty, racism, and ecological issues involving all forms of life. Some will certainly object that we cannot discuss all issues at once and that, given the limits of moral passion, we must concentrate on present and immense evils. Even granting this objecton, we can still argue for a large context with continuous moral texture so that on the one hand our understanding fully grasps the issue and on the other hand we can effectively bring our moral passion to bear on the evils we perceive. Both sides of the abortion dispute should be able to see the value of a larger context, even though they would draw different pictures of that context and infer different conclusions.

The context of "ordering life" refers back to what I described as the human vocation: the restoration of order by the animal that has broken out. Human life is the strange paradox of a nature that transcends nature. This trans-natural position requires the human ordering of life's forms in such a way that living things and patterns of life are not systematically violated. Humans cannot avoid putting their feet into delicate fabrics of life, but they can try to minimize their destructiveness by working in accord with the rhythms of nature. We should reserve the term "unnatural" for actions that directly and violently subvert the cycles of birth, growth, decline, and death as these interplay among life's forms.

From the beginning the human race has lived in the tension between artful and unnatural transformation of everything within human reach. The control of birth has always been an area where art and violence compete. Until the twentieth century, though, there was little pressure to explore the artful side, because famine, plague, and war were, among other things, forms of birth control. The modest success of the human race in controlling diseases has led to a novel problem. It took all of human history until 1900 C.E. for the first billion people to be on earth together; now a billion people are added to the total population about every twenty years. The traditional forms of birth control are no longer operative throughout the earth as a whole.

History has two equally important lessons to teach us here: that the control of birth (including abortion) has been going on for millennia, and that the twentieth century has some genuinely new aspects of this issue, including the reasons for controlling birth and the means available to do so. Unfortunately, the means have not changed as much as one might wish. Quite possibly, in twenty-five or fifty years there will be no abortion dispute because the means available for controlling birth will have been dramatically improved. However, the issue of ordering life and controlling birth is likely to last as long as does the human race.

The question of whether there should be human choice in controlling birth should not be the point in dispute. Everything is open to control by human effort, each thing according to ways that are appropriate. In a morality of goodness each thing deserves respect as sacred—that is, because it is beyond the arbitrary disposal of the human will. Each thing has its own order. One can arrange rocks in the backyard, and the ordering can be almost anything the human mind imagines. Books have a solidity one can cherish; they, too, stay put when ordered. It is another thing to chain a dog in the backyard and a still more questionable practice to put a child on a leash. Yet in certain circumstances a leash or a fence or a playpen may be the best available way for the ordering of human life.

On the question of sexuality, the human race has remained amazingly ignorant about what it is dealing with and what are appropriate forms of order. Even though moderns pride themselves on their sexual enlightenment, each child to a large extent recapitulates the race's stages of ignorance. And even if sexual education were immeasurably better than it generally is at present, there would remain big gaps between the clear knowledge of individuals about sex and the unexpected reverberations of their sexual activities. It is widely assumed that the wonder and mystery of sex have declined as modern knowledge has increased the control of sexual processes. That could be the case; but one should not assume that awe, sacredness, and mystery vary in inverse proportion to human participation, knowledge, and ordering. The original meaning of mystery is not what is unintelligible but what can always be understood further.

Some people undoubtedly treat sexual activities in a trivializing and demeaning way. Historical studies are inconclusive as to whether there is more or less of that attitude today. What I think is revealed in studies of abortion is that the vast majority of people treat sexual activity as serious, even sacred.[3] There has been no sudden and total abandonment of traditional feelings about sexual morality. One might say that the conflict in the abortion dispute is between those who see sex as sacred and those who see sexuality as sacred. The two attitudes are clearly different, but just as clearly they are not contradictory. With some adjustment on both sides, each side might come to some respect for the other rather than assuming that the other side is callous.

Those people who see sex as sacred try to protect what nature provides. A form of birth control that violently disrupts organic processes is considered immoral. Thus, if the point is to eliminate procreation in specific activities, the permanent sterilization of a man or a woman would seem unnatural. Everyone has a stake in seeing that violence is not inflicted on human generative powers. For example, everyone should be concerned whether a pill or a device does long-term organic harm as a side effect. Note that the Catholic church is often said to be opposed to "artificial" forms of birth control. On its own principles, what it is really opposed to is "unnatural" forms of control. What is unnatural is artificial, but the reverse is not necessarily true. If present forms do violence to the organism, or do violence to some percentage of individuals, the direction has to be toward better artifice. For the sacredness of sex itself, artificial and nonviolent control of birth is necessary.

Those who see sexuality as sacred start from the value of intimacy and love between the partners. The emphasis here is on the *trans* in trans-natural. Although this stance starts from an opposite emphasis, its stake in nonviolence and in the integrity of the organism is just as great. Whatever violates the love between the parties is irresponsible. Now, abstinence is obviously the most effective form of controlling birth, and it is the form implied by many arguments against other forms. But, as a general form of birth control, it would be unacceptable because it withdraws from the transformative aspect of human-nature.

Human beings are the speaking animals, the ones who can say, "I love you" with a variety of physical expressions that can include sexual intercourse. For some individuals in every culture, abstinence is a responsible choice. They remind everyone else that abstinence plays a part for longer or shorter periods in everyone's life. But to use abstinence as a generalized way to deal with control of birth would be to fail to appreciate the goodness of human sexuality, especially as integrally expressed between a man and a woman.

ABORTION AS RESPONSIBLE, TRANS-NATURAL, PRIVATE/PUBLIC

Within the context of ordering life and controlling birth, we can now focus on abortion. What does responsibility mean in this situation? Recall that discussions of responsibility often confuse the question of *responsible for* and *responsible to*. Each person ought to be responsible for his or her decisions; each person ought to be responsible to everyone 'and everything, a process that moves by expanding circles to all parties and all factors germane to the decision. This basic distinction is usually obscured in abortion debates, one side talking about *who* should be responsible for the decision and the other side insisting on *what* the responsibility is. Civil law in this case has located who is the one responsible; however, morality here as elsewhere is concerned with the what, how, why, and when as well as the who. And it is quite possible that in the bitter abortion controversies both sides are correct in their main assertions about responsibility.

To the question of who is responsible for controlling birth, the answer is: every man and woman of childbearing age is directly responsible. Indirectly, every human being might make some contribution. How a politician votes on a welfare bill might influence conditions of birth; what a schoolteacher presents in a classroom might also affect those conditions. When a couple engages in sexual intercourse, the decision of controlling birth can be worked out together; it should not be the responsibility of only one partner.

When abortion is the question, who is responsible for the decision? Nineteenth-century law, which remained in effect until the 1960s, had a clear answer: the physician. He (seldom she) was to be especially *responsible to* the "life of the mother," a phrase that allowed for considerable latitude of judgment.[4] As hospital committees in the 1950s came to scrutinize the decisions of physicians, the early changes in abortion laws were intended to clarify the physician's responsibility for abortion decisions. The feminist movement of the 1960s and 1970s, supported by the law and the courts, insisted that responsibility for the decision lies not with the physician but with the woman involved. This shift makes a lot of moral sense. The move by nineteenth-century physicians to control decisions about abortion may have had justifying reasons then, but today it is clear that the woman is the responsible party. This statement of principle is, or at least ought to be, the easy part of the problem resolvable by the court: neither the state nor the medical profession has a right to take away the woman's right to choose.

The difficult part of the problem not resolvable by a court is to whom and to what the woman is responsible. In principle, the answer is: to everyone and everything. Practically, this usually means responding to family, and friends, responding to one's own body in its total environment, and responding to historical and institutional guidelines. The support a woman receives from the man responsible for the impregnation is obviously central, although it is a part of the story often dismissed. The fact that many men fail to follow through on what they are responsible for is not simply a fact to be stated and left. The moral responsibility of the man needs to be insisted upon. The woman's choice is both a right and a burden; the man's responsibility is to make the woman's decision less of a burden. Many feminists say little or nothing about the man's responsibility, apparently fearing that such responsibility would diminish or interfere with the woman's right to choose. But this principle is a different one: the woman ought to respond *to* the man, and the man has a responsibility *for* helping the woman. An individual woman may get no tangible help out of this mutual obligation, but a general silence on the man's responsibility cannot be in the best interests of women.

A woman also responds to her social and economic situation. Whether she is seventeen or forty-one years old, whether she is married and has four children or is unmarried, whether she is financially well off or on welfare are factors relevant to a decision about abortion. To aid a woman considering abortion, moralists ought to have spelled out, better than they have so far, a spectrum of moral consideration.[5] The trivial reasons for an abortion might be not liking the sex of the fetus or not wishing to appear pregnant; the most serious reasons might be extreme fetal defects or the pregnancy's being the result of rape. In between the trivial and the traumatic are dozens of considerations of physical, social, economic, and religious factors. The failure of moralists and educators to develop such a spectrum of considerations comes from the acrimony of the present debate. Many women distrust all considerations by men on this topic. Although the suspicion may be well founded, men still have a responsibility to work with women on developing a pattern of moral considerations. This responsibility, once again, is not in competition with the woman's right to make her own decision. Women could only benefit from having available a spectrum of moral considerations. On the other side of the abortion dispute, there are the people who insist that no set of considerations is needed because abortion is wrong and therefore there is nothing to discuss. And yet very few people would not allow some exception.[6] Almost the whole U.S. population believes that aborting a pregnancy that has resulted from rape is morally allowable. Once any exception to a rule is allowed, we cannot avoid a discussion of moral factors and situations that influence general rules.

What of the "status" of the fetus? Is this not the single, unresolvable point of conflict that overrides all other moral factors? This question takes us into the second of my three concerns: the trans-natural character of human morality. Human beings do not create life; they procreate or re-produce life in a process that for all of our scientific knowledge remains a profound mystery. Every aspect of life deserves respect; the unnecessary destruction of life, human and nonhuman, is morally evil. The degree of evil varies widely, depending on the form of life and the exact circumstances of our disruption of the cycle of birth, growth, decline, and death. Plucking a daisy to put in a vase raises no moral debate; cutting down millions of trees in December to put in living rooms should perhaps raise a moral issue. Consuming a piece of Boston schrod for dinner seems morally acceptable; drilling for oil off George's Bank where the schrod are hatched is morally disastrous.

Abortion, as the word indicates, is a morally negative act. Occasionally, a woman writer will claim that there is no moral problem here at all, but the great majority of women as well as men do not agree.[7] An act of abortion obviously intrudes, interferes, and does some violence. As soon as possible, abortion should be eliminated from the ways the human race uses to control birth. There ought to be much better ways in which we transform natural processes of procreation that would eliminate the violence that abortion entails. Every act of abortion reverberates throughout the texture of human life, which is why a woman has to respond—and most women do respond—to more than her immediate feelings about being pregnant. The stake in abortion proliferation is the protection of human life against professional callousness, mindless technology, and projects of economic exploitation.

The question gets badly framed as "When does life begin?" or "When does human life begin?" Human life began hundreds of thousands of years ago. It continues to exist through the mysterious interaction of men and women, accident and providence, scientific knowledge and utter ignorance. In the stage of human life called pregnancy, there is human life becoming independent. At some point before birth, a new organism becomes capable of separate existence, although even after birth its survival depends on a community that cares for it. Respect for life ought to be provided for the stage of pregnant life. One side in the abortion dispute uses a simple syllogism: Human life should be respected; the fetus is human because it is not another species, and it is alive because it is not dead; therefore the fetus must be respected as human life. There is moral force to this simple argument, and if the whole area were not so politically volatile, everyone might accept the truth of the conclusion. There is something peculiar about a discussion in which "respect for human life" is a very problematic claim and abortion often sounds like a desirable good. The goodness of life and the undesirability of abortion ought not to be in question.

The queston can also be approached from the opposite direction—that is, from an inquiry about distinctions, forms, and stages within human life. *Some* moral difference would seem to exist between a one-hour-fertilized ovum and a five-month-old fetus. Moral arguments are nearly always arguments by analogy. We are morally certain of only a few things, one of them being that the indiscriminate killing of human beings is wrong. From a primary case of what every sane person can recognize as murder, we argue in cases of self-defense, hit-and-run driving, hunting accidents, selling heroin, political revolution, and so forth, that something is more or less like murder. The question here might be posed: Is abortion like contraception, or like infanticide? The answer would seem to be: the closer one gets to the moment of conception, the more abortion resembles contraception (some contraceptives in fact do not prevent fertilization but obstruct uterine implantation); the closer it gets to independent life outside the womb, the more it resembles infanticide.

The fact that there are no obvious lines between concepton and birth does not mean no moral lines can be drawn. We have highway speed zones where twenty-five miles per hour must be distinguished from fifty-five miles per hour. The fact that twenty-four and twenty-six miles per hour are barely distinguishable does not mean that we cannot have a twenty-five mile per hour sign. Referring to trimesters of pregnancy does not presume that two clear lines of demarcation exist at three and six months. It does suggest that very early and very late abortions are morally, as well as legally, distinguishable. If we could start from an agreement that abortion is morally undesirable and that the violence to nature should be reduced, we should be able to say of existing abortions: the earlier they are performed and the safer the conditions, the better (that is, the less bad) they are. As things are now, almost ninety percent of abortions are performed in the first three months. The 1972 Supreme Court decision has been generally effective in encouraging early rather than late abortions.[8]

This last point brings me to my third concern, abortion as a private/public activity. I have said that the most helpful way to conceive of the relation of private and public is in direct rather than inverse proportion. An important moral decision is profoundly private, and as a profound decision it is related to a wide public. But the public is not restricted to the social or governmental. Public is the visible, bodily world of men, women, and nonhumans in relation to one another and to the past. Those who are defending the right of a woman to her private decision have to be careful that they do not isolate the woman. The noninterference of the government in the decision should not be taken to mean that the public is not involved. Abortion is a very public issue, as all the controversy attests. Abortion involves several people and issues: clinics, professional staffs, money, and the disruption of life. Exclusive reliance on an ethic of rights does not place the issue of abortion into its public context.

Of what value is a right to make choices if there are no educational helps or institutional supports to private choice? For example, the parents' right to decide about the education of their children is not worth much if there are no schools; even if there are schools, the right is enhanced when there are several schools and when the parents have the money to choose among schools. Abortion no less than educaton is a public question. A woman's right to choose is an insupportable burden if there is not wide public support for her choice.

The collapse of "public" into "governmental" cuts off imagination and places an unwarranted demand on courts and legislatures. We need public policies that are not governmental policies—a point that both sides in the abortion dispute would do well to consider. On one side, people lobbying for a Human Rights Amendment to the U.S. Constitution are asking the government to settle the issue of public policy when it does not have the moral power to do so. They are right in the claim that the 1972 decision *Roe vs. Wade* was passed without a national consensus.[9] But they are inaccurate claiming that today's conflict can be solved by a new law banning abortion (except when the life of the mother is directly threatened.) No one has proposed any workable plan for how such a law would be enforced. *Roe vs. Wade* did make some distinctions, particularly in regard to the time of the abortion. It is possible that questions of when, how, where, and why could be modified, although the modifications are not mainly the government's job. Modifications of the existing law usually have the effect of discriminating aginst the poor, the less educated, and the less mobile. The attempt to restrict access could unwittingly cause later abortions, especially if the decisions becomes tied to a governmental bureaucracy.[10]

Hoping for a law that will get rid of abortion is an ineffective outlet for moral passion opposed to abortion. Even if a law could be passed, the problem would remain.

On the other side, the virorous supporters of *Roe vs. Wade* (twenty to twenty-five percent of the U.S.) should not place all their trust in governmental statute.[11] They need public support for their policies. The consensus that currently holds is a majority that is uneasy with the reality of abortion, a public that has a guilty conscience. The present law allows something to happen because no one has a logical and feasible alternative that is any better. Morally, as most women considering abortion seem to recognize, the choice is between the lesser of two evils.[12] The public issue of abortion has not been settled and cannot be settled by the government.

We need a coalition that is nowhere in sight, a coalition that would work to reduce the violent conditions and moral insensitivity that are the continuing backdrop of a disrespect for human life. An educational morality that includes religious forces ought to work at opening lines of communication and getting agreements wherever possible. The moral, religious, social question is how to transform the conditions that make abortion such a common occurrence today.

II. THE ORDERING OF LIFE AND THE CONTROL OF DEATH

In turning now to the care of the dying, I have headed this section in a way that suggests a parallel with human efforts to control birth. The parallels between controlling birth and controlling death are seldom brought out, although cases of severely deformed infants are calling attention to the relation between the two areas. For the purpose of theoretical exploration, the question of whether or not to let severely deformed infants die is not the best place to start. Unless a broader set of concerns is brought to that question, the treatment of infants may seem to be just an extension of the abortion question. That, of course, is precisely the fear of people who wish to make abortion illegal: that we are on the slippery slope that will strip personhood from many groups of vulnerable and defenseless people. Whether that movement will occur or not, the complexities of medical technology are here to stay. We have to see the large backdrop of life and death in order to judge how to apply new knowledge and new technology, be the recipient the very young, the very old, or everyone else in between.

At both the beginning and the end of a person's life there are mysterious processes that go beyond the human power to understand and control. Nonetheless, some aspects of both can be modified and sometimes improved. Some corrections can now be made of fetal development in the womb, and some drugs can relieve pain in life's last hours.

One parallel in the two areas that no one could have predicted a few decades ago has rather recer.tly surfaced. The question in the abortion debate about when a person exists has its corresponding question now at the end of life's journey. When does a person's life on earth end? Until recently, nothing seemed more clear-cut than death; and we can still easily identify a decomposing body as dead. However, in increasing numbers of cases where life continues we are not certain that we are dealing with an individual, independent, personal existence. After eight years in a coma the body of Karen Ann Quinlan was still alive, but was it any longer Karen Ann Quinlan?

As in the abortion dispute, the question seems to be one of "fact." And as with abortion, it is unlikely that judges, lawyers, and physicians are ever going to provide a conclusive answer to the factual question. In the abortion debate, the issue presses for an immediate answer because within a few months' time the passage from not-person to person occurs whether or not we can identify clear lines. On the question of death's occurrence we have the benefit of time for lengthy court cases, but also the possibility of agonizing confusion that can seem interminable.

Most discussions of controlling death are being carried out under the rubric of an ethic of rights. The individual should have the right to choose, and the government should protect that right. I and I alone am in charge of my own dying. There is a kind of heroic tone to much contemporary writing on death and dying. There may also be an obsessive attachment to talking about rights while neglecting the mystery, ritual, and simple human bonds that have been necessary to cope with the greatest of life's challenges. Most of the typical ethical writing is a relentless application of individual rights just at the place where the limits of this way of thinking become evident.

Modern systems of ethics were formed around the flight from death. The property I own and have a right to own includes my life. So long as I can possess my autonomous life, I can exercise other rights and pursue my happiness. Governments exist to protect property, especially one's right to life, a right that was under constant threat in a state of anarchy.[13] An ethic of rights has proved valuable in the modern world. The dignity of the individual has been enhanced, and protection for the vulnerable has at least sometimes been provided. In daily affairs throughout adult life we tend to speak the ethical language of rights, whether in relation to protecting our jobs, dealing with the government, or safeguarding our place in the checkout line at the supermarket. But having been formed in defense against death, the ethic of rights is of very little help when we finally have to confront dying. Ethics today is being *applied* to dying and the care of the dying, but the applications do not really fit. Dying is too central an issue of life to be one of a series of applications. And as medical technology gets more complicated, the underlying inadequacies of modern ethics can only become magnified.

The rallying cry of much contemporary writing on death is "the right to die with dignity." Sometimes the phrase is "the right to die" which may be simply shorthand or may be a different question. Does a person have a right to die? Within the ethical tradition of rights the question is a peculiar one, given that the most basic right is the right to live. No one really thinks of death as a valuable good that I am competing with others for. A right to die is really concerned with the autonomy of the will and noninterference in the individual's choices. An exclusive concern with the right to die is actually not saying much about dying and the care of the dying.

The more helpful phrase is "a right to die with dignity." This principle could open a fruitful discussion about the relation of life and death, human and nonhuman, person and environment. Dying is better considered a moral rather than an ethical activity; dying is a question of one's whole bodily self. And if any activity can be called religious, dying certainly is. Dying reveals the need for a morality of goodness in which living/dying is the central experience rather than an inexplicable last point. In a morality of goodness every being is accepted for what it is in relation to the universe of being. Here "right to die with dignity" makes sense, although the phrase would be clearer still as "right to dignity even while dying." The right to dignity can be said to be the most basic right. Each thing deserves respect, deserves to call forth a response proportionate to its place in the universe. A person invites a special relation of trust, care, and love that must not be violated. If that is the way human beings live together throughout life, then the imminence of death is no cause for eliminating dignity. Conversely, if human life is treated with little respect and dignity most of the time, we should hardly be surprised that dying is an undignified moment.

A morality of goodness that is with end (meaning) and without end (termination) faces a severe challenge in death's seeming finality. But the interrelation of all things, their presence that includes a given past and an intimated future, affirms the continuation of what we have been but in a new form beyond our visual imagination. Contemporary writing on death generally avoids any mention of religion, apparently to soothe the patient and not bring up anything fearful. Perhaps the religious imagery of "life beyond life" is embarrassingly inadequate as a conversation topic with the dying. Still, the exclusion in principle of religion is not a help. Religion may be the backdrop that a person needs to accept death as part of life, to bear with suffering as a mysterious part of life, and to recognize that death is not to be resisted at all costs. In contrast to overly heroic or slightly romanticized views of death that are promulgated today, all the religious traditions are realistic about death: it is not easy, it is not a simple fact, it is tragic. At the same time, death understood as the gateway to a new level of being can mean peaceful acceptance of our relation to the nonhuman world and to forces utterly beyond our imagination.

RESPONSIBLE DEATH

The notion of responsibility can help to clarify a morality of goodness confronted with death. Response means an answer within a continuing pattern of interaction. As in the abortion dispute, the distinction between responsible *for* and responsible *to* is crucial. Civil law and the ethic of rights concentrate on the question of *who* is responsible for a decision. This concern is praiseworthy, but lest a "right to be responsible for" turn into an impossible burden, someone has to ask about *to whom* and *to what* we are responsible. Religion's temptation is to short-circuit the whole exploration and declare that we are responsible to God. But the meaning of the word "God" is always embedded in historical realities. In a rich meaning of religious life, God is not used as a substitute for the *what* and the *whom* we respond to.

As in the abortion debate, responsible *for* is, or ought to be, the easy part of the issues around dying. And in this case, at least legally and theoretically, the answer is clear: the individual who is dying is the one responsible for decisions of treatment. I am responsible for myself and for others who cannot be responsible for themselves. These others include nonhuman realities and human beings who temporarily or permanently cannot choose for themselves. The temporary cases are decisions made for young children when disasters must be avoided. In the case of a person in an irreversible coma, the responsibility for a decision is not a temporary intercession until the person can make his or her own choices. The choice to do something that allows death to proceed is a substitution for a last human choice.

The case for our being responsible for ourselves seems not to require much theoretical defense. The alternatives are patient or physician, patient or machinery. (The relation of the patient's will to "God's will" is left open in the notion of responsible for.) In practice, physician or machinery may subtly take over for a patient. Hospitals often make the person feel like a dependent child. The physician seems to know what should be done, and the patient feels powerless. Some physicians are quite content to let that process happen, although many have no intention of subverting the patient's autonomy. The physician, in any case, has some duty to tip the balance of power in the patient's direction by making available pertinent information that can be comprehended. However, a strong sense of responsibility for one's actions takes time to develop, and some people show little of it.

Making a decision for a comatose patient is a frightening prospect for anyone, but someone has to take responsibility for the decision. If the patient cannot, the burden may fall on physician or machine. Strictly speaking, the machine does not decide, but the machine can perpetuate a prior decision if no one takes responsibility for shutting off the machine. In the past, the physician was presumed to be the one who should decide what is to be done. In many cases that is still true, but physicians have become wary of being held responsible for decisions that issue in death.

Two alternatives present themselves: the patient who is not competent to decide has left instructions about just such a decision, or else a person who is close to the patient and considers what is best for the patient makes the decision. When these two alternatives are combined, a judge or physician is more confident that justice is being done. Even when a comatose patient has left written instructions, someone has to interpret the words relative to the situation that has arisen. A person who has said, "I do not wish to be kept alive by a respirator" may have been too specific. There is other technology that may have been unknown to the patient. But a person who has said, "I do not wish to be kept alive by artificial means" may be saying something too general and may not understand the implications of the statement.

When a decision is to be made about a comatose patient, someone who cares for that person should decide. In principle, that could be anyone. If the sick person has no next of kin, we have to trust that someone will have the best interests of the patient at heart. When there is a family member, we generally assume that he or she will do what the patient would choose to do. Even there, though, sometimes self-interest and self-deception may intrude into the closest family relations; a large inheritance in the bank can distort the perception of a family member. Moral failure can always occur, but the demands of responsible morality in such a situation are clear enough.

The other part of responsibility, *response to,* has not been so well clarified by the court and perhaps cannot be dealt with there. To whom and to what are we responsible? In the ordinary flow of events we respond to a spectrum of people, things, events, causes, and institutional rules. When people get sick they understandably narrow their concerns. At least most of us at the onset of illness have a tendency to close in on ourselves and forget about other people and their problems. Some people catch a cold and are heard to say, "I want to die. I can't put up with this another minute." At times in life we each need a caring partner who can say, "Stop wallowing in self pity; you're not about to die."

Responsibility to other people includes making suggestions of moral direction. It takes nothing away from a person's right to choose when we offer him or her a spectrum of moral considerations. Even that great apostle of individual liberty, John Stuart Mill, could write, "Human beings owe to each other help to distinguish the better from the worse, and encouragement to choose the former and avoid the latter."[14] When people are seriously sick and suffering intensely, they do not need stern lectures or snap orders. But they also should not be responded to as if they had no relation to the demands of ordinary life. In the play *Whose Life Is It Anyway?* the patient criticizes a social worker for failing to reprimand him when he acted uncivilly. If criticism is not offered when criticism is due, we treat another person as a child lacking responsibility or as an incompetent adult who must be patronized. "We may subtly dehumanize patients when we do not take seriously the question of their virtues and vices, the nobility or meanness of their responses to ordeal. We act and reflect as though the patient does not have a moral life."[15]

Treating a person with dignity means talking, touching, joking, criticizing, and dozens of other activities that daily human existence entails. Respecting dignity means not making persons the objects of pity, not making them feel like aliens in the land of the living, not making them feel subordinate to machinery. A "right to die" simply loads a further burden on the autonomous will: the right to take one's own life. A "right to dignity" is a statement about contexts: contexts of human interaction in which the lonely contemplation of suicide is less frequent, contexts in which people gradually come to accept their own deaths, contexts in which a person's decision that it is time to let go of life is supported and accepted by a caring community.

When a person talks of committing suicide, it is appropriate that we intervene on the side of life. In a large percentage of cases, attempted suicide is a cry for help. Or the person sensing the need for a transformation of life goes at death in a literal and violent way. For good reasons we say that someone "commits" suicide just as we say someone commits crime. Attempted suicide should not be treated as a crime; our presumption should be that the suicidal person is temporarily unbalanced and that he or she needs help to get back to seeing that life is worth going on with. But suppose a person has carefully reflected on the matter and is determined to end his or her life.

Since the time of St. Augustine, Christianity and Western secular law have consistently condemned suicide.[16] Undoubtedly, Christianity will continue to insist that human beings are responders to life, not the owners of life. But the humans do control life to a degree by the way they respond. Obviously, some people shorten their lives by the kinds of activities they engage in. We celebrate the lives of some people who heroically sacrificed themselves for a great cause. We also sometimes stand by helplessly as someone smokes, drinks, and worries himself or herself into an early grave. But it may come to be accepted that some suicides are morally acceptable, or more likely, that deaths that were once called suicide are no longer called that. As James Hillman suggests in his classic study of suicide, perhaps God sometimes lets us know from the inside when death is appropriate.[17] Any move in this direction has to be carefully hedged by civil law lest pressure be brought upon the old and the poor to convince them that they have not a right but a duty to die.

TRANS-NATURAL DEATH

This cloudy area of what is allowable in bringing life to an end needs to be clarified with the idea of morality as trans-natural. In the past, two distinctions came into play here: *ordinary and nonordinary means of life,* and *active and passive causes of death.*

Ordinary and nonordinary means of life. Human beings have always been transforming the cycle of nature: birth, growth, decline, death. Ordinary means of staying alive include eating, sleeping, and keeping warm, activities shared with the other animals. Ordinary means also include a transforming of those activities: scientific agriculture, a sleeping pill, central heating. Only in very recent history have human beings made major interventions with complicated technology into the act of dying. Sometimes these interventions produce marvelous transformations: a person who has suffered a terrible injury is restored to full participation in a human community. Many interventions do not work; or, what is worse, they prolong the act of dying without restoring the person to specifically human activities. A leading physician said more than two decades ago, "Though cures are getting commoner, so too are half-cures, in which death is averted but disability remains."[18]

As the medical and technological issues get more complex, it is important to have the question clear. Is a "natural death" desirable? The answer depends on the alternatives: natural/trans-natural, natural/unnatural. In a coroner's report for example, the categories may be "dead from natural causes" or "died from foul play." Presumably in this language everyone wishes to die of natural causes, meaning without violent and unnatural intervention. However, if a natural death means death without any chemicals or machines being used, it is not obvious that dying in excruciating pain is preferable to receiving pain-killing drugs. As Pabst Battin warns, people who write down beforehand that they want a "natural death" may not realize what they are asking for.[19] A pain-killing drug is an artificial means, but it can also be a properly human use of artifice: one that allows the personal to transcend the declining condition of the natural.

We need a use of drugs and machines that is trans-natural without being unnatural. It is part of human-nature to try to extend life artificially. Thus, today's new problem is not well stated as "There are individuals and groups who are beginning to feel increasingly that the artificial prolongation of life is more of a burden than a benefit."[20] There is nothing wrong with an artificial prolonging of life so long as the prolonging is not unnatural. Today's problem is the artificial and unnatural prolonging of the act of dying. Humans in one sense die "like all the animals," but humans anticipate death, try to prolong life, and experience dying as a conflict between the unlimited desires of personal being and the limited movements of a natural cycle that can be modified but not rejected.

There has never been a sharp division between the ordinary and nonordinary means of life. The activities close to nature we think of as ordinary, whereas what is highly artificial is assumed to be nonordinary. But human transformation of nature makes impossible any set of things called ordinary means as contrasted to other things which are nonordinary. Physicians and judges understandably want some simple and clear guidelines about using all ordinary means to support life while being allowed not to use heroic means to keep someone alive. But the language of ordinary/nonordinary means actually hides a cluster of questions about the condition and the needs of the patient. What is the patient's overall chance of survival? What is the patient's mental condition? What are the side effects of the treatment? How is the treatment to take place? What is the cost, and is the patient's family able to bear it?[21] These kinds of questions, rather than some technically clear differentiation between ordinary and nonordinary treatment keep the person and personal activity at the center.

In some cases, what is thought to be the most ordinary means might not be if we are describing personal activity rather than things. For example, we correctly assume that eating food is an ordinary means of life. Hospitals are required to provide meals to sustain patients. However, ingestion by way of a tube put down the throat or directly into the stomach is not the human act of eating. A temporary use of nourishment by injection that restores a person to human activity is a moral good. But it is not morally compelling that a food line be kept attached for years to an irreversibly comatose patient on the principle that food is an ordinary means of life. We have instead an unnatural prolongation of dying by means of an action that bears little relation to a human being's eating food. In one of the court cases that attracted national attention, there was medical consensus that the man's comatose condition was irreversible. The family requested the feeding tube to be disconnected. The chief physician said he was not in the business of killing people. The lawyer said that a person starving to death is not dying with dignity. The Catholic priest's comment made the most moral sense; he said: "What we have here is an intervention which is not working."[22]

Active and passive causes of death. This discussion of ordinary/nonordinary means of life has already crossed over into the distinction between active and passive causes of death. A physician may not actively cause someone's death; and in usual circumstances (excluding such things as self-defense) we are all obligated to refrain from doing something that causes the death of anyone, including ourselves. In contrast, when a physician or someone else does not use every means available to keep someone alive, one could be said to be a passive cause; that is, death is allowed to happen. There is obviously some validity to this language, although it carries more weight legally than morally. It is difficult to make a court case on the basis of inaction. Whereas legal culpability is usually assigned only to the individuals who *committed* the act, the moral net goes further. If a person is stabbed on the street and no one helps the stricken person who dies, only one killer goes to jail, but many people may have some moral culpability.

Within the medical profession there used to be a crystal clear distinction. The physician's first rule was "to do no harm," which included never being the active cause of someone's death. The line between active and passive is still important, but these days it is sometimes difficult to see. A strong drug that relieves pain may also shorten the patient's life. Is prescribing a high level of the drug to be construed as actively causing death? If a machine has intervened in the act of dying, is turning off the machine the cause of death? Would it not be more accurate to say that the medical intervention preventing death has been removed and the patient is allowed to die? The death is "natural" in the sense of not being manslaughter or murder. The death is "trans-natural" in that human care has been extended to guide the cycle that leads to death. The death is not unnatural in that the body's continuation of life has not been violently interrupted by human artifice.

A person who has lived a full life may reach the point of suffering increasing medical complications. In such situations, pneumonia used to be called a "friend"—that is, the complication that finally brought on death. Today medicine can intervene to prevent the pneumonia. Is the person who in a nonviolent way lets some other "friend" complete the process the active cause of death? For example, a person who has both cancer and diabetes can allow death to occur by not taking a needed insulin shot. A recent study shows that almost ten percent of people on kidney dialysis simply stop the treatment and let themselves die. Would there be an essential difference if a person with kidney troubles, in which a high level of potassium is fatal, intentionally eats avocadoes to bring the process of dying to a close?

The moral question of active and passive causes needs situating in the context of who the person is and how the cycle of nature is being transformed. The extreme cases are clearcut: a lonely teenager putting a 357 magnum to his temple is violently intruding on the cycle of nature. In contrast, heart surgery on a child that makes possible a healthy existence is a highly active intrusion in nature but is certainly justified. In other cases a much less dramatic intervention shifts the course of nature. A person can in one sense take active charge of his or her own dying by simply saying "enough." The person has lived as long as seems right; the struggle against increasing complications no longer makes sense; a conscious good-by to family and friends is preferred to a prolonged dying under the domination of machines and sedatives.

The relevant question is whether the act is integral to the person, the community, and the environment, particularly when the person asks for help to get the means. A right to die would seem to imply that others, including physicians, have a duty to help. A right to dignity while dying implies that others should respect the wishes of the patient, including not preventing the person from dying if he or she wishes to. It leaves open the question of whether others may judge it appropriate to supply information, pills, or other material to the suffering one.

There is proper concern in the U.S. today that a physician's involvement in such planned death would radically revise the role of the physician and that the practice would be open to dangerous abuses. Despite the shady areas in deciding what is an active and what is a passive cause of death, the distinction remains crucial for physicians. He or she may need encouragement not to use all means available—that is, to let patients die when the situation humanly requires it.[23] However, the physician's resistance to using anything that actively causes death is an appropriate attitude, at least until the larger community has given far more careful thought to the legal and moral issues involved.

PRIVATE/PUBLIC DEATH

A final word about private/public morality will link up with the notion of responsibility. All important moral issues, I have argued, are widely public because they are profoundly private. In the previous section of this chapter I noted the danger of thinking that because abortion is a private decision it is not a matter of public concern.

If any act deserves to be called both private and public, it is the act of dying. As the whole person is brought to completion and the will makes a final disposition, all of that to which one is responsible resonates in the innermost recesses of one's private self. The process can best occur, however, if there is a public ritual that connects the dying person to family and friends, humans and nonhumans, past and present. In Chapter 7 I used as an example of private/public activity a well-designed funeral liturgy. Each religious group has an elaborate ceremony for the mourners that connects them to the public while allowing for private grief.

What, though, of dying itself as a private/public act? William May, in summarizing the historical study of death by Phillipe Ariés, writes: 'Until the last two hundred years dying was a public ceremony."[24] May comments that in the past people usually died at home but that today most people die in hospitals. The paradox here is that we usually speak of the family as part of the private sphere. If death moved from the family household to the hospital, did it not become more public? The answer is: not if we lose sense of the ritual that links the individual to the universe. Hospitals tend to lack *both* the connection to a public world and a sense of privacy. Ariés notes that "until the eighteenth century no portrayal of a deathbed scene failed to include children."[25] The children learned how to accept their own deaths and how generally to deal with death by seeing family members die at home.

Ariés traces the public nature of dying throughout the Christian centuries. Until the late Middle Ages the soul was related to the great events of the last day and the final judgment. By the fifteenth century, God the judge and his great court had moved into the sickroom, where the soul was exposed to and experienced its final temptations.[26] In reaction against the distortions of this later picture, God, judgment, and dying itself were removed from the center of life. A new sense of privacy seemed to require reticence about death.

The assumption was that, freed from all those religious fears, life on earth would be happier and more fulfilling. But making death a mere last point or something that happens only to others does not really fool us. The great religious drama of living/dying is replaced by intense efforts to protect individuals against intrusion. Death is banished from private meditation and is squelched as an issue to be confronted realistically in public. Is this progress? Ariés concludes: "This life in which death was removed to a prudent distance seems less loving of things and people than the life in which death was the center."[27]

Part of the moral concern for care of the dying should be the restoration of a private/public sense of dying. We cannot resurrect the Middle Ages even if we wished to. We can preserve whatever religious rituals have survived—for example, visits by hospital chaplains. We also should try to add new elements of public ritual. The Living Will, in which an individual calmly decides about some of the conditions of his or her dying, is a public ritual. The donation of organs is one of technology's contribution to connecting the dying person with the public. Ethics committees in hospitals are a public way to maintain open, humane, and responsible treatment of patients. The hospice movement, which allows more dignity to dying patients than hospitals often do, is helping to create a public sense and a ritual for dying.

I would particularly call attention to the deaths of children. Those who work with dying children may help the rest of us to discover simple rituals. Children often have an eerie sense of death that gives them a startling frankness and candor. The rituals that the very young devise will probably be more helpful to the very old than any practices devised by the middle aged. An ethic that excludes religion in principle is not likely to listen to children or to ritual as a source of wisdom. In contrast, a morality of goodness would not dictate how people should die, but it would be open to all sources of inspiration and support for the difficult journey of entrance to life beyond this life.

III. THE ORDERING OF SEXUALITY AND THE REALITY OF HOMOSEXUALITY

The third area we examine in this chapter has some parallels to the previous two, but in most respects it is a simpler story. The morality of homosexuality has not recently been transformed by technology. However, the discourse about homosexuality in the last two decades has been transformed from furtive whisperings to political statements by gay and lesbian people.[28] Many people view homosexuality as a civil-rights issue, and homosexual people are generally happy to have the question posed in those terms. In that way, the issue is clear and manageable; any group simply asking for the protections of the U.S. Constitution has the odds on its side in appealing for majority support.

An ethic of rights has immediate appeal in this case as in the previous two. A person has a right not to be discriminated against on the basis of such categories as sex, race, and age. A "gay rights movement," learning from both black and feminist movements, has been remarkably successful in the short time it has existed. Still, the movement to secure civil rights for homosexual people runs up against passionate resistance. A well-known Quaker statement from the early 1960s said "one should no more deplore 'homosexuality' than left-handedness."[29] While many people no doubt find such an approach to be eminently reasonable, it sidesteps the mystery that has surrounded homosexuality for thousands of years. Why has homosexuality been shrouded in darkness for so long, and why is tolerance by heterosexual people so difficult to achieve even today? That is the main moral issue of homosexuality.

The heading of this section relates homosexuality to the ordering of sexual life. Human beings reshape and transform the body's sexual drives. Unless there is control of these powerful forces, all other order is threatened. Heterosexual impulses are kept within strict bounds of sexual responsibility. Having a wife and children has been the usual way that men learned to be responsible—that is, responsible *for* their sexual activities and responsible *to* a clear range of sexual stimuli. Extramarital activities are extremely frequent, but they still function safely within well-defined spheres: premarital, extramarital, and even "swinging" acquired their defined meanings in relation to heterosexual marriage.

The phenomenon of homosexuality looms as a threat to the exercise of power that society calls "responsible." In that form of power an active/passive relation is clearly defined, and everyone knows the appropriate response. Michel Foucault in *The History of Sexuality* counters the view that sexuality is only a stubborn biological drive: "It appears rather as an especially dense transfer point for relations of power: between men and women, young people and old people, parents and offspring, teachers and students, priests and laity, an administration and a population."[30] Interestingly, Foucault does not include in that long list men and men, women and women. In the pairings he does list, many power shifts have been occurring, perhaps the most dramatic being the relation of men and women. The feminist revolution is a radical threat to power arrangements. Women's complaints are intelligible to most men even if the men do not agree. At least feminist agitation can be understood as attempts to modify the traditional or "natural" order.

Erotic feelings that surface within the exchanges that Foucault lists can facilitate the flow of power and stabilize the world. But because such feelings are not under the direct control of the will, they are always a threat to established channels of power. Erotic feelings toward a person of the opposite sex have a few well-defined outlets. Erotic feelings toward a person of the same sex cause confusion. The prospect can be world threatening to the person who senses internal erotic feelings that have no acceptable external form of expression. Homosexuality thus appears as an embodiment of lawlessness, a reality that must be kept as secret as possible.

Homosexual men have often shared women's plight in the sense that both groups represent a challenge to the idea that power is an exercise of will in which the stronger dominates the weaker. The accusaton against homosexual men throughout history has been that they act like women—that is, that one of them has to be the passive element in any partnership. Lesbianism did not draw the same ire throughout the centuries. It was assumed to be uncommon (most men simply could not imagine it), and it did not seem to exhibit the same level of challenge to established power relations. Today lesbianism is the "dense transfer point" between feminism and gay rights, existing in tension with both movements. As lesbianism becomes more evident and more outspoken, it could open up a quite new level of fear, confusion, and attempt at control on the part of those who until now have dismissed lesbianism as insignificant.

RESPONSIBLE HOMOSEXUALITY

A responsible morality is interested in protecting human autonomy and placing it in relation to the widest and deepest context. Sexuality as our way of being in the world can either help or hinder this responsible morality. Which it does depends on what we are responding to and how our response is shaped and formed by institutions. As Foucault suggests above, there is and should be some sexual feeling in all kinds of human exchange. If society is intensely concerned with stopping any feelings that may lead to homo-erotic expression, the range of sexual feeling is likely to be narrowed. The prohibition of feelings and gestures that someone might construe as homosexual can interfere with the formation of warm and intimate friendships. The anti-homo-sexual attitude that was directed mainly at men shows its effects in the difficulty that men have in being intimate and lasting friends with other men. Thus a paradox: one reason for society's acknowledging homosexuality is that heterosexuals would be more sexually responsible.

The right wing of Christianity is especially exercised by what it sees as a disruption of what God set up in Eden: "The old myths of the androgynous man are rejected and all ambiguity in the relationship is ordered by God. . . . Man is created for another. That other is woman. Their relationship is ordered by God.[31] This kind of argument is peculiarly abstract and is not an accurate statement about Christian beliefs. Men and women are created for a myriad set of relations, and while the writer of Genesis obviously believed that men and women should unite and procreate, heterosexual marriage is not the only relation described in the Bible. The author of the above passage uses the word "relationship" in today's faddish sense: Adam and Even had a relationship. What should be seen as a mutual relation that opens up to relations to everyone and everything collapses into a thing that can be clearly defined and securely possessed: the man and the other; the other is woman. Heterosexual marriage so defined is not very responsible in the exercise of sexuality.

Homosexuality does in fact threaten that kind of marriage and its pinched view of sexual responsibility. Gay and lesbian people understandably shy away from acknowledging this fact, preferring to operate under the protection of an ethic of rights rather than take on the whole range of issues included in a responsible morality. But civil rights will always be precarious so long as gay and lesbian people are considered a threat to the family. Arguing that homosexual love is totally neutral in relation to heterosexual love and to the family will never be convincing. The difficult but ultimately more helpful path is to argue that although homosexuality does conflict with some traditonal stereotypes of marriage and family, homosexuality offers a positive complement to marriage and family. Some of the strongest potential allies of homosexual people are childless married couples. Perhaps it is only when we acknowledge gay or lesbian couples that we will finally appreciate what thinkers of the 1920s called "companionate" marriages, those where the fruitfulness of the marriage is other than biological offspring. With that admission we might be pressed to explore better what a responsible marriage is. And heterosexual family life would be relieved of some pressures. If homosexual people did not have to pretend to be heterosexual, there would be fewer unhappy marriages. If homosexual couples were allowed to adopt children, there would be fewer unwanted children. If homosexuality could be admitted to "responsible" circles such as among physicians, clergy, and schoolteachers, there fewer terrified youngsters who have no idea where to go with their feelings of sexual strangeness.

One of the words used to characterize homosexuality has been "inversion," a relation that is upside down. When the word was applied to both gay and lesbian persons, the assumption was that their sexual life was the opposite of what it should be. Ironically, the seeming inversion that frees men from male stereotypes and women from female stereotypes can be a step toward real mutuality. Homosexual couples and the homosexual community often can teach heterosexual couples about mutual love, a willingness to share life in a variety of ways. And homosexual persons often have a wide response, including religious response. Despite the inhospitability of most churches, homosexual men and women are often deeply religious; they have, as Carl Jung notes, "a spiritual receptivity which makes them responsive to revelation."[32]

These claims can sound romanticized. They do need the support of empirical data that are not readily available. The scientific studies of the nineteenth and early twentieth centuries concentrated on the question, What causes homosexuality? If the cause could be found, perhaps the cure would not be far behind. The person who was *responsible for* his or her homosexuality was almost invisible as the psychiatrist replaced the judge in being expert on the subject. The psychiatrists, on the whole, were more tolerant in that they saw sickness rather than crime or sin. The last few decades have seen the shift from the psychiatrist to the individuals who now speak for themselves. Distortions of data remain; none of us knows ourself perfectly. But for the first time in Western history a wide range of scientific and biographical data is coming forth that will make the discussion of homosexuality intelligible. The whole human community might begin to accept what is sexually the given and might reshape the culture to be sexually healthier for everyone.

TRANS-NATURAL HOMOSEXUALITY

The charge regularly brought against homosexuality is that it is "unnatural." There is no doubt that homosexuality is non-natural or trans-natural because all human sexuality transforms nature. Anyone who claims that homosexual people do things that nature does not prescribe should spend some time discovering the variety in heterosexual practice. Of course, there are moral limits to human inventiveness in sexual activity. That limit is the unnatural, manifested by a violence that kills or maims and by severe intrusion into organic cycles of birth, growth, decline, and death. The sexual abuse of a child, for example, is unnatural; it is a violent intrusion. For many centuries, child abuse was linked to homosexual men. Comtemporary studies suggest that the percentage of child abusers is about the same among homosexual as among heterosexual men; in other words, the vast majority of child abusers are heterosexual.

Take, as another example, oral sex. Is that unnatural, or is it a part of human-nature, a continuing part of human inventiveness that shapes sexual pleasures in nonviolent ways? The answer requires some knowledge of historical and current data. The widespread prevalence of a practice does not prove anything about its being unnatural or not. Nevertheless, widespread practice, combined with a lack of evidence that the practice maims and destroys, starts the argument in one direction. If in all of human history, four or forty or four hundred people were known to have had oral sex, the burden of a long explanation would be required to show that the practice is not an unnatural aberration. But if hundreds of millions of people practice oral sex, the burden of explanation shifts to those who claim there is a violent intrusion into natural processes here. The same principle applies to masturbation. When it becomes evident that over ninety percent of men masturbate, the claim that it is an unspeakable crime against nature is going to need some supplementary data.

Here is where the late twentieth century is in an improved position regarding moral judgments. Until the late nineteenth century, homosexuality did not even have a name to be spoken in public. The coining of the strange hybrid of Greek and Latin, "homosexual," was done to name a sickness. However, from that point onward, sexual discourse was changed, with "the homosexual" as part of the permanent landscape. As Foucault writes, "The sodomite had been a temporary aberration; the homosexual now was a species."[33] The medical profession in its search for the cause and cure of "the homosexual" unintentionally helped to solidify the existence of a homosexual way of being. When gay organizations began meeting in the 1950s they often had a physician or a psychiatrist as a speaker who would explain to the audience why they were sick.[34] There may have been a masochistic element in listening to such speeches, but what was also going on was the naming of reality by one of society's high priesthoods. The small meetings of the 1950s became the large political movement of the 1970s.

The turning point in this story is the Kinsey Reports at mid-century. The material on homosexuality transformed the outlook of both homosexual and heterosexual people. What was made clear in those two reports is something that had hitherto been only implied: the difference between homosexual behavior and homosexual "orientation." Kinsey found that thirty-seven percent of men had had postadolescent homosexual experience. In contrast, four percent of men were exclusively oriented toward homosexual behavior. Both statistics were a surprise. Taken together they suggest that many men experiment with homosexual behavior and find it does not fit them. (Fifty percent of men admitted to having some erotic responses to males.)[35] The statistics also indicate that a sizeable minority—certainly several million people in this country— recognize themselves as homosexual. Heterosexual practice may be as "unnatural" for them as is the homosexual practice forced upon many men in prison. The figures on lesbian orientation and practice were lower, but the same case could be made: that there are women whose exclusive sexual orientation is same-sex love. Subsequent studies have not only confirmed Kinsey's figures but suggest that, if anything, Kinsey's figures are on the low side. One must remember about anyone's statistics on the prevalance of homosexuality that "the vice that must not be named" is not easy to count in surveys.

In both civil and church law the distinction between the person's orientation and his or her behavior became the basis for a new tolerance. "Orientation" leaves open the question of how this condition was arrived at—that is, what was the mix of genetic, social, and other factors. What the word "orientation" does indicate is that the condition is not a simple matter of free choice. Granted that people with homosexual tendencies do exist, what should be society's response? Civil laws have gone in the direction of saying, "You are to be respected as a person, the bearer of legal rights, and what you do in private is no one's business." Churches have gone in the directon of saying, "You are to be repected as a person, created by God; we do not condemn the way you are, but we cannot condone your behavior."

The Catholic church is a particularly interesting case of church response. It has always tied its sexual morality into philosophical notions about nature. Its leading thinker, Thomas Aquinas, taught that homosexuality and masturbation were more unnatural than rape or adultery.[36] He thought, of course, that rape and adultery are wrong but that they do not violate so blatantly the structure of sexual intercourse that nature establishes. Few people today would follow Aquinas all the way down that path, but Catholic teaching still reflects a similar attitude of mind.

Catholicism has maintained a strict sexual code in its official teaching: genital activity is to take place within marriage, and every act of sexual intercourse must be open to procreation. Interestingly, the acceptance of persons with homosexual orientation does not immediately pose any special problem. They are subject to the same moral code as everyone else. Thus, in many Catholic textbooks today there is a compassionate attitude toward homosexual people. Their behavior draws no special attention or condemnation. They are grouped with the widowed, the divorced, the not-yet-married, and the celibate clergy. Homosexual behavior is unacceptable because it is outside marriage.[37]

This neat distinction is not enthusiastically embraced by gay and lesbian people; however, they are generally happy to have protection of civil law and non-condemnation by the church. Many church officials have given support to civil rights legislation that includes homosexual orientation in antidiscrimination provisions. The U.S. Catholic bishops in their pastoral letter *To Live in Christ Jesus* say that homosexual persons should not suffer prejudice against their basic human rights of respect, friendship, justice (adding that "homosexual activity, however, as distinguished from homosexual orientation is wrong").[38] Some Catholic officials, however, have strongly resisted civil-rights legislation that they believe implicitly encourages homosexual activity.

The Catholic church may be in for a long struggle on this point. The ethic of rights that has guided civil law assumes a private sphere where law and morality do not intrude. The Catholic church's concern with the integrity of nature—its sacramental view of the universe—is not easily reconciled with positing a total split between orientation and behavior. In Catholic tradition, the interior needs exterior manifestation, and the exterior affects the interior. Grace is truly embodied, so the physical is not merely expression or consequence. The sacramental principle affirms the goodness of earthly, bodily, communal, institutional, and cosmic patterns. If God creates an inner drive, its outward expression is necessary and good. The outer expression will always have some restrictions because each being in the cosmos is in process of reaching some greater communion. In sexual life, the Catholic church maintains that the outer activity must be confined within monogamous marriage whose procreative possibilities are not opposed. In Catholicism, the heterosexual person has a legitimate, even if narrow, route to go for sexual activity in accord with his or her tendencies.

If there is such a thing as homosexual orientation, can the Catholic church say there is no way at all that such an orientation can be embodied? The church is here in some conflict with its own sacramental belief; an orientation that is central to a person's make-up and has no legitimate expression seems to be "unnatural." The Catholic church preserves celibacy as a life-long choice for a tiny minority who are called to it. But, a lifelong celibacy imposed upon millions of people goes against the grain of that tradition. At a protest in front of St. Patrick's Cathedral in New York City a few years ago, one sign read, "If God made twenty million of us, he must have had something in mind."

Protestant Christianity has relied more directly on the biblical text for its condemnation of homosexuality. I will not try to summarize the studies recently done pointing out the misunderstandings or at least ambiguities in the classic texts.[39] The interesting issue here is why homosexuality remains near the top of the list in things considered un-Christian when many other things receive greater condemnation in the Bible. The gospels have nothing directly to say on the matter. And it is peculiar to hear Christians citing Leviticus 10 and Leviticus 20 on this point as if they were constantly reading the Book of Leviticus for their moral guidance.

St. Paul, to be sure, was shocked by sexual practices, including homosexual ones, that he saw in the pagan world. He uses the word "un-natural" to describe practices that he thought were contrary to the way things should be.[40] He did not have the distinction of orientation and behavior, so what he says does not directly address today's issue. After all, the condemnation of people who have abandoned "natural custom" could apply to heterosexual people performing homosexual behavior or homosexual people performing heterosexual behavior. Further-more, St. Paul thought a number of things were unnatural (including some hair styles; see 1 Cor. 11:14) that were merely a matter of custom or habit.

The point is not that Christians should abandon the Bible but, on the contrary, that a biblical view of sexuality ought not to depend on a couple of isolated sentences. And today's issue of homosexuality can not be resolved with any statement or single word ("unnatural," "abom-ination") taken out of context from centuries ago. The denunciation of homosexuality is so out of proportion to anything about it in the Bible—even including texts that were mistakenly thought to refer to it—that one must wonder about the set of forces that were at work. The Bible used in this peculiar way became a main basis for con-demning homosexual behavior as unnatural. In the twentieth century, both exegetical studies of the Bible and scientific studies of human behavior have undermined the charge of unnaturalness. This conclu-sion does not justify all homosexual behavior and all elements of gay subculture. But it could get us to the main issue: a calm acceptance of people who can speak for themselves and a concerted effort to reduce violence and exploitation in the lives of all women, children, and men.

PRIVATE/PUBLIC HOMOSEXUALITY

The gay/lesbian rights movement is a striking case study in the am-biguity of "private" and "public." As in the defense of a woman's right to choose abortion, the danger here is in complacently accepting the split between two spheres, the private (individual and sometimes family) and the public (with heavy emphasis on government). The widely ac-cepted distincton of orientation and behavior readily fits this separation of private and public sectors of reality.

Gay and lesbian leaders will sometimes argue that homosexual re-lations should be private (not interfered in by the government) and at other times argue that homosexual relations should not have to be kept private (clandestine). The confusion does not originate from these statements but from the history of the private/public relation. In the historic transition we now seem to be in, homosexual relations may be a main key to getting a newly integral meaning for private/public. When private is equivalent to family household, we do not have a deep-enough meaning of privacy; when public means governmental policies, we do not have a wide-enough meaning of public. Homosexuality challenges both fronts of this modern separation of two realms.

On the side of privacy, the sexual life should be recognized as part of the sacred interior life of the person. It need not be displayed for any organization; it ought not to be controlled from outside, except where some restrictions are necessary for public order. Generally, the responsible ordering of sexual life belongs to persons responding to persons. The government ought to legislate against rape and other acts of violence. Laws may also be necessary to cope with the spread of diseases sexually transmitted. But such things are not a reason for the wholesale control or suppression of sexual practice. Government and church organizations become involved in regulating heterosexual marriage mainly because of the possible offspring. Thus the government has less reason for involvement in homosexuality because there is no problem with the control of birth.

On the public side, sexuality needs public forms that are visible and readily accessible. Sexuality flows through encounters of men and women, men and men, women and women. Art, fashion, sport, religion and, alas, warfare are public rituals of human sexuality. The gay or lesbian person does not always have to be talking about sex in public any more than a black person always wishes to talk about being black. But black, female, gay, and other important variations of being human should not be invisible. A school child does not necessarily need instruction on homosexuality, but knowing about the existence of gay and lesbian schoolteachers, people who are not going to be fired for simply acknowledging who they are, is important for all children. A young person who gradually discovers his or her homosexual orientation should not have to say "I'm sick; I'm alone."

The contribution of gay and lesbian people to the arts is widely known, but in the past their sexual status had to be played down. Occasionally, a great artist would flaunt the fact of sexual deviation, at the risk of mental health and social ostracism. Would there not be more fruitful and happier lives among artists, schoolteachers, clergy, physicians, football players, and members of other professions if individuals were not forced to cut off part of the self, worrying that they are going to be exposed? Heterosexual people sometimes complain, "Yes, I'm tolerant, but why can't they be like us in regard to public display?" When people have suppressed an important part of their life, they often have to overstate the case in reaction. But it must also be said that we are nowhere near righting the balance or allowing into advertisments, public rituals, and artistic materials the proportionate place of homosexuality. Public heterosexualism is so omnipresent as to be invisible.

Consider the case of marriage. It is a powerful public institution that every heterosexual person accepts as a given. Homosexual lovers ought to have available a public support for their relations. Public, it should be recalled, means not just governmental or social (other individuals) but visible space that creates a sense of historical stability. Gay and lesbian people are accused of being promiscuous, of jumping from one partner to another. Two things can be said in response. First, although promiscuity runs high among some gay men, we have no reliable statistics to compare gay/lesbian promiscuity with that of the rest of the population. Second, it would hardly be surprising to find that the homosexual relations are less stable and enduring. Policies of both civil and church society encourage instability. In a context of social hostility, John Boswell notes, "The most effective defense against opposition will lie in fleeting and clandestine relationships which do not attract attention or private suspicion."[41] In other words, the result is neither a private life nor a public life.

During the last few decades a visible subculture of gay life has appeared not only in San Francisco and New York but in most large cities. "Gay" is the proper adjective; that is, it is a world of men. Lesbian women seem more often to be finding a public setting in rural places where the cultural surroundings are different. To some people this visible culture of gays and lesbians is a sign of the collapse of civilization; to others it is a proof of progress in modern tolerance. Most likely, both of these extremes are inaccurate, or at least it is too early for firm conclusions.

The gay subculture is able to flourish in untidy societies where the grip of governmental authority is loose. But a community or nation cannot live on looseness alone. We need some unity to our public life so that tolerance is a positive conviction rather than a result of governmental ineptitude and public confusion. We need many forms of public love; we need public concern for the environment; we need public organizations that are not arms of the government. For whatever reasons, gay and lesbian people have generally been more aware than heterosexual people of the need for community, the arts and cultural values. The moral question of homosexuality, therefore, is not one of tolerating a group that now finds public respectability. Instead the gay/lesbian movement can be seen as an attempt to create or re-create the meaning of public for everyone.

CHAPTER 9

Teaching Morally

Having examined a morality of goodness that is responsible, trans-natural, and private/public, and having illustrated this morality in the previous chapter, we can turn once again to the twentieth-century concern with moral education. I have claimed that today's moral education has both too narrow a meaning of "moral" (equating it with an ethic of rights) and too narrow a meaning of "education" (equating it with schooling for children). An educational morality has to include all the forms of life that educate. One of these forms is the religious life, but it has generally been excluded from the twentieth-century meaning of moral education.

Two of the main questions in moral education have been "Can we teach morality?" and "Is there a system of moral development?" The modern answers have been no to the first, yes to the second. There is a certain logic to the answers: we need not teach, cannot teach morality, because development occurs "naturally." Nonetheless, this combination of answers creates a paradox. Moral education is assigned to schools, but the schoolteacher is warned against trying to teach morality. Children are thought to have an inbuilt impetus toward thinking in a moral way. Thus, the schoolteacher's job is to devise techniques and exercises to unblock this natural development.

In this chapter and the following one I address the two basic questions of teaching morality and of moral development: "Can we teach morality?" and "Is there a system of moral development?" I give a positive answer to both questions, although my notion of lifelong moral development, drawn in part from religious sources, bears little resemblance to the moral development described by Lawrence Kohlberg. As for teaching morality, I do not begin with classroom instruction. I think it quite evident that we are taught morality by parents, friends, co-workers, and others. I also think that some aspects of morality can be taught in classrooms by schoolteachers prepared to do so.

The uneasiness that quickly surfaces at the idea of teaching morality reveals a confusion about the idea of teaching itself. The question prior to whether we can teach morality is: How does one teach *morally?* If one can teach morally, then all of one's teaching, not just the teaching of morality, might contribute to the moral development of learners. Seldom in moral education or in any educational literature is teaching itself examined. One might get the impression that teaching is so obvious an idea that it does not require intellectual exploration; instead we have teacher "training."

Underlying the evasion of the topic of teaching is the well-founded suspicion that it is an unavoidably moral act. Teaching seems to involve a kind of influence and control that is difficult to justify in any theoretical way. When Ivan Illich attacked the school in his tract *Deschooling Society*, he equated (school) teaching with corruption.[1] His attack was outlandish, and he offered no workable alternative. What he did succeed in doing fairly easily was pricking some guilty consciences. Society and its schoolteachers were and are unsure about the morality of teaching.

The peculiar ambivalence associated with teaching is captured in the striking introduction to Jacques Barzun's *Teacher in America:*

To be sure there is an age-old prejudice against teaching. Teachers must share with doctors the world's most celebrated sneers, and with them also the world's unbounded hero-worship. Always and everywhere, 'He is a teacher' has meant 'He is an underpaid pitiable drudge.' Even a politician stands higher, because power in the streets seems less of a mockery than power in the classroom. But when we speak of Socrates, Jesus, Buddha and 'other great teachers of humanity,' the atmosphere somehow changes and the politician's power begins to look shrunken and mean.[2]

Barzun's is a powerful but, I think, a prejudiced view of teaching that dichotomizes the activity of teaching into words of power over children by a lowly bureaucrat and words of powerful charismatic figures preached to the millions. There are some connecting links between the two poles: male figures, commanding words, dominative power. But is there no ordinary form of teaching done by women and men apart from this dichotomy? Barzun's next paragraph provides some direction:

The odd thing is that almost everybody is a teacher at some time or other during his life. Besides Socrates and Jesus, the great teachers of mankind are mankind itself—your parents and mine. First and last, parents do a good deal more teaching than doctoring, yet so natural is this duty that they never seem aware of performing it.[3]

Having brought up this "odd thing" that could open the door to an analysis of teaching, Barzun immediately reverts to using "teacher" in such a way that parents and most human beings have little share in the word.

Barzun's wild dichotomy allows us to avoid facing the moral question about teaching. On the one hand, we assume that little children need controlling by someone. And while parents have an inherent right to tell children what to do, we also allow the schoolteacher the power to tell children what to think. On the other hand, we acknowledge that there are "great teachers" such as Jesus and Socrates who know more than any of us. They tell us what is good for us, and if we had any sense we should probably follow their prescriptions, but we do not. The moral question that remains about teaching is: What justifies the directive and controlling power of anyone who presumes to teach anything?

TO TEACH IS TO SHOW HOW

In describing the act of teaching, the best starting point is the word's Old English etymology: to teach is to show how. To teach means to show people how to do something. But there are many ways of showing, many things that can be shown, and many settings in which showing can occur. One should note that age has no inherent connection to a theory of teaching. True, reflecting on children has a certain appropriateness, particularly children below five years old. A theory of teaching has to be realistic and meaningful for all individuals of the human species. The very young, the very old, the physically or mentally handicapped, and other vulnerable members of the human race are good tests for theorizing about teaching. In practice, though, most theoretical statements about teaching are merely reflections upon children who can reason and are in the classroom setting.

Teaching is what any human being can do for another: show him or her how. Does it extend beyond the human world? This meaning of teaching does have its beginnings in the practices of complex nonhuman animals. Like the word "community," teaching is a human reality but one that should not exclude other animals. Teaching guides and transforms bodily life as life presents itself. In showing a human being how to do something, one must never forget that one is still among the animals, where words have only limited effect.

Teaching, I wish to argue, is bodily activity in a human group. A pattern is presented in such a way that the learner can assimilate what is offered and can respond in some way. The response of the learner should influence the next step in teaching. Although there is a peculiar satisfaction for both teacher and learner in mastering a particular skill, the process of teaching and learning is "without end." One might also say that teaching and learning are without beginning, in that the process is occurring before a particular teacher and a particular student take up a particular task. Teaching is embodied in the community's life. What is communicated at any moment is not necessarily what the teacher is consciously teaching. Theories of teaching usually make much of intentionality. While I would agree that intentionality plays some part in teaching, the main intentional elements may have become embodied throughout generations of teaching. When an adult tells a fairy tale to a child, the teaching transcends the particular adult's intention. Something similar happens in all storytelling and in the performance of rituals. The "showing how" goes beyond the direct control of both teacher and student.

Religious history is a helpful source for understanding *how* teaching occurs. Despite the differences among religions, there are some remarkable commonalities regarding teaching. A community of adherents "hands over" the teaching that consists of a way of life guided by interpretation of sacred texts. An individual who claims to be a teacher is tested against the whole community, dead members as well as living. Authority resides in the community's way of life, so a teacher can claim only to *re-present* the tradition. A saying attributed to Muhammed is a claim made by each religion: "My community cannot be in error." Errors creep into particular formulations, but, by definition, that is not where the true community is.

Modern times began with a revolt against the very idea of tradition and against an authority residing in tradition. On what ground does a teacher stand in the era of modern enlightenment? The usual answer has been: reason alone. But reason has not proved to be so readily accessible and so comprehensively applicable as the gentlemen of the eighteenth century assumed it would be. Babies still need training; book learning is still tedious. Artistry still requires discipline, nations still mask self-interest, and perfectly reasonable people still deceive themselves. If the wise, the learned, and the skillful have no communal support for sharing their accomplishments with those who lack learning, wisdom, and skills, then brutal and dehumanizing forms of achieving order are eventually necessary. One form that this takes is the "charismatic" leader, as Max Weber named the phenomenon. If isolated individuals cannot bear the burden of reason and choice, they may be strongly attracted to powerful figures who teach self-destruction.

Two things make teaching unpalatable to modern attitudes. One is its premise that we are not all equal; the other is its requirement of discipline. Teaching is an activity between unequals: the one who is teaching has what others do not have. Teaching aims at creating equals, but it begins with being directive. An initial trust is therefore required. Something of great value cannot be conveyed in sixty seconds and sometimes not in six months. That is why the teacher may say that you will understand the teaching only as you change your behavior and begin to practice a discipline of life. But in modern society we are encouraged to do only what strikes us as reasonable, an attitude that provides no firm basis for trusting a way of life and its teachers.

"Tradition" means "handing over"; a close relative is "transmission," a word that is maligned in educational literature. Transmission can be a useful metaphor for indicating what a community does through its representatives: pass on the best it has to the next generation. Of course, some teachers, including schoolteachers, have the task of challenging aspects of the transmitted materials. Each teacher reshapes what is handed on within a traditioning or transmitting process. As a teacher shows how to do something, the handing over must have room for creative responses that alter the shape of the tradition. The learner can then be shown, not things to mimic, but activities with structures of meaning that open beyond themselves.

PREACHING AND THERAPY

One way to explore the nature of teaching is to study the role of speech in the act of teaching. I look at two extremes of the spectrum, preaching and therapy, before turning to classroom instruction, which shares some characteristics with both of these extremes. I then turn to parenting, friendship and religious guidance as forms of teaching that draw upon preaching, therapy, and classroom instruction.

In many forms of teaching, speech has the function of choreography. The teaching is a showing how the body moves. Words come in for the directions: hold the fingers this way, breathe from down here, add one clove of garlic. In choreography, human speech and written texts give directions for moving the body. But when speech emerges in interpersonal exchange, political judgment, literary art, scientific inquiry, and philosophical discourse, it strains against its choreographic role in the act of teaching. Speech bends back on itself, and the verbal directives themselves become the "subject matter." Teaching is about reshaping movement, and language itself can be seen as a human movement.

Preaching, therapy, and classroom instruction are forms that teaching takes when language reflects back on itself. Each of these three has an important contribution to make to the life of the speaking animal. And each threatens to undermine the whole range of teaching when it tries to take over as the only way to teach. Although classroom instruction more than the other two preempts the *word* "teaching" for itself, preaching and therapy make their own claims to be ultimate guides and final judges of how we should live.

Preaching. Preaching is a form of teaching that is well suited to an ethic of the good. If people already know what is good for them, good for human nature, what they need is someone to exhort them to strive for the good. The language is already determined by texts established centuries ago. The great preacher's contribution is "style," the ability to fashion the words in such a way that an audience passionately responds.

Preaching is almost totally anathema in the modern world. No one except ecclesiastics openly admits to doing it. In Philip Rief's curt summary of the issue, "Preaching is not teaching, except in a church."[4] It is considered a terrible accusation to say of someone that he or she is preachy or is sermonizing. When we are no longer confident that there is a good common to all human beings, we find it irritating to listen to someone who presumes to know what is good for us and who therefore badgers us for failing to do what is obviously the right thing to do.

Theories of moral education in the twentieth century have been defined in opposition to preaching. "To teach morality," writes Durkheim, "is neither to preach nor to indoctrinate; it is to explain."[5] But are these the real alternatives for the meaning of teaching? In academic circles, "explaining" takes the form of fifty minutes of talk at the front of lecture halls. The format of lecturing usually lacks the ritual elements of preaching and is directed at reason rather than emotion. The explanatory speech is a rational reduction of the form of preaching. Academic scholars are often very certain about what is good for us: rational explanations.

If the rational side of preaching is still with us, one might suspect that preaching's emotive elements are also close at hand. One does not have to go any farther than the television set, where the best examples of preaching are not the Sunday-night evangelists but the incessant commercial "messages." Television advertising is a striking example of preaching that is aimed at emotional reaction. We may not know the ultimate good for human beings, but we know we would feel better with a laxative that works, with beer that tastes good and is less filling, and with an automobile that apparently improves one's sex life. Nothing in the television world is given more attention than the production of these twenty or thirty seconds of art. The right phrase can mean millions of dollars overnight.

What a whole people condemns is often what they are addicted to. Since we believe that preaching is out of date and lives on only in church, we are vulnerable to the influence of great preachers who know how to hypnotize with words. If reason and emotion are split apart, reason being assigned to lecture halls and scholarly papers, a corrupted form of preaching with constant appeal to self-interest takes over our social, political, and economic life. It does little good to denounce such preaching; the denunciation is only one more example of preaching.

The more effective way to deal with our corrupted forms of preaching is to acknowledge that preaching is one valid form of teaching and to encourage preaching in its appropriate contexts. People might be embarrassed by the word "preaching" being applied to a television journalist's reporting on famine or a politician's speaking obvious truths to a nation resistant to hear. Nonetheless, journalists or politicians would often do better if they let their words flow forth from bodily presence without the pretense that they are merely sharing ideas or answering questions. The great politicians know how the sermon works; they know that their words can change the self-perception of millions of people. Unlikely characters such as Adolf Hitler or Reverend Jim Jones get a place in history books for mesmerizing people with sermons. But the positive possibilities are evident in the speeches of Roosevelt or Churchill, King or Gandhi.

Preaching is an appropriate part of a morality of goodness. Each thing is good, and goodness is what overflows from the center of things. For human life, what can overflow is speech. The real preacher does not give his or her audience only what they want to hear as determined by last week's opinion poll. The preacher may not even wait for an audience. "To him who hears me, I wish him well," said Meister Eckhart, "but as for me, I would have preached at the collection box."[6] Eckhart's great mystical insights are not in his scholarly Latin treatises but in sermons preached in the vernacular German. We have access to these sermons because dedicated nuns took notes. Sermons do not exist on paper, because preaching is personal presence in which words gush up at the center of life to force movement.

Christianity is a particularly preachy kind of religion, tracing its origins to a man who apparently spent his days going about preaching. Jesus' preaching was in the context of and in tension with the highly ritualized Jewish religion of the time. Jesus of Nazareth was one of many Jewish reformers who used the power of words to challenge, to upset, to point beyond existing institutions. The Christian church developed preaching into an art form. Despite its domestication within the institution, the form could be subversive when embodied in Savonarola, Eckhart, Luther, Wesley, or Edwards. An important test for Christian preachers is their respect for the Judaism that to this day remains the context for and the restraint upon Christian urging to transform the world.

Should the Christian church have institutionalized preaching and expected that people could be programmed to preach every Sunday at eleven A.M.? Institutionalizing important human realities, whether art or preaching or sex, guarantees continuance over time but cannot guarantee consistent high quality. Since church preachers cannot always produce the best of the form, they should observe some general restraints. They should be relatively brief; they should keep to commenting upon a text; they should leave out the ornate phrases that so easily flow in churchy settings. Most important, the preacher should not nag people, carping at their failure to do this or that. A morality of goodness struggles with evil, failure, and sin by trying to get more goodness to overflow itself.

Most sermons in church need not be masterpieces, but they should keep this art form alive. It is a form in which one person uses words with a kind of delicious attentiveness. Preaching is testimony that speech matters, that it is ultimately important. A sermon can subvert every formulation of speech, but it affirms the reality of speech itself. Preaching should therefore be filled with wit and irony, turning upside down what is assumed to be normal morality, the morality of complacency and self-congratulation.

Therapy. At the other end of the teaching spectrum is therapy. In this form of teaching, speech is seldom used as a directive. Therapy turns speech against speech and tries to strip away the outer covering that hides the hurts and prevents the healing. Therapy is a particularly appropriate form of teaching in an ethic of rights. And in a culture that largely identifies the moral life with the protection of individual rights, it would not be surprising to find that teaching and therapy are equated.

Therapy has an extremely high reputation in the modern world. Healing through personal exchange and nonverbal ritual has always been recognized as part of the moral life. However, in the twentieth century, therapy has been institutionalized as a kind of secular version of priesthood. In religion the priestly action mediates salvation (a word meaning health). The contemporary therapist acts to restore power to the organism so that the individual may exercise her or his autonomy. The therapist's activity is a kind of non-action, a willingness to accept the client without moral judgment. By listening more than by speaking, the therapist provides direction and healing. The only good the therapist is sure of is the autonomous will of the client.

Nevertheless, what is praised without critical challenge is in danger of becoming an addiction that envelops all other activities. That sick people need therapeutic help is clear enough; that all educational forms should become forms of therapy is dangerous. At present, the idea of teaching is suspect; workshops and seminars are likely to have "facilitators" rather than teachers. In reacting against teachers—by which is usually meant preachers who tell us what to think—we are in danger of being controlled by the assumptions of therapy. We come to think that any words are true if they make us feel good. One statement is as good as the next because words are ultimately unimportant.

Adult-education literature is a striking example of the triumph of therapy. The word "teaching" is often excised, and it is regularly asserted that adults will not sit still for a course with theoretical substance presented by a schoolteacher. Adults, it is claimed, are interested only in problem solving: marital problems, weight problems, car problems, tax problems. Needs assessment and problem solving are what you need to facilitate adult-education programs, and the students always have to be participating in solving their own problems. A therapeutic culture is a very comforting world for rich and powerful people who have individual problems to be solved, but it leaves poor and powerless people with few resources with which to change the system that oppresses them.

A denunciation of therapy would have no effect at all; therapy would simply absorb the words used to denounce. The corrective to therapy's tendency to take over all teaching is to acknowledge the value of therapy but to complement it with other forms of teaching. A morality of goodness in which each thing is allowed to be itself puts high value on therapy. We need quiet healing everywhere in the world. Sometimes the best thing that happens in classrooms, whether with children or adults, is that people feel better about themselves. But in the long run people will be more helped if therapy is usually the indirect result of classroom education, not the main activity. When the alternatives are therapy and violence, all education is on the side of therapy. But when the choice is between therapy and theory, classrooms have to go with theorizing as their main reason for existence.

These days a theoretical use of speech has to be defended. Words can be used to get understanding and then to change a situation. As therapy envelops a culture, though, words are used not to provoke but to soothe, particularly to adjust people to their situations. Sigmund Freud was concerned that his theory of psychoanalysis would be taken over by the medical profession, which would reduce it to a therapy. Freud said that he practiced therapy for two reasons: to understand his theory better and to make a living. His fear that psychoanalysis would be reduced to a therapy for those who could afford its high price has not proved groundless.[7]

Among religions of the world, Buddhism is the preeminently therapeutic one. Whereas Jesus was a preacher, Gautama took as one of his names "the silent one." Buddhism is almost totally devoid of theoretical speculation. A question such as "Who made the world?" simply does not register. Buddhism exists as a set of techniques that are responses to suffering. By penetrating beyond the superficial level of ordinary consciousness, Buddhism tries to get at the roots of human suffering. By grappling with the human condition in this way it discovers a commonality with all living things.

In Buddhism, talking about our problems is seen as a problem of its own. Language is cut out by a surgery far more radical than any found within Western religion. "Language is resorted to in order to serve as a wedge in getting out the one [language] already in use; it is like a poisonous medicine to counteract another.[8] The famous *koans* of Zen Buddhism are puzzles that have no rational answers. But from meditation on these puzzles the student's mind breaks through to what is beyond speech. With the help of a guru who is a therapist-teacher, the self is liberated from its existence and readied for confronting nothingness.

Christianity and Buddhism might have something to learn from each other on the topic of language. Christianity tends to equate teaching with preaching in its clericalized churches. Buddhism, with its absence of doctrines, sermons, and moralizing, has an immediate attractiveness these days. In fact, it may fit all too well into a therapeutic takeover of Western culture. Both Christianity and Buddhism could use a serious encounter with the classroom. Both religions have valuable moral insights that the culture needs, but if these religions are to be heard they have to enter theoretical analysis, not as dictators but as contributing partners.

CLASSROOM INSTRUCTION

Teaching in school, far from being the only form or the prototypical form of teaching, is a peculiar way to go at the activity of teaching. On one side, it is as verbal as preaching. Not only is it carried on largely *by* words; it is largely *about* words. On the other side, it is as nonjudgmental as therapy, not trying to change an individual's behavior. It is very directive in its use of words, but the directives are not aimed at evoking a decision to change one's life.

Classroom instruction is a strange form of human activity, always threatened with vacuity because it mainly consists of talk about talk. To teach is to show how, and in classrooms this means to show how to speak. A preacher assumes that the language is a given and that the task is to move the hearers to act. The schoolteacher assumes that language itself is in question and that, except for a hope to change language, moving people to action is not intended. Like a therapist, the classroom instructor cannot prescribe but can only advocate. An advocate appears with a brief and engages in plausible interpretation; the case is won only with the accompanying response of the hearers. The therapist achieves an objectivity of judgment by allowing the client to present the words, the therapist neither suggesting nor judging those words. The classroom instructor tries to be objective by drawing upon many voices from the larger community and then advocating a pattern of speech.

Objective can mean unbiased, fair, and based on evidence. It can also mean the exclusion of a human subject. In math or physical sciences, the first meaning entails the second; that is, unbiased evidence eliminates the subjective as far as possible. But most of the time we reach an objectivity of evidence not by excluding a human subject but by bringing in several of them. Researchers are checked by other people's research. A judge is helped to judge fairly by knowing there are higher courts. Schoolteachers are kept objective by having faculty colleagues and responsive students.

The chief moral requirement for the act of classroom instruction is to limit the direct advocacy for change to changing language. No one has the right to intrude on another person's mind. We have to be able to get out of the way of powerful opinions about the right way to live. Every schoolteacher ought to work within self-imposed restrictions. Legally, a schoolteacher can get away with all kinds of preaching and therapy, which are generally not appropriate for the classroom. The schoolteacher cannot avoid being invloved in moral advocacy. But the public character of language is the schoolteacher's protection; it allows her or him to be challenged from all sides. The schoolteacher brings to the classroom encounter whatever tools of scholarship she or he has. So also do the students bring their own ways of speaking; even an illiterate student or a mentally retarded student has some say in language.

Language can be placed between the covers of a book to exist as an object. We recognize that a book has a life of its own beyond the control of its author. But a book will influence only the minds of those who choose to read it. Language in a classroom should also be placed on a table between teacher and student. Advocating a change of that object, that particular pattern of speech, does not directly entail changing the convictions of the student. The student is invited to take part in a conversation and discover ways of speaking that he or she may choose to adopt.

The idea of "putting language on a table between us" may sound like an esoteric project fit only to be used with graduate students. Actually, the younger the students, the more important such an approach is. University students and other adult students are better able to recognize unwarranted intrusions and moral manipulations. They provide objectivity because they are usually not bound to be there and they have their own formed convictions. Elementary school students are most in need of protection, of having the means to step back from a forceful opinion by an adult who has power over them. A child is legally required to be in the classroom, and courts provide almost no protection of privacy for children while they are in school. The schoolteacher of the young should avoid whatever goes directly at the emotions of the child. Nevertheless, if and when the classroom becomes an environment of trust, students voluntarily reveal some of their feelings in what they say. Feelings are always present in classrooms but they should not be the direct object of the teaching or the reality that instructors seek to change.

The classroom instructor's starting point is not "I'm knowledgeable and you're ignorant. My job is to tell you (or preach to you) the truth."

Neither is the instructor's starting point "You, the students, already have truth within. My job is to arrange you in groups and to use therapeutic techniques that will reveal the inner truth." Rather, the starting point is: "We both have a share of truth insofar as experience has already taught us. Neither of us has a fully adequate language for that truth. My job is to advocate a better language than you now speak." The claim to "better language" by the instructor has to be continually reexamined in light of both a wider human community and the response of these particular students.

I think that the most exciting, interesting, and effective instructors do in fact operate under these guidelines. People remember as a "great teacher" someone who may have been a bit quirky but who definitely was a person with convictions. The teacher provoked thinking that altered one's life, but paradoxically he or she seemed not to care what you thought so long as you could articulate your convictions. Passion was let loose in the classroom, although passion was not the object of the teacher's attention. Strange subjects such as Cicero, early church history, chemical solutions, or Shakespeare took on monumental importance.

The instructor is forced into all sort of tricks to re-create the subject in the student's mind. If language were assumed to be already set, then the subject matter would be what was said by Isaac Newton, Thomas Aquinas, or Max Weber. But if all language is questionable, the teacher has to keep asking questions of the "subject matter," not just to test whether students have the answer but to go beyond the current knowledge of both instructor and student. Good schoolteachers convey a double impression: mastery of the subject through detailed preparation, and an open mind expecting to learn something new in the act of teaching. One of William James's students described his classroom teaching thus: "He always left the impression that there was more; that he knew there was more; and that the more to come might throw a very different light on the matter under discussion. He respected the universe enough to believe that he could not carry it under his own hat."[9]

The moment-to-moment activities of good classroom instruction cannot be charted in detail. The competent instructor prepares carefully and then acts out of instinct. Even the most experienced instructor, who has learned a lot by trial and error, can never predict exactly what will happen. Response is integral to the activity, so success can never be guaranteed on any particular occasion, at least not the success the instructor was hoping for.

In the middle of a class discussion an instructor has to calibrate what an expression of his or her opinion will do to the discussion. Over a long time the instructor cannot avoid stating opinions, but they do not constitute the subject matter. No subject matter should be out of bounds for classroom consideration, and no one's convictions, including the teacher's, should be silenced. Students need not agree with the opinions of the instructor.[10] Any good instructor loves to have students who can disagree and hold their ground in an intelligent argument.

Such classrooms often have a sense of playfulness.[11] Language allows for a testing of its limits and a playing with its possibilities. Instructors spend some of their time conveying information, but that is better done these days by books, films, and computers. Classrooms are for playing with that information. To schoolteach is to play with language, seriously but not solemnly discovering new ways to think and to imagine. If classroom instruction is done morally with self-imposed restriction to linguistic advocacy, the results are endless questioning, abundant playfulness, and intellectual curiosity.

Where "teaching morally" is the school's way of acting, the question of teaching morality (or teaching ethics) can be raised. Systematic reflection on the moral life is appropriate in any school, although generally speaking the older the students, the more substantial the reflections. In the university or professional school the course is likely to be called the "teaching of ethics." A morality of goodness recognizes the value of teaching morality or teaching ethics. The school is asked to do its part by stimulating reflection on the moral life and providing a language to discuss moral problems.

Teaching morality in schools might begin with reflecting on the concrete conditions of student life. What about the doses of patriotic sentiments indicated through such rituals as saluting the flag? Or consider that spontaneity of speech is unusual in schools; schools impose an order well beyond what is needed for the school's functioning. Or what about the moral tenor set by sports teams with cheerleaders and athletic scholarships? The point is not to preach against any of these things but to develop a moral language to question them. Some controversy might follow—which need not be a bad thing. The eventual study of ethics in a systematic way would then have less tendency to become an abstract system with little connection to ordinary life.

TEACHERS AND MORAL TEACHING

Throughout the preceding sections I have spoken of the *act* of teaching, my concern being the restrictions necessary to preaching, therapy, and classroom instruction so that they are morally good activities. Teaching as an act is, of course, embodied in a person who is not always performing that activity. The one person can and usually does engage in several kinds of teaching. A therapist may instruct a class in psychology, treat a client, or tell her child to behave. A church minister may preach to a church congregation on Sunday morning, teach a theology class in the seminary on Monday morning, and comfort a grieving widower on Tuesday morning. A schoolteacher often does all three kinds of teaching in the course of a day: teaching five class periods, monitoring the cafeteria, and calming an upset child. The idea of professional role is generally helpful for distinguishing between the times one is teaching according to one's professioinal preparation and the times one is teaching in other ways.

One of the drawbacks in the schoolteaching profession is that the act of provoking the mind in classrooms is engulfed by other duties. That is especially the case when schoolteaching is identified with the teaching of children. The culture thinks of teaching as an activity of school-teachers and thinks of schoolteachers as custodians of children. In the middle of the nineteenth century the culture shifted from an ethic of the good to an ethic of rights. Correspondingly, schoolteachers passed from being schoolmasters training children in required subjects to schoolmistresses nurturing children in a wide area of needs. A profession of schoolteaching whose specific activity would be to challenge the intellects of adults and children has not been firmly established.

Most of the world's teaching is not done by clergy, psychotherapists, and schoolteachers. Rather, the activities of preaching, therapy, and instruction are engaged in by everyone. Parents and relations, friends and colleagues, supervisors and co-workers, teach every day, most of the time in ways that are not consciously reflected upon. People move from one form of teaching to another, and so long as the form is appropriate they teach morally. Any parent who does not abandon his or her vocation is regularly practicing preaching, therapy, and instruction. From birth, a child is swaddled in nonverbal rituals that nurture, comfort, and encourage his or her autonomous development. From the time a child can do anything dangerous, parents warn, cajole, command, and otherwise deliver short sermons. From the time the child begins to use its reasoning powers, the parent gives pedagogic instruction in select areas. The three kinds of teaching generally decline as the child gets older, but the teaching does not necessarily stop. Many parents are still teaching from their deathbeds in all three ways.

Teaching by parent, friend, or anyone else is moral when it is *responsible, trans-natural,* and *private/public.* As with the three issues examined in Chapter 8, we can test the morality of teaching by applying these characteristics of a morality of goodness.

Teaching is moral when it is *responsible*—that is, when it answers to the situation. Each situation has its own factors that govern the appropriateness of the teaching activity. A Christian preacher can assume that his or her audience is there to hear a sermon on Christian living. A psychotherapist in charging a fee for services sets up a contract of responsibility. A schoolteacher teaching people who are not legally free to be elsewhere has the advantages and disadvantages of a captive audience. Being morally responsible as a teacher means not forgetting the relational context within which one is showing someone how to do something. Every teacher must begin by asking, Why are these people gathered here?

Moral responsibility for a teacher also means respecting the learners and listening for their responses. Teaching involves teach-learn-teach-learn, and so on without end. In physical acts of showing how (teaching a child to ride a bicycle or teaching someone to swim), the teaching and learning are so immediate to each other that one can barely distinguish the two activities. The direction and the response are instantaneous, and teaching constantly adapts to the bodily movements of the learner. When the project is complete, the teacher and the learner have a common feeling of success or failure.

As speech breaks loose from its choreographic function, teaching can be said to be occurring even if no one is responding, but that meaning of teaching is chimerical. A good teacher is always picking up responses and adapting to them even if he or she is doing all the talking. A preacher whose message does not depend on what the congregation wants to hear still works with the rhythm of the audience and its murmurings. This is most evident in black churches, where the preacher might get "Amen, brother" as a response. A schoolteacher needs independence of mind, but all the techniques of classroom instruction require some kind of audience participation.

An effective schoolteacher will generally finish the response to a question by inviting a further response to the answer just given. Parents and friends carry out such a procedure just by continuing to be parents and friends. Moral guidance occurs not by giving solutions to moral problems but by being one pole in a conversation to clarify what we are each responsible for. A religious tradition places the whole conversation in a context of rituals that link human and nonhuman, present and past. Each human response is part of an unimaginably rich tapestry of teaching and learning throughout generations.

The *trans-natural* character of human-nature is evident in the act of teaching. Nature gives the potential for teachableness, and the complex animals teach their young to survive and to adapt. Over a long time some aspects of nature are transformed. The human animal, the wild animal that has broken out, cannot survive at all without teaching. Using speech as choreography, the humans transform nature more radically and more rapidly than other animals.

Because the human animal can abstract speech and consider it on its own, there arise preaching, therapy, and instruction. Each of these three breaks out of nature, so there is danger of doing something unnatural. A person who speaks for two hours while his or her listeners sit on hard benches can turn preaching or schoolteaching into an unnatural act. A therapy that does not allow sufficient time for bodiliness and will to be integrated can turn unnatural. The body must never be forgotten in teaching even though speech can be abstracted from bodiliness.

To teach morally is to use speech in ways that lead to a reduction of violence in the world. A parent or friend who shows a way of life in which the drives of bodily emotions are gently brought into order is contributing to a human transformation of the natural. An ethics course in a school should provide a larger vision of how nature is to be transformed without violence.

Finally, moral teaching is *private/public*; teaching morally means relating the private inner self and the large public world. A teacher has no right to intrude upon the center of anyone else's soul. Not even a parent has that right, let alone schoolteacher, church minister, or government official. A teacher is one who shows how, but it is up to the student to take it within. If someone refuses to learn, that is his or her prerogative. A teacher may come back many times, holding out the offer of something valuable to learn. Only when the response comes from within, from a sense of responsibility *for* one's own learning and a responsibility *to* the teaching, can the process of teaching-learning occur.

As in the issues studied in Chapter 8, teaching is public in the very act of being private. Teaching is bodily visible and takes place in the medium of public language. A preacher brings to bear ancient texts in their relation to contemporary life. A schoolteacher mediates the language of a wider community of scholars. A therapist brings the healing of bodiliness, memory, and relations to other people. A parent or a friend is the connecting link to a public life for the individual. To teach morally is to enlarge the imagination, clarify language, and open the door to the future.

An old adage says "Any teacher who can be replaced by a machine should be." Real teaching, in schools or elsewhere, will never be replaced by machines. It is true that machines can now do much of the subsidiary part of education, making available vast stores of information. But the moral issue in education can be solved only with human teachers. An attempt to avoid moral questions in education can lead to a machinelike attitude on the part of teachers. The way to avoid moral coercion in teaching is to know both one's own convictions and the limitations inherent in teaching.

A teacher can invite another into a dialogue of meaning and can try to make learning conditions as propitious as possible. However, what happens in teaching is always a surprise and a mystery. A teacher cannot take credit as the "cause" of someone's learning; the mystical tradition has more insight on this point than most modern studies of education. That is, we are not responsible for the goodness of other people, and likewise we need not feel guilty about their shortcomings.

This double attitude of assuming neither credit nor blame could lead to careless indifference in teaching. Properly understood, though, it provides a freedom to respond to whatever the situation calls for and leads to a zest for being a teacher. Teaching should liberate both teacher and student, giving them the joy of participating in the flow of life in a way that gently controls the human reshaping of our lives together.

CHAPTER 10

Toward Moral Integrity

Until the mid-nineteenth-century, educatonal writers presumed that it is possible to teach morality. It was the job of parents and schoolmasters to inform the young about human nature and to see that the young observed the rules of right conduct. In the second half of the nineteenth century a dramatic shift began to occur, the effects of which we are still trying to cope with. The teaching of morality was removed from the schoolteachers, and while schools try to maintain some code of conduct, no one is very confident of having the grounds for saying this is right and that is wrong. And one would have to be optimistic to think that the teaching of morality is being adequately handled at home. Parents share in the culture's confusion over the basis of morality.

The idea that has come to fill the gap is moral development. If neither parent, schoolteacher, church, or government knows enough to educate the young in morality, where is the basis of moral stability to be found? The answer is: an inborn structure that guarantees moral progress for the individual if we can clear away encumbrances to it. The idea of moral development in the twentieth century functions as the secular substitute for providence, predestination, and heavenly salvation. There is no final reward to life and no invisible hand guiding us there. Nevertheless, we can progress morally by coming to see that everyone has a right to his or her choices. Such progress occurs particularly as the young person develops rational skills. Moral development, it is assumed, begins about age five or six and continues until the late teens. It is a mental progression aided by the discussion of values and hypothetical dilemmas.

Christian writers have reacted to the challenge of the idea of development either by rejecting the whole idea or by trying to keep it in its place. That place is usually a step below faith or grace or whatever defines the higher life. This way of positing the relation between secular and religious categories often seems to satisfy both parties. The secular developmentalists are willing to allow the claim that there is a higher way and then simply disregard whatever is said from that quarter because it is based on faith. On their side, Christian writers claim that they do take seriously the idea of development, although they also claim to have a greater insight because of their faith. The chance for a valuable dialogue is lost because the image of higher and lower access to truth is unchallenged from either side. The moral insights of Augustine and Aquinas, Luther and Calvin, Francis and Eckhart, Berrigan and Merton are not confronted in the writing on moral development because they are presumed to belong to the realm of faith. The liberal principle that we need *both* development and religious conversion is more a restatement of the question rather than an answer to the relation between the secular use of development and the Christian use of religious categories.

Not all Christian writers are willing to grant that development is a good idea so long as it is complemented by Christian categories. On the evangelical right of Christianity what counts is conversion to a new life. For example, Eric Gritsch, commenting on Luther's description of the Christian life as death and rebirth, writes: "Such a view of Christian formation conflicts with Western culture's 'natural pedagogy' of anthropological concepts of potentiality, development and self-realization. . . . Luther perceived such a pedagogy to be the greatest temptation to become self-righteous, to trust the ability of one's inner self rather than having faith in God's work."[1] Gritsch repeatedly uses the word "development" as the key to this natural pedagogy, which, far from being a helpful means, is perceived as the greatest temptation. Here, at least, the issue is joined. The right wing of Christianity recognizes the threat of the modern view of development. The two ideas of development and conversion cannot simply be juxtaposed. Perhaps, however, the two can be related in a way different from either liberal or evangelical assumptions in Christian writing. Before easily accepting or totally rejecting the modern view of development, the religious person should reflect on its history and imagery.

HISTORY AND IMAGERY OF DEVELOPMENT

Surprisingly little is written on the idea of development itself. Or perhaps it is not surprising that a notion so central to a whole era is simply taken for granted. It is an idea that shows up in almost every field of study today, one of those optimistic modern terms that nearly everyone wants a share of. Its two closest relatives are "progress" and "evolution"; "development" avoids the presumptuous connotations of the former and the biological limitations of the latter. "Development" can be used to comprehend both individual and cultural change. While its pretensions are more modest than those of "progress," "development" still suggests a change for the better. Thus, the issue of *moral* development is not peripheral to development itself, because to move from a worse to a better stage implies standards by which someone knows what is good and bad or what is good, better, and best. One might go so far as to say that all theories of development are theories of moral development.

The two groups that most frequently use the term "development" are psychologists and economists. Each group is almost totally oblivious to the other group's use of the term. Ostensibly, there is no direct connection between the psychological and the economic meanings of development. However, an underlying connection between the two usages is an intriguing possiblity. Are theories of economic development products of a certain kind of psychological development? Are theories of psychological development the product of one part of the economically developed world? Perhaps some day someone will be able to write the story of the development of development.

For the present, the field of developmental psychology tends to assume that it invented the idea of development. Psychology departments offer courses presumptuously called "Human Development." The implication is that not only psychic but personal, moral, religious, and any other kind of development is to be discovered and described by psychology. But it is not clear today that development is the preserve of psychologists. Indeed, one might argue that psychology came rather late to the idea of development and that psychology today does not hold the controlling interest in the term.

Psychology's main competitor for ownership of development is economics. Michael Novak asserts that development is an idea invented by Adam Smith in 1776.[2] Smith's *Wealth of Nations* propounds the idea that we can indefinitely expand wealth by organizing and investing resources. The process, which is guided "as if by an invisible hand," has no endpoint of perfection but nonetheless betters the human condition. Even if Adam Smith is not given all the credit, one can make a strong case for tracing the modern idea of development to the economic revolution of several centuries ago. In this perspective, developmental psychology is an application of the idea of development. The application to psychological data may be warranted, but one should not forget a larger context and a longer history for the meaning of development.

When we speak of moral development there is no obvious reason why it should be seen as belonging to psychological development. But in the half century since Piaget's *The Moral Judgment of the Child*, moral development has increasingly been defined as a psychological, an epistemological, or a "cognitive" question. The name of Lawrence Kohlberg has become almost synonymous with moral develpment. But when Kohlberg is pressed on the issue, he admits he cannot measure moral development. He claims to measure stages of moral reasoning, but it might be said more precisely that he measures stages of reasoning about hypothetical moral dilemmas. Although Kohlberg acknowledges that the link between this scale of measurement and other categories of moral activity is at best unclear, both he and his followers slip into talking of their work as one of measuring moral development.

Moral development should be related to all the fields that use the word "development." In ways that are not easily measurable, moral development has some connection to physical, social, political, religious, and other kinds of development. And, of course, economics being so central to development, one must ask about the correlation of moral development and economic development. To ask about this relation may seem to be a silly question, but perhaps it is just an embarrassing one.

The nineteenth century was not averse to drawing a direct correlation between moral development and wealth. Many Christian churchmen joined the chorus, one of the most famous Christian preachers saying bluntly what others only suggested: "No man in this country suffers from poverty unless it be more than his fault—unless it be his sin."[3] In 1901 the Rt. Rev. William Lawrence wrote in "The Relation of Wealth to Morals": "In the long run, it is only to the man of morality that wealth comes. We believe in the harmony of God's universe. . . . Only by working along the lines of right thinking and right living can the secrets and wealth of Nature be revealed."[4]

There were reformers in the nineteenth century and there are many more today who are inclined to turn Lawrence's picture upside down. Karl Marx in the earlier period and Latin American theologians of today see the poor as holding the pivotal role in the struggle for a morally just world. The New Testament portrait of Jesus would seem to be on the side of those who see an inverse relation between moral development and riches. However, before letting economics govern the picture in either way, other kinds of development should have their say.

Economics tends to engulf every other meaning, including the psychological meaning, of development. It does so by supplying the controlling image for the direction of development. The image is so all-pervasive in U.S. culture that we hardly notice it as an image at all. I refer to the image of growth, or more exactly, growth without limit. Development as applied to both the culture and the individual had to have a quasi-religious meaning to replace providence and heaven. No one wishes to worship anything less than the infinite. That quasi-religious meaning is the image of the unlimited potential of the individual and groups of individuals once they are freed from a preordained end-point. Growth without limit stipulates a direction while avoiding closure to the process.

John Dewey's educational writing was often attacked for being vague on the topic of growth. But Dewey knew what he was doing; he was simply a little ahead of his time in the psychological implications of development. Dewey's progressive education could have been called growth education. "There is nothing that education is subject to save growth," writes Dewey, "and nothing that growth is subject to save more growth."[5] Later critics wanted to know "growth in what?"[6] Dewey had not overlooked this question. He knew that in questions of "objectives" one had to say growth in knowledge or growth in employable skills. But as for education itself, the direction can have no endpoint and can be described only as growth in growth.

When Dewey started writing in the late nineteenth century, the economic scene was still one of individual entrepreneurs and small companies. Individuals amassed fortunes, and companies sought to turn a profit. There was still a sense of limit to dealings in the business world. The modern corporation had its beginnings about 1890. Since then the legal limit on the corporation has been overwhelmed by the spread of national and subsequently trans-national corporations. This new economic phenomenon often seems illogical when judged by the old standards of selling a product and making a profit. By the 1970s, John Kenneth Galbraith could write, "The corporation is a form of association whose fundamental impetus is to grow. . . . Growth is its basic orientation, continued growth without any purpose or end beyond sheer growth."[7] As Dewey had foreseen, growth in profits, plants, or products cannot satisfy the modern thirst for development; growth in growth is what provides a quasi-religious exhilaration to life.

On the psychological side, the words "growth and development" often function as a single phrase. With reference to young children the phrase makes considerable sense. As a part of child psychology, development was seen to depend partially on physical growth. The child's mental capacities would generally have a better chance of developing in a healthily growing body. Piaget called himself a genetic epistemologist, someone interested in the organic basis of rational thought.

In recent decades with the interest in adult development, the idea of development has broken loose from child psychology. Development throughout adult life requires a rethinking of the way psychology originally talked about development. But such reappraisal has not occurred, because "adult development" and "lifelong development" are attractive phrases that do not stir up opposition. The bridge from the old to the new meaning of psychological development is the cultural favorite: growth. In popular psychology since the 1960s no word is more prominent than "growth." The interest is not so much growth in knowledge, love, or commitment to a partner, but growth without limit. "The Human Potential movement saw the growth impulse as so powerful and compelling that it could only be resisted by willful repression. Thus, to deny growth was worse than lazy, it was a perverse and destructive expenditure of energy in the service of an obsolete emotion—guilt."[8]

During the last two decades there has also arisen some resistance to the image of growth as adequate to guide personal and cultural forms of development. Two main sources of that resistance are feminism and ecology. At least some of feminism sees the need for a new partnership of women and men rather than a competition to see who can outgrow whom. And particularly in economic terms, women's lives around the world are deleteriously affected by the obsession with growth.[9] As far as ecology is concerned, Dewey's statement that "growth is subject to nothing but growth" is literally insane ecologically. Growth is but one element in the cycle of nature; a harmony and balance of forces are necessary if the ecological system is to prosper. "What we can be sure about is that nothing grows forever, because the environment has a limited carrying capacity for living organisms."[10]

The concerns of feminism and ecology lead back to the question of religion's relation to development. The question can again be asked: Are the religious idea of conversion and the modern meaning of development compatible? My response is that not only are they compatible but that they require each other. Some sense of conversion is needed to provide development with an alternative to both unlimited growth and an endpoint. Conversely, the religious idea of conversion needs to be rescued from the assumption that God enters vertically into an individual life. Instead of a single dramatic point of conversion, the moral life is one of continual conversion. This idea does not exclude the possibility that one or several moments in life are especially formative. Even then, however, conversion is a circling back on oneself and a recapitulating of life at a deeper level. Similarly, development is a movement of responding that deepens the personal center of response while broadening the area to which response is made. Moral development requires conversionary development or developmental conversion.

Religions that emphasize conversion often speak of a "new man." Their claim is easily dismissed by moral philosophers, psychologists, and social scientists. In the most literal sense, the claim is obviously false; no one totally abandons his or her previous history. Eventually, one must find an integrity to all of one's life, accepting the past that one might be ashamed of as part of the present. Nonetheless, the language associated with dramatic revelatory insight and courageous moral decision reminds us that human beings are capable of surprising even themselves. People are sometimes able to marshal extraordinary moral virtue that does not seem to flow from their past. And, alas, the surprise can be in the other direction. Religions constantly warn that regression as well as progress is possible. People who have a reputation for great virtue can fail badly when a touch of heroism is called for.

An ethic of the good collapses the idea of development into steps toward a goal. An ethic of rights trusts in unlimited growth as the context for everyone's choosing as he or she pleases. A morality of goodness has no preestablished limits to individual development, but it has a sense of aesthetic harmony and of the need for restriction based on responsibility. Development of the person means being responsible *for* oneself in response *to* the total environment. Development is a transformation of what nature offers, but it does no violence as we try to reshape living forms. And development's result is a deeper privacy and a wider public for the world of human activity.

Religion, instead of merely adding to this process of development, is a force of resistance from within. Religion for the most part is a simple and concrete reminder that all idols, including the idol of growth, are to be rejected. Through ritual and doctrine, religions declare: This is not God; that is not God. Religion has both direction and open-endedness. "Toward God is thy limit," says the Quran, giving a direction but not an endpoint.

AGES/STAGES OF MORAL DEVELOPMENT

Contemporary literature on development and moral development refers to stages within the whole process. Like the word "development," "stage" is sometimes assumed to be a word invented by Piagetian psychologists. But the idea that life has stages runs throughout the world's literature and is especially prominent in religious literature. The Christian mystic, for example, speaks of purgative, illuminative, and unitive stages in the mystical journey. From those three categories, individual writers have offered variations on the stages for describing the spiritual life.

In *The Moral Judgment of the Child,* Piaget has three stages for the moral development of the child. For the young child, moral rules are absolutes and imposed from the outside; Piaget calls this heteronomous morality. When the child gets older; rules appear to be under the control of the human will and at the service of the human community. Morality is now autonomous, based upon perceptions of equality and social cooperation. Piaget points to a third stage that would include love, compassion, and forgiveness.[11] However, Piaget did not feel competent to chart this third stage because it involves other things besides the growing rational powers of the child. Piaget is therefore of limited help for theories of lifelong development, both because he has little to say about adults and because of what his system does say about the very young: that a child before the age of five is simply amoral because it is incapable of making moral judgment.

Lawrence Kohlberg has tried to fill out Piaget's system with more stages and with scientific measurements. Kohlberg has six rather than three stages, but they are still focused on age five or six up to the teenage years. He has belatedly come to acknowledge that the experiences of adult life seem to be a necessary condition for exercising advanced moral reasoning. Like Piaget, Kohlberg has little to offer about adult life and is totally silent about children before age five or six.[12] The silence is no accident; the system is so defined as to make the very young child premoral or amoral.

A developmental system that studies logical capacities can chart progress along a straight line. The stages of the system are hierarchical, invariant, and sequential. In the set a, b, c, the element c is higher than b, while b is higher than a; c always follows b and a; c follows a and b in that order. When applied to moral issues and children, a child's reasoning powers follow this straight line of development. Piaget's third stage cannot emerge before stages one and two in that order. Kohlberg's stages have to move through his pre-conventional, conventional and post-conventional levels of morality.

This image of an arrow forward or a ladder upward conflicts sharply with warnings of religion: "Let him not be overconfident and say 'this virtue I have already mastered successfully, it can never leave me.' There is always the possibility it may."[13] Moral reasoning moves in stages that are hierarchical, invariant, and sequential, but moral development is a much more complex affair. It involves a continuing recapitulation of the past in service of an ever-precarious synthesis in the present. There is some sequence in that old age requires a middle age and a youth to precede it. But overall, the steps of development are, as Maria Harris puts it, not steps up a staircase but steps in a dance.

Everyone goes through all the stages of moral development in the course of a lifetime. Some lives shine brightly for the rest of us, many lives follow a meandering path, and some lives appear to be tragic failures. However, it would be arrogant to pronounce with certainty that a particular individual is a total moral failure. The New Testament and other religious documents warn that the people who are the big moral failures are not the obvious sinners who are condemned by their fellow human beings. Real moral failure involves a process of self-deception, a topic I will come back to shortly.

Age and stage are very closely related, although they do admit of some distinction. One gets to each age of life by simply staying alive. One gets to each stage of moral development by responding to what life offers at every age. Thus everyone get to every stage but not equally well. Education is what should fill the gap between age and stage, showing us how to respond so that each age is the best we can make it. Moral development begins at birth, if not earlier, and continues at least until our dying breath. At each step of the way, moral education should accompany moral development.

Whatever is good education is moral education. The principle may seem too obvious for stating, but people often assume a wide gap between moral education and the rest of education. Moral education has come to mean a special set of dilemmas to which young people should address their reasoning. At the right age and in the right setting, such discussions can undoubtedly be *part* of moral education. But moral education also occurs through care of children, play, instruction, friendship, political debate, and quiet reflection. Whatever reshapes these activities to enhance their meaning and lead us to the next step in life deserves the name moral education.

The moral development of the very young child brings out the interrelation of all ages. One cannot describe the moral development of infants without referring to the moral development of parents and grandparents. Parenting a child is one of life's great moral adventures, and so is the "childing" of one's parents. Moral life is shaped by our responses to a matrix of relations. The responses in the relation of adult and child are not equal, but the process can still have a degree of mutuality. We often underestimate the infant's power of receptivity to moral influence. However, the parent usually has some sense of this receptivity, and the grandparent may have an even greater sense of it.

Our era will probably go down in history as the time when the deep bond between the very young and the very old was rediscovered. A grandparent and a grandchild often share a bond of mutuality that is of inestimable value in moral development. The vulnerability of both the old and the young is a test for the rest of society, which is often obsessed with domination and productivity. A theory of moral education has to include an old person sitting quietly with a child. How older people are treated in a particular society can profoundly affect the moral development of the very young. "A society which does not provide sufficient gratifications for the elderly will be an unhappy society for the young as well as the old. If the old are not gratified, nobody can accept the prospects of age with equanimity."[14] For the very young, moral development consists mainly in what is received as a gift. The modern secular world does not know what to do with this fact that fits neither an ethic of the good nor an ethic of rights. It can seem grossly unfair that at life's crucial beginning stage the individual whose life is in question is not in control. All that he or she can do is respond within the given set of relations. Within a morality of goodness,the small child is a revelation of the human condition rather than an exception to the normal situation when individuals control their own destiny. For a morality of goodness, life does not consist of self-will and choice among limitless options; it is response to what life has already formed for us. Modern ethics can make no rational sense of this picture. The exclusion of religion eliminates not only dogmatic systems of rigid morality but also a sense of wonder and receptiveness at the center of life.

A grateful attitude when one is very young makes it possible to accept external guidance later on. Moral development involves a commitment to a code of conduct. Most people who have received generous and affectionate care do not experience moral codes as a terrible daily ordeal. Rather, acting in accord with standards of civil behavior is a token return for all that parents and culture have freely provided.

Learning to observe rules of conduct is an important part but not the whole story for children and teenagers. William James, when asked how to increase the ethical efficiency of the school, answered: "I should increase enormously the amount of manual or 'motor' training relative to the book work, and not let the latter predominate till the age 15 or 16."[15] In the context of recent discussions of moral development, James's reply must strike many people as bewilderingly irrelevant. But within the educational morality discussed here, his answer is not strange at all. James is calling attention to the fact that morality involves a bodily response to a community's way of life. Ethical thinking will be vacuous unless it is reflection from within well-developed physical relations.

The physical training of the young in play as well as in work is needed for moral development. Boys have traditionally had open to them a wide range of physical work and sports programs. But for many young women, new opportunities for physical work and competitive sports have only recently opened. The federal government's Title Nine, which guarantees equality for girls and boys in school athletic programs, was a step forward in moral as well as physical development. Feminist writers as early as Mary Wollstonecraft in 1792 had seen the importance of physical training for women.[16] It took a long time for the government to see the point, and the government may yet backslide from its commitment to financial equality. However, the corner has probably been turned, so women's athletic programs are not likely to disappear. What remains is to see that all boys and girls, not just a privileged elite of trained athletes, have opportunities for exercise, physical training, and competitive sports.

Physical development need not be at the expense of study, as William James's words may seem to suggest it is. The doctrine of a "sound mind in a sound body" in an earlier era was not far off the mark for moral development. The prototype of the relation between study and sport need not be college football with its cynical attitude toward academic life. There is no inherent reason why physical training programs should not help a young person's studies. Similarly, work-study programs or the kind of service work recommended in the Carnegie study *High School* can enhance academic learning.[17]

A wholehearted response to life is the chief moral issue for youth. The response includes the physical, mental, social, spiritual, and vocational. If their elders do not always approve of the particular forms that this response takes, let the elders voice their concerns and criticism without undercutting the enthusiasm of youthful response. The young cannot give up their selfishness if they have not achieved a sense of self. They need encouragement to commit themselves to the particulars of life: someone or some few people who can be cared for and loved;

some one thing or a few things that awaken a vocation to work. "To get a boy committed to some worthwhile activity such as chemistry or engineering is no less part of his moral education than dampening down his selfishness."[18]

Here is where religion can trip over itself precisely because it has something to offer to morality. Christianity in particular has often been thought of as a religion for youth. Adolescence as a distinct age in life arose in part as the time when one would undergo a religious conversion. The seventeenth-century Puritans had thought that conversion could occur as early as eight years of age.[19] The enlightened nineteenth century recognized that "loyalty to Christ" could not be chosen until the teenage years.[20] What should have become evident in the twentieth century is that the religious challenge to selfhood is chiefly aimed at middle age. Few things are so dangerous as mature judgments adopted by immature minds. Christianity has a strong penchant for preaching selflessness to the young, but they could do with less preaching and more instruction about morality. They could also use some therapy for their volatile emotional lives before they jump into well-defined religious commitments.

Conversion, as was pointed out earlier, is not a one-time leap at age eight, eighteen or eighty-eight. Conversion denotes the recurring movement of return to the self in its deeper relations. Of the many conversionary movements in the course of life, it is at mid-life that one is likely to encounter the extreme paradox of religion: you can save your life only by losing it. Such strange sayings can be appreciated only by a person who has a sense of what it means to acquire a self. Only in *mid-life* is one faced with the decision of letting go of a self that is the result of many decades of hard work.

Conversion need not take a religious form in the sense of appealing to the Beatitudes or to Buddhist meditation practice. However, the language of mid-life reversal does take on religious-sounding phrases. For example, a group of therapists between thirty-five and forty-five years old, after a series of meetings that moved from peer supervision to personal therapy, concluded: "At this time, one must give up the normal defenses of early life—infinite faith in one's abilities and the belief that anything is possible. The future becomes finite, childhood fantasies have been fulfilled or unrealized. . . . The reality of one's limited life span comes into sharp focus, and the work of mourning the passing of life begins in earnest."[21]

Male mid-life crisis has become a fashionable topic of this era. The word "conversion" seldom appears in this literature, but a circling back on one's youth and a renewal of one's relations to wife, children, job, and parents is needed. Most of all, the man who has begun to question everything has to come to terms with his own mortality and the vulnerability of his own body. This mid-life experience can be sudden and quite unexpected. If he can let go and die to the image of his youthful self, better years await him. If he only holds on and holds back, he can drive himself into despair, as did Gant in *Look Homeward, Angel:* "He was fifty, he had a tragic consciousness of time; he saw the passionate fullness of his life upon the wane and he cast about him like a senseless and infuriated beast."[22]

There seems to be a significant difference between men and women on this point. At least until now, mid-life crisis as a dramatic "de-illusionment" has been mainly a male phenomenon. Women's crises apparently have not been as concentrated: they have begun earlier and have spread throughout a wide range of middle-age years. Perhaps in the future, middle-age experience will come to be more similar in men's and women's lives (women are closing the gap on the heart-attack rate). Or, it may be that physical and social differences will continue to dictate the crises at different times and in a different rhythm. In either case, the idea of a middle-age conversion or conversions should not be overlooked. An educational morality that is not closed to the resources of religion is better able to understand such crises than a moral development relying almost entirely upon rational thinking and autonomous will.

While middle age is the time for radical reorientation in moral development, old age is a time for solidifying one's gains. By the time one arrives at old age, one has usually encountered serious illnesses, parents and friends have died, the job is not so important, children are beyond direct control. For the first time since childhood, a very simple moral attitude becomes possible. One is grateful for what has been and is contented with the day's lot. Despite harsh social conditions that may be present and despite the decline in physical strength that is inevitable, many people report that old age is one of the happier parts of their life. Paul Claudel's attitude at age eighty might not be so unusual: "Some sigh for yesterday! Some for tomorrow! But you must reach old age before you can understand the meaning, the splendid, absolute, unchallengeable, irreplaceable meaning of the word 'today'."[23]

Younger adults often imagine the old as grasping at time while the years roll by faster and faster. No doubt some older people do feel they are running out of time. Such a feeling is what Erikson calls despair, the flight from death because it represents the end of the world.[24] People who have lacked receptiveness in childhood, discipline in adolescence, and reconciliation in middle age will find it difficult to accept the conditions of old age. Our modern theories that pretend that life goes straight up to better times are no preparation for old age and the imminence of death. Modern theories of development picture life as an elevator to the roof of a high-rise building; what they fail to say is that you get pushed off the roof when you get there.

People who do not assume movement up the ladder to success need not fear despair at the top. Those who have lived in deep and wide responsibility, taking responsibility for their own decisions and responding to bodiliness, time, and community, will respond in old age as they have previously responded. Wisdom, writes Erikson, "is detached concern with life itself in the face of death. It maintains and conveys the integrity of experience in spite of the decline of bodily and mental functions."[25] The integrity that Erikson speaks of as the virtue of the last age is entrance into deeper communion with all time and all bodiliness. Time is not flying by if one's attitude is a deepening receptivity to all time. Abraham Heschel in his later years wrote, "He who lives with a sense for the presence knows that to get older does not mean to lose time but rather to gain time."[26] The dreams of the old are both memories of the past and submersion in the present.

Deep rootedness in the present is the only trustworthy place for the visions of the future. The visions of youth that we think of as expansive are usually narrow, focused as they are along straight lines toward goals. In old age the lines do not run that way; neither arrows forward nor ladders upward dominate the imagination. But the notion of responsibility remains as important as ever.

We need settings for the old that encourage responsibility in two particular ways: with the young and with the old who are most in need. The older person has a vocation to share the wisdom of age with the young. There is some danger here of romanticizing the wisdom of the old as if they suddenly became speculative philosophers at age seventy. The wisdom of the old lies more in their simple attitude of acceptance and quiet reflection. The old provide memory for the young; even when the wires in the brain get crossed and recent memories get confused, the reality of longer memory is still invaluable.

As for helping others more in need than themselves, we need settings that do not patronize the old and force them into a second childhood. Like the young who wish to minister and not just be ministered to, the old need to be challenged to help others. "They have just as much of an obligation to serve their fellow human beings as they had at any other stage of life."[27] Reflection, prayer, and physical presence are possible in any age. They are necessary in every age as resistance to the human temptation toward self-centeredness and self-pity.

TRUTHFUL INTEGRITY

Finally, what guides the process of moral development not as endpoint but as all-embracing context? In Chapter 5 I said that development is in the direction of a just world—that is, one in which everything can be itself in relation to the whole cosmos. Standing in the middle of this movement is that paradoxical creature, the human animal, whose vocation is to respond to everything and to be responsible for whatever cannot decide for itself. Each human being goes beyond nature, either moving the world a little closer to justice through reconciliation or else making the world more unjust through the use of violence. Development toward a just world depends precariously upon the human individual and his or her willingness to act as nonviolent caretaker of what is and guide of what is coming to be.

The human being is the animal that anticipates its death and is tempted to dismiss its responsibility to everything and everyone. Why struggle for a just world if I am not going to enjoy it? It can seem more pressing to build up barriers to ward off death. And so layer upon layer of self-protection moves death from the center of consciousness. The danger is that in fleeing from death, which is at the center of life, the human individual withdraws from life. The incapacity to die is ultimately an incapacity to live. Every human being, writes Simone Weil, "secretes falsehood as a way of avoiding death." What is therefore needed to guide the person's moral development is truthfulness of life.

The philosophical ideal of self-knowledge has been praised at least since the time of Socrates. No one writes essays in support of self-ignorance. But religions warn that the choice between knowledge and ignorance can be misleading. Northrop Frye notes that Christian history has distrusted both gnosticism and agnosticism.[28] While Christianity and other religions encourage us to find out the truth about our own lives, they warn us that we are likely to be deceived about truth itself. We cannot be sure of the truth of anything else unless we attend to the problem of self-deception.

Human life has innumerable layers of illusion created because of its need to protect the fragile ego. Any sudden attempt to pierce through every obstacle to the naked truth is almost certain to create additional layers of self-deception. Only with a lifetime of patient attentiveness and nonviolent receptiveness to what is real can the truth slowly emerge out of the tangle of illusion and counter-illusion. To give up lying does not mean settling into enjoyment about the truth of oneself. As one begins to be freed from self-deception, the experience opens up new dimensions that were previously closed to the light. The sorrows and the sufferings of the world become more evident as self-deception is lessened. Any rejoicing in the truth is done in the midst of sorrow.

Modern society can be described as obsessively concerned with true statements yet barely able to comprehend what is meant by a truthful life. Nowhere is the concern for truth-telling greater than in the United States. People expect that in advertisements and politics the sellers will abide by clearly stated rules of truth in packaging. You can be put in jail for many years if you commit perjury. At the time of Watergate, much of the rest of the world looked on with amusement or disbelief as teams of investigators asked: What did the president know and when did he know it? Like the character in Beckett's play *Krapp's Last Tape*, the truth of one person's life was sought— in fact is still being sought— by studying the words on a tape recording.

It is easy to ridicule this U.S. obsession with truth-telling. But more than a few governments in the world could use a dose of concern for truth-telling, symbolized by such things as the rights to free assembly and to freedom of the press. The U.S. is admirable in insisting on "openness" even if that sometimes leads to bizarre incidents. The press does not accept anything that has the least scent of censorship or "prior restraint," even in the midst of subtle negotiations or the conducting of military operations.

The United States in this regard is revelatory of its origins in the eighteenth-century Enlightenment. Truth-telling became a paramount concern at that time in history, and the concern for true statements has not abated since then. The best explanation for this modern concern is provided by Hannah Arendt: "The loss of certainty of truth ended in a new, entirely unprecedented zeal for truthfulness—as though man could afford to be a liar only so long as he was certain of the unchallengeable existence of truth and objective reality, which surely would defeat all his lies."[29] Arendt is describing here a shift in the locus of truth: from a quality of life in a community of trusting people to a function of statements made by individuals or machines.

The ancient religious traditions, as Arendt implies, had played somewhat loosely with the literal truth. There is a time for making true statements and a time for supporting the community. The Talmud allows one to sing of the "beautiful and graceful bride" even if she is lame, blind—or has a beard.[30] Thomas Aquinas allows for a whole realm of false statements to people who have no right to the truth from us.[31] "Buddhist tradition goes even further in understanding truth as relative; it cites the analogy of a father trying to coax his children from a burning house by using whatever statements will succeed.[32]

Compare these religious examples to Kant's ethic of rights. For Kant, one may not refuse the truth to a murderer who is asking directions to his intended victim. In modern ethics, as Kant recognized, the fragile system of ethical principles is built by human beings, and it is undermined by every human failure to speak the truth clearly and literally.[33] Nineteenth-century educators were extremely agitated over stories for children that depicted animals speaking. Since such statements are not true, the child's moral development would be corrupted.[34]

Sissela Bok's Lying: Moral Choice in Public and Private Life illustrates the powerful but narrow concern for truth-telling in modern ethics.[35] At the beginning of the book she refers to the great mystery of truth that classical philosophy and religion have dealt with. By page 6 she clears up the "conceptual muddle," distinguishing between "the moral domain of intended truthfulness and deception and the much vaster domain of truth and falsity in general." Bok henceforth assumes this distinction between moral truth and epistemological truth.

Like most writers on ethics, Bok wishes to keep her distance from religion, even though she quotes liberally from religious writers of the past. She is particularly concerned about religion's claim to possess a revelation from God, a claim that can lead to a persecution of others.[36] Although a claim to *possess* revelaton is indeed dangerous, revelaton may still be a key to understanding truth. The meaning of revelation should not be abandoned to fundamentalists. In early Greek thought, revelation was the very name of truth. Lying, therefore, was concealment in the dark. Bok's exclusive concern with "deceptive statements" obstructs any profound understanding of truth as a quality of the real and a central demand of the human vocation. Bok concentrates on the intention to deceive others, but she is oblivious to religion's message that lying to others is a never-entirely-successful attempt to deceive oneself.

In contrast to Bok's epistemological and moral meanings of truth, medieval thought distinguished between ontological and logical truth. Every judgment of the human mind involves logical truth, which is important because it is a measure of our lives. Logical truth is a human participation in the truth of being or reality. The modern era, of course, distrusts all talk about "being" or "objective reality." Nevertheless, the question of truth as a personal experience of something real is one of the few possible bridges between premodern and modern philosophical worlds. In trying to get beyond the dilemma of either isolated subject or objective data, twentieth-century thought cannot avoid new questions about truthfulness as a relation involving the person. An exclusive concern with deceptive statements and the intention to deceive isolates lying from personal truth, political power, and any larger context of human interaction. With such a narrow focus, the greatest violations of truth may not be noticed at all.

As a different approach to lying, consider Dietrich Bonhoeffer's "What Is Meant by 'Telling the Truth'?" Bonhoeffer is concerned that speech between human beings be genuine. "When words become rootless and homeless, then the word loses truth, and then indeed there must inevitably be lying."[37] Lying does not usually happen because someone intentionally sets out to deceive. We lie because we have not learned how to be truthful with our lives. Telling the truth requires an understanding of the situation in which we find ourselves and of the relation of all parts of our life to that situation. One speaks truth to the extent that one's life is in touch with what is real.

Many people who enunciate abstract truths actually lie about their own lives because there is no self-revelation in their words, no revelation of "being" as experienced relation. In one sense, nothing is easier to do than to make true statements; one simply conceals whatever is important. There is a form if insanity that consists in making statements that are literally but vacuously true. Soren Kierkegaard tells of a man who, wishing to prove he was sane, hung a little globe on his belt, and every time it bounced he said: Bang! The world is round. He could not understand why he was put away as insane. Kierkegaard thought there were people who told no lies because their lives were empty of meaning and their statements did not really mean anything.[38] Statements that are both true and take us somewhere are not easy to make. They require more than a resolve not to make false statements.

Bonhoeffer's particular concern was identifying a kind of truth-telling that does violence to the truth. A propostion may be truthful in the abstract yet not serve the cause of truth. "For the cynic the truthfulness of his words will consist in his giving expression on each separate occasion to the particular reality as he thinks he perceives it, without reference to the totality of the real; and precisely through this, he completely destroys the real."[39] The man who is proud of "telling it like it is" carries no burden of guilt even if his words destroy reputations and friendships. He would no doubt scoff at the idea that his blunt and honest truths are a way of evading any serious grappling with the truth in all its ambiguities.

Bonhoeffer's essay on truth is nicely undergirded by Herbert Fingarette's *Self-Deception*.[40] For Fingarette, the self is a kind of community. The members of the community that have their own independent engagements are reason, feeling, aim, and so forth. Self-deception is a failure to reach a synthesis among the members of the community. Fingarette would agree with Bonhoeffer that the truth has to be learned—that is, the truth about one's engagements in the world that precede our rational reflection. A person who is deeply engaged may avoid spelling out the meaning of those engagements because that would mean accepting greater responsibility.

A little self-deception exists in everyone, but the man or woman who performs heroic deeds and has a reputation for virtue is most in danger of self-deception for a person with a real self is capable of deceiving that self. In religious traditions the great saint and the great sinner are close together. The moral genius can go either way, so no one can claim to be virtuous before death. In *The Brothers Karamazov*, the devil, asked whether he ever tempted the holy men who prayed for seventeen years in the wilderness, replies: "My dear fellow, I've done nothing else. . . . They can contemplate such depths of belief and unbelief at the same moment that sometimes it really seems they are within a hair's breadth of being turned upside down."[41]

Medieval philosophy had the important category of willful or culpable ignorance. One who is willfully ignorant has maneuvered himself or herself behind legitimate concerns and personal reputation. Willful ignorance is still a key to the moral meaning of truth, even if it usually does not convict in court. Corporate executives and politicians frequently use ignorance as a ploy so that they will not be legally responsible for the actions of their underlings. The information that comes from the top of the pyramid is all about virtuous living and courageous decisions. No lies need be told when one is ignorant, but the truth is lacking if the ignorance is part of a pattern of self-deception.

An accusation of moral turpitude directed at a self-deceived person will be ineffective. It will probably sound ridiculous and will only further hide the problem. Such a person needs someone who will tactfully and persistently examine in detail the texture of his or her life. The counselor to the self-deceiver, says Fingarette, must manifest "unswervingly dedicated reliability and dispassionateness."[42] It is often easier to feel tolerance toward criminals than toward a powerful, seemingly virtuous person who is living a lie. But for the sake of that person and his or her contribution to the good of the human race, a humane tolerance is called for.

This meaning of truthfulness suggests that the moral development of a person is not a straight-line sequence. We keep circling about the unreachable center of our lives from which thinking, feeling, and deciding emanate. Individual virtues are acquirable: we can train ourselves in courage, sobriety, or just judgment. However, the constellation of a virtuous life is always precarious. Personal moral development consists in the lessening of self-deception in a community of men, women, and nonhumans.

If we return to two of Sissela Bok's concerns in *Lying,* they are illuminated by this approach to truth. Bok is puzzled by the fact that physicians often do not tell the truth to dying patients.[43] The fact is that they often evade the truth by silence, which in Bok's definition is not a lie. Studies suggest that at least eighty percent of dying patients wish to know the truth. Are physicians reading other polls? Do they not believe these polls? It is more likely that physicians have difficulty facing up to the limits of their profession and to their own personal mortality. Physicians are not moral monsters who set out to deceive their patients. They are like the rest of us; or, in Fingarette's framework, they are likely to be more engaged and more responsible than most people. But when your vocation is to save lives and when one hundred percent of your patients eventually die, the impulse to self-deception is extremely powerful. The physician either has to find a meaning in death or else build a wall against mortality. The most amazing self-deception can be found among people who regularly see death but who have convinced themselves that "fortunately I'm powerful, so I'll never die." An ethic of rights that concentrates on the patient's right to know cannot get at this problem. We need a morality that moves in the direction of communication and communion, one that allows death its limited rights.

A second concern of Bok that I note here is lying to children. On this point, Bok moves away from her own rational principles. She thinks that the immature and the incompetent should not be manipulated for their own best interests. "Rather than accepting the common view, therefore, that it is somehow more justifiable to lie to children and to those the liars regard as being *like* children, special precautions are needed not to exploit them."[44]

Here Bok transcends her rationalistic tendencies and makes contact with religious traditions that see truth and childlikeness as closely related. Jesus was particularly severe in judging those who scandalize a child. The Christian gospel sees the revelation of truth in the most unlikely places: the lives of the powerless, the dispossessed, the vulnerable. The very young and the very old are close to a truth that must be listened to by the middle-aged. The issue is not simply telling the truth to the powerless. It is, rather, the discovery that the powerless have a profound truth to teach: that our lives are not our own to be possessed and wielded for gain, but that everything is to be received with gratitude and enjoyed in communion.

In summary, personal moral development is a lessening of self-deception in a community of men, women, children, and nonhumans. We can contribute to that development mostly in indirect ways. We can work to bring about environments where the revelation of truth and the reconciliation of opposites have some chance of occurring. We can reshape the forms of life that the past has passed on to us, occasionally giving a sermon or instruction to help along the mostly nonverbal activities that govern life. It is not our responsibility to finish the task, but it is our responsibility to refuse to withdraw from participating in the transformations of history.

Notes

CHAPTER 1: MORALITY AND EDUCATION

1. Arthur Lovejoy, *The Great Chain of Being* (Cambridge: Harvard University, 1936).
2. Ludwig Wittgenstein, *Tractatus Logico-Philosophicus* (London: Routledge and Kegan Paul, 1971).
3. Ludwig Wittgenstein, *Philosophical Investigations* (New York: Macmillan, 1953).
4. William Butler Yeats, "The Circus Animals Desertion," in *The Poems of W. B. Yeats* (London: Macmillan, 1949), Vol. II.
5. James Rest, "Basic Issues in Evaluating Moral Education Programs," *Evaluating Moral Development*, ed. Lisa Kuhmerker (Schenectady: Character Research Project, 1980), p. 4.
6. *Ibid.*, p. 9.
7. Emile Durkheim, *Moral Education* (New York: Free Press, 1961), p. 3.
8. W. Cantwell Smith, *The Meaning and End of Religion* (New York: Macmillan, 1962), p. 41.
9. Durkheim, *Moral Education*, p. 19.
10. Jean Piaget, *The Moral Judgment of the Child* (New York: Collier, 1962).
11. John Dewey, *Democracy and Education* (New York: Free Press, 1966), p. 76.

CHAPTER 2: AN ETHIC OF THE GOOD

1. Aristotle, *Nichomachean Ethics* 1094a, 1–5.
2. Reiner, Schürmann, "Withering Norms: Deconstructing the Foundation of the Social Sciences," in *Social Science as Moral Inquiry*, ed. Norma Haan and Robert Bellah (New York: Columbia University, 1983), p. 191.
3. Aristotle, *Metaphysics* 1072a–1072b.
4. See Ronald Beiner, *Political Judgment* (Chicago: University of Chicago, 1983).
5. Pico Della Mirandola, *On the Dignity of Man* (Indianapolis: Bobbs-Merrill, 1965), pp. 4–5.
6. *Ibid.*, p. 5.
7. Aristotle, *Nichomachean Ethics*, 1176b; Frederick Copleston, *Aquinas* (Baltimore: Penguin, 1955), p. 211.
8. Thomas Spragens, *The Irony of Liberal Reform* (Chicago: University of Chicago, 1981), p. 197.
9. Quoted in Durkheim, *Moral Education*, p. 169.
10. Jeremy Bentham, "An Introduction to the Principles of Morals and Legislation," in *A Bentham Reader*, ed. Mary Mack (New York: Pegasus, 1969), pp. 78–144.
11. The phrase for which Bentham is best known actually originated with Francis Hutcheson, *Inquiry Concerning Moral Good and Evil* (London: John Bohn, 1850), sec. 3, ch. 8.

12. John Stuart Mill, "Bentham" and "Utilitarianism" in *Essays on Ethics, Religion and Society* (Toronto, Routledge and Kegan Paul, 1969), pp. 75–116 and 203–60.
13. Frank Knight, as quoted in Fred Hirsch, *Social Limits to Growth* (Cambridge: Harvard University, 1976), p. 61.
14. Bertrand Russell, as quoted in Hirsch, *The Social Limits of Growth*, p. 135.
15. Hirsch, *Social Limits of Growth*, pp. 32–54.
16. *Ibid.*, p. 135.
17. Adam Smith, *The Wealth of Nations* (New York: Modern Library, 1937), p. 14.
18. Friedrich Nietzsche, *The Genealogy of Morals*, ed. Oscar Levy (New York: Russell and Russell, 1964), p. 121.

CHAPTER 3: AN ETHIC OF RIGHTS

1. Mill, "Utilitarianism," pp. 203–260.
2. Immanuel Kant, "Of the Metaphysics of Morals," in *Critique of Practical Reason and Other Works* (New York: Longmans, Green, 1927), p. 9.
3. Daniel Maguire, *The Moral Choice* (Minneapolis: Winston, 1978), pp. 156–57.
4. George Grant, *English-Speaking Justice* (Notre Dame: University of Notre Dame, 1985), p. 86.
5. John Locke, *The Reasonableness of Christianity* (Stanford: Stanford University, 1958), p. 67.
6. Kant, "Of the Metaphysics of Morals," p. 38.
7. John Dewey, *Theory of the Moral Life* (New York: Holt, 1960), p. 74.
8. Kant, "Of the Metaphysics of Morals," p. 47.
9. Peter Singer, "Ten Years of Animal Liberation," *New York Review of Books*, Jan. 17, 1985, pp. 46–52.
10. See Mary Midgely, *Beast and Man: The Roots of Human Nature* (Ithaca: Cornell University, 1978), p. 46.
11. Charles Birch and John Cobb, *The Liberation of Life* (Cambridge: Cambridge University, 1981), p. 150.
12. *Ibid.*, p. 151.
13. Midgely, *Beast and Man*, p. 351.
14. John Locke, *Some Thoughts Concerning Education* (Cambridge: Cambridge University, 1922), p. 31.
15. John Locke, *Of Civil Government: Second Treatise* (Chicago: Regnery, 1955), p. 10.
16. John Rawls, *A Theory of Justice* (Cambridge: Harvard University, 1971).
17. *Ibid.*, p. 506.
18. *Ibid.*, p. 396.
19. *Ibid.*, p. 23.
20. *Ibid.*, p. 12.
21. Michael Sandel, *Liberalism and the Limits of Justice* (Cambridge: Cambridge University, 1982), p. 131.
22. Rawls, *A Theory of Justice*, p. 140.
23. *Ibid.*, pp. 264–65.
24. *Ibid.*, p. 550.
25. *Ibid.*, p. 128.
26. Sandel, *Liberalism and the Limits of Justice*, p. 98.
27. *Ibid.*, p. 41.

CHAPTER 4: A MORALITY OF GOODNESS

1. Durkheim, *Moral Education*, p. 100.
2. David Hume, *An Enquiry Concerning the Principles of Morals* (Chicago: Open Court, 1900), p. 121.
3. Aristotle, *Physics*, 198a–198b.
4. Plato, *Republic*, 509.

5. *Ibid.*, 516.
6. *Ibid.*, 517.
7. Plato, *Timaeus*, 30.
8. Pinchas Lapide, *Jewish Monotheism and Christian Trinitarian Doctrine* (Philadelphia: Fortress, 1981), p. 65.
9. *Ibid.*
10. See Robert Wilken, *The Christians as the Romans Saw Them* (New Haven: Yale University, 1984), p. 85.
11. Plotinus, *The Enneads* (London: Faber and Faber, 1969), VI, 9, 10.
12. John Rist, *Plotinus: The Road to Reality* (Cambridge: Cambridge University, 1967), p. 225.
13. Plotinus, *Enneads*, III, 2, 6.
14. *Ibid.*, VI, 9, 11; V, 8; V, 5, 8.
15. Lovejoy, *The Great Chain of Being*, p. 92.
16. *Debar R.*, II: 10.
17. Rist, *Plotinus: The Road to Reality*, p. 117.
18. Reiner Schürmann, *Meister Eckhart: Mystic and Philosopher* (Bloomington: University of Indiana, 1978).
19. Thomas Aquinas, *Summa Theologica* (New York: Benziger, 1947), Ia, 3, prologue; John Caputo, *Heidegger and Aquinas* (New York: Fordham University, 1982), p. 259.
20. Thomas Aquinas, *Summa Theologica*, I–II, 110.
21. Lovejoy, *The Great Chain of Being*, p. 84.
22. Thomas Aquinas, *De Potentia*, 5:4.
23. *De Veritate*, 4:2; see David Burrell, *Aquinas* (Notre Dame: University of Notre Dame, 1979), pp. 146–56.
24. *Summa Contra Gentes*, 4:19; Burrell, *Aquinas*, pp. 157–61.
25. *De Veritate*, 22:2.
26. Quoted in Hans Waldenfals, *Absolute Nothingness* (New York: Paulist, 1980), p. 61.
27. Jacques Maritain, *The Degrees of Knowledge* (New York: Scribner, 1959), p. 326.
28. Matthew Fox, *Breakthrough: Meister Eckhart's Creation-Centered Spirituality* (Garden City: Doubleday, 1980), p. 36.
29. *Ibid.*, p. 48.
30. *Ibid.*, p. 325.
31. Author of The Cloud of Unknowing, *A Letter of Private Direction* (New York: Crossroad, 1981), p. 20.
32. Rufus Jones, *Some Experiments in Mystical Religion* (New York: Abingdon, 1930), p. 112.
33. Ernest Bloch, *Atheism in Christianity* (New York: Herder and Herder, 1972), p. 65.
34. Fox, *Breakthrough*, p. 224.

CHAPTER 5: RESPONSIBLE MORALITY

1. Nietzsche, *Genealogy of Morals*, p. 8.
2. Max Weber, "Politics as a Vocation," in *From Max Weber: Essays in Sociology*, eds. H. H. Gerth and C. Wright Mills (New York: Oxford University, 1958), pp. 77–128.
3. See Pinchas Lapide, *The Sermon on the Mount* (Maryknoll: Orbis, 1986).
4. John Howard Yoder, *The Politics of Jesus* (Grand Rapids: Eerdmans, 1972), pp. 98–99.
5. *Ibid.*, p. 171.
6. *Ibid.*, p. 158.
7. Carol Gilligan, *In A Different Voice* (Cambridge: Harvard University, 1982).
8. In *Social Science as Moral Inquiry*, p. 40.
9. Carol Gilligan, "The Conquistador and the Dark Continent: Reflections on the Psychology of Love," in *Daedalus*, 113 (Summer 1984): 79.
10. Robert Bellah and others, *Habits of the Heart* (Berkeley: University of California, 1985), p. 304.

11. *Ibid.*, pp. 13–17.
12. *Ibid.*, p. 16.
13. Midgely, *Beast and Man*, p. 217.
14. G. K. Chesterton, *Orthodoxy* (Garden City: Image, 1959), p. 48.
15. Mary Douglas, *Natural Symbols* (New York: Vintage, 1973), p. 73.
16. H. Richard Niebuhr, *The Responsible Self* (San Francisco: Harper & Row, 1963).
17. See Murray Sayle, "KE 007: A Conspiracy of Circumstance," in *New York Review of Books*, April 25, 1985, pp. 44–54; Alexander Dallin, *Black Box: KAL 007 and the Superpowers* (Berkeley: University of California, 1985).
18. Hume, *An Enquiry Concerning the Principles of Morals*, p. 17.
19. Sandel, *Liberalism and the Limits of Justice*, p. 35.
20. Grant, *English-Speaking Justice*, p. 174.
21. Carol Gilligan, "Justice and Responsibility: Thinking about Real Dilemmas of Moral Conflict and Choice," in *Toward Moral and Religious Maturity*, ed. Christiane Brusselmans (Morristown: Silver Burdett, 1980), p. 248.
22. Plato, *The Republic*, #336–56.

CHAPTER 6: TRANS-NATURAL MORALITY

1. Samuel Gorovitz, *Doctors' Dilemmas* (New York: Oxford University, 1982), p. 171; Paul Ramsey, "The Medical Ethics of In Vitro Fertilization," *American Medical Association*, 220 (June 1972): 1346–50; 1480–85.
2. Gorovitz, *Doctors' Dilemmas*, p. 172.
3. Midgely, *Beast and Man*, p. 260, footnote 11.
4. Wilken, *The Christians as the Romans Saw Them*, p. 85.
5. Perry Miller, *Errand into the Wilderness* (New York: Harper Torch, 1964), pp. 48–98.
6. Basil Mitchell, *Morality: Religious and Secular* (New York: Oxford University, 1980), p. 85; see also Carl Becker, *The Heavenly City of the Eighteenth Century Philosophers* (New Haven: Yale University, 1932), p. 53.
7. Jean-Paul Sartre, *The Flies* (London: Hamish Hamilton, 1946), pp. 96–97.
8. Henri de Lubac, *The Mystery of the Supernatural* (New York: Herder and Herder, 1967); Karl Rahner, *Theological Investigations*, vol. 1 (Baltimore: Helicon, 1961).
9. Thomas Paine, *The Rights of Man* (New York: Dutton, 1951), p. 113.
10. Chesterton, *Orthodoxy*, p. 144.
11. Midgely, *Beast and Man*, p. 26.
12. G. E. Moore, *Principia Ethica* (Cambridge: Cambridge University, 1903), ch. 1.
13. John Boswell, *Christianity, Social Tolerance and Homosexuality* (Chicago, University of Chicago, 1980), p. 166.
14. Alfred Kinsey, *Sexual Behavior in the Human Male* (Philadelphia: Saunders, 1948) and *Sexual Behavior in the Human Female* (Philadelphia, Saunders, 1953).
15. Midgely, *Beast and Man*, p. 79.

CHAPTER 7: PRIVATE/PUBLIC MORALITY

1. Hannah Arendt, *The Human Condition* (Chicago: University of Chicago, 1958), pp. 38–49.
2. *The Federalist Papers* (New York: Simon and Schuster, 1974), #10, 45, 48.
3. Arendt, *The Human Condition*, p. 34.
4. *Ibid.*, p. 23.
5. *Ibid.*, p. 39.
6. John Wikse, *About Possession: The Self as Private Property* (University Park: Pennsylvania State University, 1977), p. 16.
7. Edmund Morgan, *The Puritan Family* (New York: Harper Torch, 1966), p. 25.
8. Hannah Arendt, *Between Past and Future* (New York: Viking, 1961), p. 188.
9. Christopher Lasch, *Haven in a Heartless World* (New York: Basic Books, 1977).
10. Arendt, *The Human Condition*, p. 40.

11. *Ibid.*, p. 57.
12. Edward Norman, *Christianity and the World Order* (New York: Oxford University, 1979), p. 79.
13. "Private Religion, Public Morality," *New York Times*, Oct. 5, 1980.
14. Cornel West, "Religion, Politics and Language," in *Christianity and Crisis*, Oct. 15, 1984, pp. 366–67.

CHAPTER 8: THREE MORAL ISSUES

1. Kristin Luker, *Abortion and the Politics of Motherhood* (Berkeley: University of California, 1984), p. 181.
2. Beverly Harrison, *Our Right to Choose: Toward a New Ethic of Abortion* (Boston: Beacon, 1983), p. 132.
3. Luker, *Abortion and the Politics of Motherhood*, p. 178; see also Mary Segers, "Abortion and Culture: Toward a Feminist Perspective," in *Abortion: Understanding Differences*, eds. Sidney and Daniel Callahan (New York: Plenum, 1984), pp. 229–52.
4. Luker, *Abortion and the Politics of Motherhood*, p. 40.
5. Seeger, "Abortion and Culture: Toward a Feminist Perspective," p. 250.
6. Gilbert Steiner, *The Abortion Dispute and the American System* (Washington, D.C., Brookings Institute, 1983), pp. 65–66.
7. Barbara Ehrenreich, "Is Abortion Really a Moral Dilemma?" *New York Times*, Feb. 7, 1985, p. C2.
8. Christopher Tietze, *Induced Abortion: A World Review* (New York: Population Control, 1981).
9. Steiner, *The Abortion Dispute and the American System*, p. 84.
10. Mary Ann Lamanna, "Social Science and Ethical Issues: The Policy Implications of Poll Data on Abortion," in *Abortion: Understanding Differences*, eds. Sidney and Daniel Callahan (New York: Plenum, 1984), pp. 1–23.
11. Luker, *Abortion and the Politics of Motherhood*, p. 227.
12. Gilligan, *In A Different Voice*.
13. John Locke, *Of Civil Government. Second Treatise* (Chicago: Regnery, 1955), p. 90.
14. John Stuart Mill, "On Liberty," in *John Stuart Mill: Selected Writings*, ed. Mary Warnock (New York: Meridian, 1962), p. 206.
15. William May, *The Physician's Covenant* (Philadelphia: Westminster, 1983), p. 80.
16. M. Pabst Battin, *Ethical Issues in Suicide* (Englewood Cliffs: Prentice Hall, 1982).
17. James Hillman, *Suicide and the Soul* (New York: Harper, 1975), p. 32.
18. Theodore Fox, quoted in Daniel Maguire, *Death by Choice*, 2nd ed. (Garden City: Doubleday, 1984), p. 3.
19. M. Pabst Battin, "The Least Worst Death," *Hastings Center Report*, April, 1983.
20. Hans Küng, *Eternal Life?* (Garden City: Doubleday, 1984), p. 165.
21. Jonathan Glover, *Causing Death and Saving Lives* (New York: Penguin, 1977), pp. 196–97.
22. The case of Paul Brophy; from interviews on "20/20," Dec. 5, 1985.
23. Sidney Wanzer and others, "The Physician's Responsibility Toward Hopelessly Ill Patients," *New England Journal of Medicine*, April 12, 1984, pp. 955–59.
24. May, *The Physician's Covenant*, p. 82.
25. Philippe Ariés, *Western Attitudes Toward Death* (Baltimore: Johns Hopkins, 1974), p. 12.
26. *Ibid.*, pp. 34–36.
27. Philippe Ariés, *The Hour of Our Death* (New York: Knopf, 1981), p. 306.
28. In this section, the words "homosexual," "gay," and "lesbian" are used as adjectives. Generally, "homosexual" is used to refer to the individual's sexual orientation or behavior; "gay" in referring to men and "lesbian" in referring to women are used for communal, political, and cultural references.
29. Alistair Heron, *Toward a Quaker View of Sex* (London: Friend Home Service Committee, 1963), p. 21.

30. Michel Foucault, *The History of Sexuality, vol. 1: An Introduction.* (New York: Vintage, 1980), p. 103.
31. Don Williams as quoted in Jerry Kirk, *The Homosexual Crisis* (Nashville: Thomas Nelson, 1978), p. 50.
32. Carl Jung as quoted in John McNeill, "Homosexuality, Lesbianism and the Future," in *A Challenge to Love: Gay and Lesbian Catholics in the Church,* ed. Robert Nugent (New York: Crossroad, 1983), p. 62.
33. Foucault, *The History of Sexuality,* p. 43.
34. John D'Emilio, *Sexual Politics, Sexual Communities: The Making of a Homosexual Minority in the United States 1940–70* (Chicago: University of Chicago, 1983), pp. 18–30.
35. *Ibid.,* pp. 34–35.
36. Thomas Aquinas, *Summa Theologica,* II–II, q. 154, a. 11–12.
37. Gabriel Moran, "Education: Sexual and Religious," in *The Challenge to Love,* pp. 159–73.
38. *To Live in Christ Jesus: A Pastoral Reflection on the Moral Life* (Washington, D.C.: US Catholic Conference, 1976), p. 19.
39. See Boswell, *Christianity, Social Tolerance and Homosexuality;* John McNeill, *The Church and the Homosexual* (Kansas City: Sheed, Andrews and McMeel, 1976); Tom Horner, *Jonathan Loved David: Homosexuality in Bible Times* (Philadelphia: Westminster, 1978); Walter Wink, "Biblical Perspectives on Homosexuality," *Christian Century,* Nov. 7, 1979, pp. 1082–86.
40. Rom. 1:26–27.
41. Boswell, *Christianity, Social Tolerance and Homosexuality,* pp. 26–27.

CHAPTER 9: TEACHING MORALLY

1. Ivan Illich, *Deschooling Society* (New York: Harper & Row, 1971).
2. Jacques Barzun, *Teacher in America* (Boston: Little, Brown, 1945), p. 10.
3. *Ibid.*
4. Philip Rief, *Fellow Teachers* (New York: Harper & Row, 1973), p. 2.
5. Durkheim, *Moral Education,* p. 120.
6. Quoted in Fox, *Breakthrough,* p. 85.
7. Sigmund Freud, *The Question of Lay Analysis* (New York: Norton, 1959); see also Russel Jacoby, *Social Amnesia* (Boston: Beacon, 1975), p. 123.
8. D. T. Suzuki, *Mysticism* (Westport: Greenwood, 1975), p. 53.
9. Ralph Barton Perry, *The Thought and Character of William James* (Boston: Little, Brown, 1935), vol. 2, p. 704.
10. B. V. Hill, *Faith at the Blackboard* (Grand Rapids: Eerdmans, 1982), pp. 105–21.
11. Northrop Frye, *The Great Code* (New York: Harcourt, Brace, Jovanovich, 1982), pp. xiv–xv.

CHAPTER 10: TOWARD MORAL INTEGRITY

1. Eric Gritsch, *Martin—God's Court Jester: Luther in Retrospect* (Philadelphia: Fortress, 1983), p. 182.
2. Michael Novak, lecture at the annual convention of the National Catholic Educational Association, April 4, 1984.
3. Quoted in Henry May, *Protestant Churches and Industrial America* (New York: Harper Torch, 1967), p. 69.
4. William Lawrence, "The Relation of Wealth to Morals," in *God's New Israel,* ed. Conrad Cherry (Englewood Cliffs: Prentice Hall, 1971), p. 246.
5. Dewey, *Democracy and Education,* p. 51.
6. Richard Hofstadter, *Anti-Intellectualism in America* (New York: Vintage, 1963), p. 373; Boyd Bode, *Progressive Education at the Crossroads* (New York: Newson and Co., 1938), p. 83.
7. John Kenneth Galbraith, *The New Industrial State* (Boston: Houghton Mifflin, 1967), p. 257.

8. Barbara Ehrenreich, *The Hearts of Men* (Garden City: Anchor, 1983), pp. 96–97.
9. See Irene Tinker, "The Adverse Impact of Development on Women," in *Women and World Development,* eds. Irene Tinker, M. B. Bransen, and M. Buvinic (New York: Praeger, 1976).
10. Birch and Cobb, *The Liberation of Life,* p. 38.
11. Piaget, *The Moral Judgment of the Child,* p. 323.
12. Lawrence Kohlberg and Edward Fenton, "The Cognitive Developmental Approach to Moral Education," *Social Education,* 40 (April 1976): 213–16.
13. *The Living Talmud,* ed. Judah Goldin (Chicago: University of Chicago, 1957), p. 86.
14. Robert Katz, "Jewish Values: Sociopsychological Perspectives on Aging," in *Toward a Theology of Aging,* ed. Seward Hiltner (New York: Human Sciences Press, 1975), p. 141.
15. Quoted in Michael Sadler, *Moral Instruction and Training in the Schools* (Longmans, Green and Co., 1908), p. 94.
16. Mary Wollstonecraft, *The Rights of Woman* (New York: Dutton, 1929), pp. 23–57.
17. See Ernest Boyer and others, *High School: A Report on Secondary Education in America* (New York: Harper & Row, 1983).
18. Richard S. Peters, "Concrete Principles and the Rational Passions," in *Moral Education: Five Lectures* (Cambridge: Harvard University, 1970), p. 40.
19. Morgan, *The Puritan Family,* p. 174.
20. Joseph Kett, *Rites of Passage* (New York: Basic Books, 1977), p. 204.
21. Winslow Hunt and Amnon Issacharoff, "History and Analysis of a Leaderless Group of Professional Therapists," *American Journal of Psychiatry,* 132 (Nov. 1975): 1164–67.
22. Thomas Wolfe, *Look Homeward, Angel* (New York: Modern Library, 192), p. 20.
23. Quoted in Katz, "Jewish Values: Sociopsychological Perspectives on Aging," p. 146.
24. Erik Erikson, *Childhood and Society.* 2nd ed. (New York: Norton, 1963), p. 269.
25. Erik Erikson, *Insight and Responsibility* (New York: Norton, 1964), p. 133.
26. Abraham Heschel, "The Older Person and the Family in the Perspective of Jewish Tradition," in *Aging and the Human Spirit,* eds. Carol LeFevre and Perry LeFevre (Chicago: Exploration Press, 1981), p. 42.
27. Arthur Fleming, White House Conference on Aging, 1971, cited in Eugene Bianchi, *Aging as a Spiritual Journey* (New York: Crossroad, 1982), p. 161.
28. Frye, *The Great Code,* p. 67.
29. Arendt, *The Human Condition,* pp. 277–78.
30. Jacob Petuchowski, *Our Masters Taught: Rabbinic Stories and Sayings.* (New York: Crossroad, 1982), p. 96.
31. Thomas Aquinas, *Summa Theologica,* II, 2, 110.
32. See Sung Bae Park, *Buddhist Faith and Sudden Enlightenment* (Albany: State University of New York, 1983), p. 51.
33. Immanuel Kant, "On a Supposed Right to Lie from Benevolent Motives," *Critique of Practical Reasoning and Other Writings* (New York: Longmans, 1927), pp. 361–66.
34. Bernard Wishy, *The Child and the Republic* (Philadelphia: University of Pennsylvania, 1968), pp. 51–52.
35. Sissela Bok, *Lying: Moral Choice in Public and Private Life* (New York: Vintage, 1978).
36. *Ibid.,* pp. 5–6.
37. Dietrich Bonhoeffer, *Ethics,* ed. Eberhard Bethge (New York: Macmillan, 1965), p. 367.
38. Soren Kierkegaard, *Philosophical Fragments* (Princeton: Princeton University, 1962), p. 235.
39. Bonhoeffer, *Ethics,* p. 370.
40. Herbert Fingarette, *Self-Deception* (New York: Humanities Press, 1969), p. 85.
41. Fyodor Dostoyevsky, *The Brothers Karamazov* (New York: Signet, 1957), p. 585.
42. Fingarette, *Self-Deception,* p. 143.
43. Bok, *Lying,* p. 241.
44. *Ibid.,* p. 230.

Index